AF248780

Law, Reason, and the Cosmic City

Law, Reason, and the Cosmic City

Political Philosophy in the Early Stoa

Katja Maria Vogt

OXFORD

UNIVERSITY PRESS

OXFORD

UNIVERSITY PRESS

Oxford University Press, Inc., publishes works that further
Oxford University's objective of excellence
in research, scholarship, and education.

Oxford   New York
Auckland   Cape Town   Dar es Salaam   Hong Kong   Karachi
Kuala Lumpur   Madrid   Melbourne   Mexico City   Nairobi
New Delhi   Shanghai   Taipei   Toronto

With offices in
Argentina   Austria   Brazil   Chile   Czech Republic   France   Greece
Guatemala   Hungary   Italy   Japan   Poland   Portugal   Singapore
South Korea   Switzerland   Thailand   Turkey   Ukraine   Vietnam

Copyright © 2008 by Katja Maria Vogt

Published by Oxford University Press, Inc.
198 Madison Avenue, New York, NY 10016
www.oup.com

First issued as an Oxford University Press paperback, 2012

Oxford is a registered trademark of Oxford University Press

All rights reserved. No part of this publication may be reproduced,
stored in a retrieval system, or transmitted, in any form or by any means,
electronic, mechanical, photocopying, recording, or otherwise,
without the prior permission of Oxford University Press.

Library of Congress Cataloging-in-Publication Data
Vogt, Katja Maria, 1968–
Law, reason, and the cosmic city: political philosophy in the early Stoa /
Katja Maria Vogt.
p. cm.
Includes bibliographical references and index.
ISBN 978-0-19-532009-1 (hardcover); 978-0-19-992224-6 (paperback)
1. Stoics. 2. Political science—Philosophy. 3. Political
science—Greece—History. I. Title.
B528.V64 2007
188—dc22   2007003542

1 3 5 7 9 8 6 4 2

Printed in the United States of America
on acid-free paper

To my parents

Acknowledgments

I would like to thank my colleagues at Columbia University for their encouragement and support of this project. My special thanks go to Wolfgang Mann: I have benefited enormously from his advice and many conversations about ancient philosophy during the past years, as well as from his extensive comments on several versions of the manuscript. The readers from Oxford University Press provided very valuable comments, more extensive and well-meaning than I could have hoped for. Their notes have been very much appreciated and made me think more thoroughly through the spectrum of perspectives readers might bring to this book. John Cooper, David Sedley, and Gisela Striker have each furthered the book by generously taking time for discussion of some of my ideas, which helped me arrive at a more precise understanding of what I wanted to say. I would also like to thank Stephen Menn, who commented in a very constructive way on the second chapter. Stephanie Beardman kindly read the fourth chapter and gave very insightful comments. Elisabeth Scharffenberger has been extremely generous in helping me translate some particularly difficult passages in Philodemus.

To Columbia University I am indebted for the Chamberlain Fellowship in 2006, which made it possible for me to devote myself fully to completing this book. A Summer Research Grant from Columbia University in 2004 enabled me to present and discuss earlier versions of the first two chapters with Francesca Alesse, Anna Maria Ioppolo, and Emidio Spinelli at La Sapienza in Rome. Their feedback has been very valuable to me. I have presented an "ancestor" of some sections of the first chapter at talks at a conference in Bonn, Germany, and at the New School in New York and would like to thank both audiences for questions and feedback.

An earlier, and in some ways different, version of my discussion of the role of the Sceptics in transmitting Stoic political philosophy has appeared in the *Zeitschrift für Philosophische Forschung* (2005). An article on a core piece of testimony on Stoic cosmopolitanism was published in *Antike Philosophie Verstehen* (2006); this earlier article addresses some particulars about this fragment that I am not taking up in the same way in this book.

My interest in Stoic ethics goes back to a seminar I took in 1992 with Michael Frede and Gerhard Seel. I learnt much at this seminar, and am especially grateful to Michael Frede, whose way of engaging with ancient philosophy has been inspiring to me. I am also indebted to Friedo Ricken, my teacher in Munich, whose tireless and precise feedback on earlier projects, and whose attitude as a scholar have deeply shaped my work. During my time at the Humboldt-Universität in Berlin, Christof Rapp offered me the opportunity to coteach a graduate seminar in which I presented some of my research on Stoic ethics; I am grateful to him for the invitation to do so and for his continued support of my work over many years. Michael Bordt kindly invited me to teach a graduate seminar on Stoic ethics in Munich when the book manuscript was nearly completed. His own interest and the very well-prepared group of students who attended the class made it a wonderful occasion for me, and a valuable one for testing some of my ideas in front of a lively audience.

Patrick Glauthier, Andrew Hall, Erica Meltzer, Christiana Olfert, and Jonathan Rick have helped me prepare the manuscript for publication; I am grateful for their willingness to take on this task, and to perform it as well as they did.

Finally, my deepest thanks go to Jens Haas, for his stern and unwavering criticism of everything I write.

Contents

Law, Reason, and the Cosmic City

Introduction

Early Stoic political philosophy is famous for adopting a cosmopolitan perspective. The Stoics do not confine their discussion to the constitution of one particular state, but instead focus on the *community of all human beings*. Early Stoic philosophy is further associated with the origins of what eventually developed into the natural law tradition. The Stoics envisage a *law that applies to everyone*, a law that is fundamentally different from the various laws that regulate life in particular political states. The Stoics thus seem to develop two ideas—cosmopolitanism and the notion of the common law—that have been of major importance in the history of political thought.

At the same time, attempts to present the early Stoics as cosmopolitanists and early proponents of a natural law theory might run the risk of reading the texts too anachronistically. Do not the Stoics, when they discuss life in the world as our 'city' (polis), propose an ethical ideal of life in agreement with nature, rather than a cosmopolitanist theory in any recognizable sense? And do they not identify the law with Zeus? Especially with a view to the physical side of Stoic thought on the law and the cosmic city, we are well advised to hesitate and emphasize the ways early Stoic political thought is foreign to later traditions in political philosophy. But at the same time, we should not neglect those aspects of the Stoic theory that *are* relevant to later developments in political philosophy, and that make original contributions regarding questions that we still view as important to this field.

The early Stoics may justly be counted among the ancestors of natural law theory. One basic respect in which the Stoic conception of the law is related to later thought on natural law is that, according to the Stoics, the common law *applies* to all human beings and has a status that is on an altogether different plane from the particular, historical laws of any given state. If we take this to be the core intuition of natural law theories, then we should refer to the Stoics as important early proponents of such a position. But the Stoics also identify the law with Zeus, conceived as a *corporeal god*. This idea certainly drops out of the natural law tradition. Further, natural law theory is arguably concerned with a *body of laws*, while, as I shall argue, the Stoics are not. According to the Stoics, the law is something like a 'force of nature.' It is prescriptive, but not in the way a body of rules is. What the law prescribes that we do is what Zeus commands us to do. But, according to Stoic physics (i.e., natural philosophy), Zeus *is* reason—the prefect reason of the cosmos. To act lawfully is to act as perfect reason commands, and the task of becoming virtuous is the task of acquiring perfect reason oneself, so that our decisions for action are lawful commands issued to ourselves. The prescriptions of the law are thus not set up by a divine authority for us to adhere to, neither as a code of laws nor as particular prescriptions. The agent who deliberates perfectly—be it a god or a human sage—issues commands to herself when deciding what to do, and these commands have the status of law.

Similar considerations apply to Stoic cosmopolitanism. The Stoics develop ideas that are of great philosophical interest, and that are in various ways related to later conceptions, but they are not offering, in any straightforward way, an 'early version' of theories we are familiar with through later traditions. The Stoics *are* cosmopolitanists. They are not, however, cosmopolitanists in the sense of calling for the establishment of either a worldwide state or worldwide political institutions. The city in which all human beings live need not be created; it *is* the world. The 'cosmic city' is not an ideal; it is a reality. Like Stoic thought about the law, Stoic cosmopolitanism is, to some extent, a physical and a theological theory. The cosmos is inhabited by *all* rational beings who live in it, including the *gods*. But the Stoics are still cosmopolitanists in a sense that is relevant to more recent thought on these matters. They argue that *all* human beings are bound together by *belonging to the same city*, and thus they propose that there is a community of all human beings in a very substantial sense. This community goes beyond the idea that all human beings have, as human beings, one way of leading a good life, and also beyond Aristotle's observation that, even when we meet a total stranger, we feel somehow related to him, in a way that is due to the mere fact that he, too, is a human being.

It is a well-known idea in political philosophy that the boundaries of states delimit those to whom we owe a special kind of concern, or even any concern at all. In a sense, the Stoics rely on this idea. According to them, we must understand that we *already* live in one state together with all other human beings; they propose that we consider the concerns of all others who live with us in this world as relevant to our actions. Each human being is a different part of the cosmos. The boundaries of family and city in the ordinary sense matter with respect to where, precisely, we happen to be placed, and this is relevant to which particular action is appropriate for us at a given moment; however, they are not boundaries of what needs to be considered in deliberation. Appropriate action is action that takes the concerns of all human beings to be relevant considerations. The virtuous agent takes a worldwide perspective, and at the same time, in a given situation, she regards her particular roles and her station in life as relevant to her actions.

Stoic cosmopolitanism is neither an 'impartialist' nor a 'partialist' theory. Like other ancient philosophers, the Stoics think in terms of *affiliation* with others. It is through an *affective* and *relational* disposition that we act as we should, and the task of virtue is to acquire this disposition. Like Plato, the Stoics propose a way to extend our affiliation. In their case, however, the scope is not that of a particular city, but that of the cosmic city. And Stoic thought on the emotions has significant implications for the vexing question of whether one *can feel* affiliated with everyone. Emotions are, famously, not part of the ideal life as conceived by the Stoics. We are to overcome all emotions (*pathê*), and thus, affiliation of the ordinary kind, which goes along with grief, pride, desire, and so on. The ideal of affiliation with all others envisages an affective disposition, but a *perfectly rational* one, to be understood in terms of the good feelings (*eupatheia*) of the sage. The Stoics ask us to give up on the partial, 'emotional' affiliations that structure so much of our political lives. But their ideal is not that we take an *unaffiliated*, 'neutral' stance toward everyone. It is to be *as* affiliated with the most distant Mysian (as an ancient critic puts it) as with our relatives and compatriots, but to be so in a way that is based wholly on reason.

Stoic cosmopolitanism and the Stoic conception of the common law differ in significant ways from later theories that use similar terminology. To some scholars, however, the Stoic conceptions seem to be not only partially foreign to later political thought, but really not part of *political* philosophy at all. If cosmopolitanism is about a large living being, the cosmos, with us as its parts, and if the common law is a physical force pervading it, then what could these conceptions possibly contribute to political thought? Are the Stoics, then, proposing *physical* theories? We may rephrase this concern, focusing on the ethical side of these ideas. If Stoic cosmopolitanism is about an ideal of being a perfect part of the world and about adherence to the law by striving to perfect one's reason, are these conceptions not most plausibly understood as proposing ideals for individual agents? Either way, it may appear difficult to see how early Stoic thought on law and the city is political philosophy of a recognizable sort.

It is worthwhile to pause and ask what should legitimately count as political philosophy. In scholarly debates on Stoic philosophy, it sometimes seems as if we had only two options. Either we ascribe a political theory about the ideal constitution, the best laws, and the just state to the Stoics, or we subscribe to the view that, ultimately, the ideal of living in the cosmos as its citizen is an ethical ideal, concerned with the good life of an individual agent, an ideal that is tied to a physical theory of the cosmos as a living being. But why should a theory only be called 'political philosophy' if it is concerned with the best (i.e., ideal or just) constitution and laws? If this is the conception of political philosophy we presuppose, then, according to the interpretation I shall defend, the early Stoics indeed do not pursue political philosophy. These questions do not seem to be their central concerns. However, it does not seem to me that we should take this view of what deserves to be called political philosophy.

The early Stoics work out conceptions that, while differing in important ways from more familiar ideas in political philosophy, address *questions* we regard as central to this field, questions about the scope of our political concern and the nature of law. I shall offer an interpretation that considers early Stoic thought on the cosmos as a city, and on the common law, as a genuine contribution to *political* philosophy. This interpretation, of course, would be implausible if it were stipulated that early Stoic political philosophy be an independent and clearly delineated field within Stoicism. It is a commonplace in the interpretation of ancient philosophy to point to the deep connection of ethics and political philosophy. Like Plato or Aristotle, the Stoics discuss political ideas without actually marking a sharp distinction between ethics and political philosophy. What is more, the Stoics are famous for putting forward theories that are *all* interrelated in very fundamental ways, and that all rely on a set of core conceptions such as reason, nature, and wisdom. The key notions of Stoic political thought—law, reason, nature, cosmos, god—are in fact highly relevant to *all* of Stoic philosophy. I shall thus attempt an interpretation of early Stoic political philosophy as a typical field of Stoic thought, a field that is deeply tied to other areas of Stoic philosophy. More specifically, I shall argue that early Stoic political philosophy contributes significantly to our understanding of the Stoic conception of *wisdom*, the relationship of theology and ethics as the Stoics see it, as well as the Stoic theories of appropriate action and of how we are to regard all others as belonging (*oikeion*) to us.

An important purpose of this book thus is to *relocate* early Stoic political philosophy—from the margins of what we perceive as early Stoic philosophy to a position closer to its center. The testimony regarding early Stoic political philosophy begins to make much more sense, and proves to be considerably more interesting, once we see how intricately it is connected with core Stoic ideas about wisdom, appropriate action, affiliation with all other human beings, god, and reason. And the core conceptions of early Stoic political philosophy—the conception of the *common law*, and the conception of the *cosmic city*—are much more plausibly interpreted if we do not think of them as located in some side-branch of Stoic philosophy, seemingly disconnected from the rest of Stoic thought, but rather as ideas that are integral to our understanding of such central concepts of Stoic philosophy as nature, cosmos, wisdom, and reason.

But why should one be tempted to sideline early Stoic political philosophy in the first place? When we survey the testimony on early Stoic political philosophy, it seems that the Stoics were at least as interested in issues like incest and anthropophagy as in the notions of the city and the law. They seem to have put forward numerous views that their contemporaries considered shocking and shameful, and that their own followers within the Stoic school sought to delete from the records. If we attempt to assess the status these *disturbing theses* (as I shall call them) had within Stoic thought on the basis of the amount of information we have about them, it may seem that they are at the heart of Stoic philosophy—that they tell us what life in the cosmic city is like. The worst caricature that can be constructed from this is roughly the following: the Stoics envisage an ideal city, and life in this city is centrally characterized by the eating of human flesh, marriages within families, and other such scandalous arrangements.

Some scholars who do not find attractive the idea of the Stoic sage enjoying meals prepared from human flesh, marrying his mother, not bothering to properly bury his parents, and so on, have attempted to get around the disturbing theses by attributing them to a Cynic phase of Zeno or to Zeno's youthful foolishness when writing his *Republic*. If this approach were justified, we could just leave these matters aside and turn directly to a discussion of the Stoic conceptions of the law and cosmic city. But while such strategies for dealing with the disturbing theses go all the way back to antiquity, they do not hold up. Chrysippus proposes the same kinds of ideas, and so does Zeno in books other than his *Republic*.

In chapter 1, I offer a reassessment of the disturbing theses. They portray neither the institutions of an ideal city nor the rules for life in it nor the kinds of actions that are indifferent because only virtue 'counts.' While it is easy to make such interpretations seem implausible to begin with—by presenting them in this somewhat overstated way—it is not so easy to see in detail why these interpretations, and a range of related views, misrepresent some fundamental aspects of Stoic ethics. As I shall suggest, testimony on early Stoic political philosophy has a quite fascinating and at the same time highly distorted history. This history is due in part to the polemical strategies of authors like Philodemus, but, most important, to an accident of transmission. However, this accident is interesting in its own right, at least insofar as we conceive of Hellenistic philosophy as shaped by the engagement of the different 'schools' with each other. The Sceptics took an extraordinary interest in Stoic claims about how it might be unproblematic to eat one's own amputated leg or to marry within one's family.[1] Such claims can

---

[1] I shall use the term *Sceptics* to refer both to Pyrrhonian and Academic Sceptics. However, we shall mostly be concerned with Pyrrhonian Sceptics.

be put next to the lawless ways of life of creatures like the Cyclopes. They lend themselves outstandingly well to Sceptic arguments that draw on the crassness of this or that idea about life—both because they conflict with appearances, understood as 'our normal life,' and because they conflict with practically all other philosophical views about the good life. What could be better suited for the Sceptic who wants to induce suspension of judgment on how to live? The disturbing theses make their appearance not in one but in numerous Sceptic arguments that lead to suspension of judgment on questions about the good life. And as a result, we have—compared to how little we have on nearly everything else in early Stoic philosophy—abundant testimony on these matters.

Schofield identifies the Sceptic origin of the bulk of the sources on the disturbing theses.[2] Even though Schofield himself does not draw this conclusion, his study, I shall suggest, opens the way for assessing the disturbing theses as misrepresentative of the theoretical core of the Stoic theory. Once we see how vital reference to the disturbing theses is to Sceptic suspension of judgment on questions about the good life, we can understand where we should situate these claims. They are more important in Sceptic than in Stoic philosophy. The history of the testimony suggests that some of the disturbing theses were nothing more than *examples and illustrations* in the Stoic texts themselves, but that they became integral to philosophical *argument* for the Sceptics.

Nonetheless, we do need to explain how the Stoics can claim that courses of action that seem horrific to their audience are unproblematic. However, it is one thing to consider such views as the core of a theory and quite another to think that, in the end, the theory will have to be interpreted so as to make room for such claims. This assessment leads us into the Stoic theory of appropriate action (*kathêkonta*). As I shall argue, a claim like 'it is not out of place to φ' needs to be understood as 'there can be a situation in which it is appropriate to φ.' It does *not* mean that to φ is generally permissible, 'morally indifferent,' or prescribed. The thesis that the disturbing theses need to be related to the theory of appropriate action is not new. But scholarly work about early Stoic political philosophy often proceeds on the assumption that we have a solid understanding of

---

[2] *The Stoic Idea of the City* (London: Cambridge University Press, 1991).

this theory. However, the way we interpret early Stoic political philosophy depends on the actual *details* of our reconstruction of this doctrine, not just on an overall understanding of some of its main ideas. In chapter 1, I offer a first, brief sketch of Stoic thought on these matters. The details of what it means to consistently act appropriately, and thus wisely, are then pursued throughout the rest of this book.

Discussion of the disturbing theses also invites reflection about Stoic *method*, and this will help to set up a framework for some of the assumptions of my overall interpretation. One needs to explain how the disturbing theses, if they play but a secondary role, could have gained at least enough initial prominence to have been picked up by the Sceptics. As I shall argue, the Stoics' predilection for presenting their views in a way that is deliberatively *counterintuitive* prepares the ground for the Sceptics' exploitation of Stoic 'monstrosities.' Like the Stoic paradoxes, the disturbing theses aim at emphasizing the revisionary nature of Stoic philosophy.

Yet one of the disturbing theses is quite obviously different from the others: Zeno says that only the sages are citizens, friends, relatives, and free, while all others are personal and public enemies, slaves, and alienated. It is evident how this claim could appear just as revolting as the idea of eating one's own leg—it makes parents and siblings into enemies, and practically everyone into a slave. But the structure of this thesis is different from claims about anthropophagy or incest: at this point Zeno is explaining the notion of *wisdom*. In epistemology and ethics, the figure of the sage, and thus the notion of wisdom, are the Stoics' core tools for developing their theories. It is through the figure of the sage that we see which impressions one should assent to; we understand what opinions and emotions are by learning why the sage does not have them; it is through the conception of the sage that the Stoics explain things such as how appropriate and correct action differ. By claiming that only the sages are citizens, friends, relatives, and free, Zeno declares that being a citizen, a friend, a relative, and free are *achievements of reason*—to perfect one's reason *is* to become a citizen, a relative, a friend, and free. I begin to explore this core thesis of early Stoic political philosophy in chapter 2.

The first component of Zeno's thesis, that only the sages are citizens (S), directly leads us into a central question in the interpretation of

Zeno's *Republic*, and (as I argue) of early Stoic political philosophy in general: does the claim that only the sages are citizens mean that Zeno's ideal city is a city of sages? Most scholars have thought that the answer must be yes. Even though it is slightly odd to think of a little city of sages somewhere in the cosmos, and similarly odd to think of a few sages scattered over the world as somehow making up their own city, it has seemed to scholars that (S) decides the question. How else could only the sages be citizens, if not insofar as there is a city of sages? As I shall argue, the Stoics employ a complex set of intuitions about cities. In one sense, a city consists of its citizens, and similarly, the city the Stoics discuss is constituted by those parts of it that have perfect reason. But in another sense, citizenship is the *best* status that is available in a political community in which many others also live who have a *lower* status. All human beings who are not wise have this lower status—they belong to the community the cosmos comprises, but they are not its citizens. To be a citizen is to have, as it were, the *full* status of belonging to the city. The cosmos as a city has citizens: the sages and gods. But there are also those who belong to the city without being its citizens, those who merely inhabit the city and have a lower status within it.

According to Plutarch, Zeno says that *we should regard all human beings as our fellow-citizens* (H). This piece of testimony is very controversial; it does not fit in with the view that Zeno envisages a city of sages. Together with the fact that Zeno is not attested to have spoken of a 'cosmic city,' this apparent discrepancy has led some scholars to think that early Stoic political philosophy undergoes a development—Zeno conceives of a city of sages, whereas Chrysippus thinks of a cosmic city. But on the interpretation of (S) that I shall offer, we can see that (S) and (H) are consistent. Only the sages are citizens of the cosmos. But all human beings are each other's fellow-inhabitants of the cosmos, or citizens in a lesser sense. There is, as I shall argue, no need to assume that Chrysippus discusses a different kind of city than Zeno (even though, of course, their views are likely to have differed, in emphasis and in detail). Throughout early Stoic philosophy, there seem to be *both* a concern with being a perfect part of the world—the aspect of the theory which is addressed in (S)—*and* a concern with a worldwide community of all human beings—the aspect that is discussed in (H).

As I shall argue, the task of seeing all others as one's fellow-inhabitants of the cosmos is deeply related to the task of *oikeiôsis* or affiliation. It is through (H) that Stoic political theory addresses how one should try to see *all* others, and how one should relate to them. And it is through (H) that we can come to understand a further dimension of *oikeiôsis*: we should not only come to see all others as 'belonging to us,' but we should come to see them and us as parts of a single *community* regulated by a *common law*. To live by this common law, as we shall see, is to act consistently as reason commands. Reason commands appropriate action, and appropriate action deals with things like health, life, wealth, strength, and their opposites, that is, with the things that, according to the Stoics, are indifferent, but have *value* and *disvalue*. Indifferents are irrelevant to happiness, but they are *relevant to action*. They provide us with considerations for deliberation. Once we fully understand how we are to see others, we can see that the lawful life takes not only *our own* health or illness, wealth or poverty, and so on into account but also the health, illness, wealth, poverty, and so on of *all that belongs to us*, that is, of all human beings. In this way, the common law quite literally 'ties others to us'; it makes consideration of their concerns pertain to us, because, ultimately, they are *our* concerns. In chapter 2, I discuss the worldwide community that the Stoics envisage. But since human beings can make progress with respect to virtue and wisdom, and can eventually perfect their reason, one can be a member of this community in different ways. But one is its *citizen* only as a being with perfect reason—a sage or a god.

Thus in chapter 3, I turn to the sages and the gods. In order better to understand what (S) means—that only the sages are citizens, friends, relatives, and free—we must, I suggest, discuss some basic questions about the Stoic conception of *wisdom*. And since not only the sages but also the gods are wise, we must also study the conception of *citizen-gods*. Chrysippus famously says that Zeus is, with respect to virtue, not superior to any human sage, and that in fact, Zeus himself is wise. However, while the gods are wise, they are not sages—they are physically different kinds of beings. And because this is so, we cannot reduce talk of the citizen-gods to talk about the sages. We need to engage *both* with the conception of sages and with the conception of citizen-gods.

The Stoics reserve practically every form of expertise for the sage—the sage is the only soothsayer, priest, judge, magistrate, king, and so on. The thesis that only the sages are citizens, friends, relatives, and free follows the same pattern. Claims of this kind, I shall argue, both explicate the notion of wisdom and relocate and reinterpret the relevant term in the theory of the soul. Whatever it is that is ascribed solely to the sage is one *application* of his perfect state of mind or one aspect of what it *means to be wise*. Accordingly, the Stoics reinterpret these terms drastically, but not without preserving some continuity between the conventional and the technical use of the term: to be a citizen is, both in Greek poleis and in the cosmic city, to be a full member of the community. To be a relative is, both in the traditional and in the Stoic sense, a relationship of belonging. The claim that only the sages are relatives means that only they *fully belong* to the cosmos or to what is best about the cosmos—reason.

This idea of a full integration with the reason of the cosmos, and a 'full belonging' to it, is obviously difficult. Human beings are parts of the cosmos, no matter what they do. So what does it mean to become, as it were, a better part of the cosmos? It is at this point that I turn to the Stoic conception of citizen-gods. While scholars do not deny that the Stoics talk of the gods as citizens, they do not explore this *as a claim of physics*. And we might think that if early Stoic political philosophy is indeed about such obscure ideas as citizen-gods, we are unable to see how we could possibly gain anything philosophically interesting from studying it. However, the interpretation I propose tries to make a case for finding the conception of citizen-gods and its physical details illuminating. The gods— that is, *corporeal portions of Zeus*—provide us with a model of what it means to be fully integrated into nature. Some of the Stoic gods are the planets. They are exemplars of 'self-action' (*autopragia*): they move by their own reason in a way that is fully in tune with the order of nature. And they are, in a complete sense, parts of the perfect reason that pervades the cosmos. In them, we have a physical model of what the Stoics mean when they speak about a lawful life and an 'easy flow of life.'

We now have an idea of how the Stoics conceive of the cosmos as a city. The world is an inhabited place and a place that is regulated by the law. The conjunction of these two ideas makes the world a city. This city creates a community of all rational beings who live in it, that is, all human beings and the gods. But it also sets up an ideal for us: to become one of its full citizens. The law regulates the cosmos, and thus it ties all human beings together. But the law is identified with *perfect reason*, not with reason. A human being who is not wise does not live up to the law; she does not live a lawful life. The ideal of citizenship is thus also an ideal of being able to live lawfully. But what does this mean?

In chapter 4, I turn to the Stoic conception of the common law, and I suggest that it is best approached through the Stoic identification of law and reason. The cosmos is perfectly reasonable, as is the sage. But human beings, if they have not achieved wisdom, are not—they have reason, albeit in a way that, compared to perfect reason, is deficient. They are rational insofar as they have acquired, by natural processes, so-called preconceptions, and thus a basic orientation in the world. To be rational is to have preconceptions, notions that are in need of much refinement, but that nevertheless provide a basic grasp of things. To be rational also means to be able to 'move *by* oneself.' The actions of a human being are set off by assent to impressions that present courses of action as appropriate (or: 'to-be-done'). Human beings can assent or not assent to such impressions, and thus decide for or against doing something. And before they assent to an impression that presents a course of action as 'to-be-done,' they consider the taking and rejecting of indifferents, and assent to impressions about the situation they are in. To make progress toward reason, virtue, or wisdom is to improve one's understanding of the role of things that are relevant to action within a natural life. The wise person, who *has* mastered this understanding, assents only to impressions that present courses of action that are *in fact* appropriate. By assenting to these impressions, *her* reason issues a command to *herself*, and, as a prescription of *perfect* reason, this command has the status of law.

The bulk of chapter 4 is devoted to the question of how precisely the law, as the Stoics conceived it, is prescriptive. The interpretation I offer has two components. First, the sage's assent has, insofar as it issues from the consistent disposition of perfect reason, a law-like quality. Perfect reason is law, insofar as every decision made by a perfectly reasonable being (in the sense of: a being with perfect reason) has the status of law. Second, the law is *substantive*, insofar as the sage's assent is based on an understanding of the facts of nature that matter to human action. It is substantive in a way that is exactly parallel to the way reason is substantive. To be rational is to have naturally acquired notions of how things are (the preconceptions), and to be perfectly reasonable is to have perfected these notions, so as to have achieved a full understanding of things. To be rational with respect to action is to have naturally acquired notions of what is relevant to action, and of what we should concern ourselves with in deliberation. To be perfectly reasonable is to have perfected these notions. The lawful life is the life in agreement with nature, and our interpretation of the Stoic conception of the law must recognize the substantive side of this ideal.

With this interpretation, I am challenging two approaches that have figured prominently in recent debates about the Stoic conception of the law. One of these, which I call the rules-interpretation, argues that the law is prescriptive insofar as it consists of laws or rules, and thus is something like a legal code. This approach does not, I shall argue, do justice to the ways the Stoics discuss appropriate action: it is particular actions, not types of actions or pursuits of valuable things, that are appropriate. The competing approach, which I call the prescriptive-reason interpretation, recognizes this fact and focuses on the way the sage's reason prescribes particular actions. This interpretation, however, neglects the substantive side of the Stoic theory. As I shall argue, the Stoics do not envisage laws or rules, at least not as elements of ideal deliberation (nor as part of the progressing fool's deliberation, since the progressor should aim at being wise). But they do offer a substantive account of how we should live—an account that is spelled out through their theory of value.

As I shall argue, the law, as the Stoics conceived it, is prescriptive in two ways—with respect to the normative force of decision-making and with respect to the way it prescribes the relevant considerations for action. In each decision for action, the agent tells herself what she should be doing; if she is wise, the command her reason issues has the status of law. But the sage's decision is also perfect with respect to the deliberative route that leads up to her decision for action. The sage is perfect in taking into account everything that counts as a relevant consideration, in 'selecting and deselecting' indifferents. Things that are of value and disvalue—that is, health, wealth, life, illness, poverty, death, and so on—are these indifferents, and they provide the relevant considerations for action. It is important to note that not only the *agent's* health, illness, wealth, poverty, life, death, etc., make up these relevant considerations. Rather, the health, illness, wealth, poverty, life, death, etc., of all those who *belong to* the agent matter. It is at this point that we can see how the Stoic conception of the law is interconnected with the conception of the cosmic city: to act lawfully and in a manner that is in agreement with nature includes considering everyone as belonging to oneself, and thus regarding everyone's concerns as relevant to oneself.

The law is a law by nature. Nature guides us, from the moment of birth, to acquire early notions of what is harmful and beneficial, and what is appropriate; it is part of the development of coming to live a natural life to refine these notions. The law is also by nature insofar as it is a natural force, identified with reason, which pervades the cosmos. But the epithet the Stoics choose for the law is not 'natural.' Rather, they talk of the *common* (*koinos*) law. The law is common insofar as what is of value and of disvalue for human beings are facts about human life within the cosmos. While each agent needs to deliberate in any given situation with a view to whatever is relevant to the particular situation, all agents are nevertheless tied together by one substantive guide on what kinds of things are to be selected and deselected. *We can only follow the law by becoming wise ourselves.* Even though the law is identified with Zeus, that is, the reason of the cosmos, Zeus (or reason) does not set up a law external to us for us to adhere to. The task is not to understand what the reason of the cosmos, *as distinct from one's own reason*, commands. The task is to become a fully integrated part of the reason of the cosmos, in order to command to oneself lawful action in each and every decision for action.

By identifying the law with the reason of the cosmos, the Stoics return to one of the oldest political questions of antiquity: how do a life according to nature and a life according to the law relate? This question is perceived, as we may observe in a wide range of Greek literature, as engaging with the *value* of law and, at the same time, as concerned with the deficiencies of each particular law, deficiencies that arise from the generality of law and the contingencies of culture and historical circumstances. Anyone who defines the end (*telos*) as life in agreement with nature, as the Stoics do, and who is well versed in these debates, as the Stoics certainly are, must address the question of how life in agreement with nature relates to the law. According to the Stoics, life in agreement with nature *is* life in agreement with the law. The natural life is not a *lawless* life, or an extrapolitical life, in the sense of a life outside of the political community of the polis. Rather, life in agreement with nature is the only truly lawful life, and it *is* a life in a city—the only real city. The Stoics argue that an agent who does not recognize the laws of her particular city as what ultimately determines the appropriateness of actions does not opt 'for nature' and 'against the law.' Rather, she recognizes that nature itself sets up a law for us to adhere to, and that this law is common to all human beings. This law does not break down into a legal code, but like a legal code, it determines for every nontrivial action whether this action is appropriate or not.

Before I begin to argue for this view, a few words on the protagonists of this study. I shall be concerned with the early Stoics, and most important, Zeno of Citium (334/3–262/1 BCE), the founder of Stoicism, as well as the second and third major figures of Stoic thought, Cleanthes (331/0–230/29 BCE) and Chrysippus (c. 281–c. 208 BCE). At times I shall turn to later Stoics, either because they seem to present ideas that are, at least partly, in agreement with earlier Stoic thought— as is the case with Diogenes (c. 240–c. 150), who was a student (or student's student) of Chrysippus, and Hierocles (fl. c. 100 CE)— or because certain texts have been taken to be relevant to the interpretation of earlier views, as is the case with some writings by the first-century Roman Stoic Seneca. Not a single treatise by one of the early Stoics is preserved, and research on their work is fraught with well-known difficulties. It is an obvious and conscious simplification to talk about 'early Stoic philosophy.' Zeno, Cleanthes, and Chrysippus are standardly considered its main figures. However, some other Stoics, like Sphaerus (third century BCE), may have been quite important, too, while still others, like Aristo (c. 320–c. 240 BCE), a student of Zeno, disagree on substantive points and thus might have shaped the development of Stoic thought by provoking further discussion.[3]

---

[3]The Stoics do not seem to have had a 'school' in the sense of property they owned. And they thus might not have had 'heads of the school' in quite the same way other so-called schools did. Zeno, Cleanthes, and Chrysippus thus are probably not 'successors'

Cleanthes, Chrysippus, and other Stoics seem to understand themselves as adherents of Zeno's views. But it is difficult to tell whether, at some points, they merely *present* themselves in this way. A Stoic might do a wide range of things while referring to Zeno: he might spell out a Zenonian tenet in more detail, rephrase it in what he takes to be elucidating terms, develop a new metaphor, integrate a response to an objection by refining the theory, offer an original theory of his own that he takes to be in agreement with the other parts of the theory that have already been developed by Zeno, and so on. Thus, when we speak of an 'orthodox' Stoic view, this must be done with caution. A view that is in agreement with Zeno's philosophy might substantially add to it, and it might, while still taking itself to be in agreement with Zeno's thought, be a 'defense' of it that modifies the earlier doctrine. This is one of the ways we should, I think, envisage development within early Stoicism. Another point to consider is that the individual Stoics seem to have had different philosophical interests and thus seem to have put more or less effort into this or that field in philosophy; and perhaps, related to this, we should also assume that they had what one might call different 'philosophical temperaments' (consider Chrysippus's pronounced interest in logic, which is, in the sources, sometimes tied to his love of puzzles and technical intricacies). Finally, thinkers as productive and original as Zeno and Chrysippus might well have changed their minds on some issues over the course of their lives. If we had, for example, several of Chrysippus's treatises, we would surely argue about the development of his thought, just as we do with other major ancient philosophers.

Thus to talk about early Stoic philosophy is a simplification not just because it assumes that (at the very least) three impressively creative thinkers agree on all major questions but also because it assumes that none of them ever changed his mind about anything of relevance. These assumptions are quite artificial, and this needs to be kept in mind at every step. But rather than emphasizing

---

as the heads of such an institution. Rather, they seem to have succeeded each other as leading figures of a school of thought. For a detailed and critical discussion of the various views that have been taken on this matter in the course of scholarship on Hellenistic philosophy, see Ivor Ludlum, "Two Long-Running Myths: A Centralized Orthodox Stoic School and Stoic Scholarchs," *Elenchos* 24 (2003): 33–55.

the artificiality of a notion of early Stoic philosophy, I shall proceed on the understanding that this is a worthwhile construct—because it allows us to work on an overall understanding of the major elements of this philosophy. For the most part, I shall assume that we can sensibly work with such a notion of 'early Stoic philosophy'—if we are prepared to step back from it whenever this seems necessary, leaving room for different versions of a theory, differences in emphasis, changes in perspective, and responses to counterarguments that modify specific aspects of the theory.

1

The Disturbing Theses

Some of the best known texts on early Stoic political philosophy talk about incest and anthropophagy. The Stoics apparently recommend these practices, and dismiss courthouses, traditional education, the institution of marriage, and the importance of burial ceremonies. These are some examples from a range of highly revisionist claims that stand out in the reports on early Stoic political philosophy. However, to anyone who reads these reports within the broad context of Stoic philosophy—and that means anyone who studies Stoic logic, physics, and ethics, and not just the part of ethics that is devoted to political philosophy—it may seem obvious that these claims cannot be the core of *any* field of Stoic philosophy. No matter how prominent they are in the sources, they seem far too specific and concrete to be so central. As far as we know, the study of abstract conceptions—such as nature, god, and reason—is central to all of early Stoic thought. Specific courses of action are mentioned in order to *illustrate* more theoretical explanations of, for example, what it means for human beings to live in agreement with nature. Some Stoic treatises on appropriate action may have consisted largely of discussions about particular courses of action; but even these treatises would build on more general ideas on reason, nature, and so on. Thus many scholars who have devoted much time to the study of early Stoic philosophy have hesitated to deal with the scandalous claims about incest, anthropophagy, and so on that are apparently at the core of early Stoic political philosophy. It would be too out of character for the Stoics to focus, in any field of their philosophy, on such concrete claims.

However, the testimony on these theses—which I call the disturbing theses—plays such a central role in what we know about early Stoic political philosophy that one must either neglect this field or engage with them.[1] As I argue, the study of these claims is very well worth our time. First, it opens the path to reconstructing what I take to be the central teachings of early Stoic political philosophy, teachings that develop the conceptions of the cosmic city and the common law.[2] Our analysis of the disturbing theses bears directly on—and determines, to some extent—how we interpret Stoic thought on the law and the city. Second, the study of these claims helps to shed light on Stoic method—on why, and in what ways, the Stoics highlight the revisionist nature of their ethical theories. Third, such study leads into discussion of wisdom and appropriate action, which, as we shall see, is crucial for the interpretation of early Stoic political philosophy.

The disturbing theses are, for the most important part, reported by Sceptics.[3] The Sceptics are philosophers in their own right, even when they compile long lists of dogmatic claims that, cut out of their context, look like doxography. As I shall suggest, we must take the time to understand how the Sceptics put the disturbing theses to work *within their own philosophy*. The disturbing theses help the Sceptics formulate key arguments for suspension of judgment on whether there is an art of living and on whether there is anything shameful. Not only do the Sceptics *compile* scandalous Stoic theses,

---

[1]Marie-Odile Goulet-Cazé calls these claims, in a nicely suggestive and brief way, the Kynica of the Stoics; *Les Kynica du stoïcisme*, Hermes Einzelschriften vol. 89 (Stuttgart: Franz Steiner Verlag, 2003). But, as I will point out in much detail, the apparent closeness to Cynic philosophy is by no means the most important feature of these claims.

[2]According to the sources, Zeno does not use the notion of the cosmic city. As I will argue, this does not commit us to positing an important shift between Zeno's and Chrysippus's views.

[3]Polemical discussion by other philosophers, Philodemus most important among them, contributes to these theses' fame. However, it is the Sceptics, not Philodemus, who report a wide range of them, and thus have effectively produced the image of early Stoic political philosophy as centering around these claims. Malcolm Schofield was first both to suggest that all four key texts go back to Sceptics and to emphasize the importance of this fact; *The Stoic Idea of the City*, (Chicago: Cambridge University Press, 1991). I am enormously indebted to Schofield's work. He argues that the sources all go back to *Pyrrhonian* Scepticism. Since I shall argue that the Stoic theses have been utilized in a variety of Sceptic arguments, and since I am not sure we can fully trace the history of these arguments, I use the term 'Sceptic' in a broader sense, as I mentioned earlier, to refer both to Academic and Pyrrhonian Scepticism (even though I shall mostly be concerned with Sextus, and thus with Pyrrhonian Scepticism).

thus creating the misleading impression that Zeno and Chrysippus might have written treatises in which these claims were presented in a similar, continuous fashion, but, what is more, some of the Sceptic arguments depend on the impression that these compilations are *Stoic accounts of the art of life*. Once we see that this might be an effect of the Sceptic aim—generating a quite absurd 'art of life' out of whatever 'shocking' ideas they can find in a large array of Stoic texts—we might hesitate to take the phrasing of the claims at face value.[4]

Scholars disagree on whether we should think that the law according to the Stoics is something like a legal code (consisting of laws or rules). If the disturbing theses are general claims on what is permitted, what is to be done, and what has no place in a good life, they provide evidence for the idea that the Stoics propose substantive rules regulating specific spheres of life.[5] But if they are not, and this is what I shall argue, then we might be left without *any* examples of such rules.[6] There are not many contexts in which the Stoics discuss particular ways of acting, and the claim that the Stoic law translates into rules is much more difficult to defend if the disturbing theses cease to be a key point of reference.

As I shall suggest, the disturbing theses are most plausibly interpreted as reflecting Stoic thought on wisdom and as illustrations of more abstract arguments about appropriate and lawful action. Theses

---

[4]I have offered an earlier, much briefer, and in several respects different version of my interpretation on the disturbing theses in "Gibt es eine Lebenskunst? Politische Philosophie in der frühen Stoa und skeptische Kritik," *Zeitschrift für philosophische Forschung* 59 (2005): 1–21, where I defend the view that the common denominator of the Sceptic arguments that frame the lists of disturbing theses is a contrast between theory and everyday life; this emphasis no longer seems to me to be at the core of Sextus's arguments. Further, I did not yet see how the fact that the Sceptics present the Stoic claims as an account of the good life bears on the *phrasing* of the theses, which I now think is a significant and misleading feature of the lists.

[5]They might also provide indirect evidence for the claim that the Stoics conceive of rules: They might formulate *exceptions* to rules (see chapter 4).

[6]Interestingly, even the Sceptics are aware of this. In PH 3.245–249 and M 11.189–196, Sextus argues as if the Stoic art of life could be described through the disturbing theses. But in other places he says that, for the Stoics, the art of life is wisdom, and he goes on to explain that there is no action (in the sense of: no type of action) that is specific to the sage, because anything can be done by sage and fool alike, given that the only difference is that the sage does it from wisdom. See M 11.181 and 199–209.

such as 'education is useless' or 'temples need not be built' should be read in the context of thinking about what being educated and piety *really* are—these are facets of being wise. Theses about incest, anthropophagy, and so on illustrate how, for the Stoics, no type of action is generally forbidden. Zeno and Chrysippus point out that we tend to draw distinctions where there are no relevant differences (i.e., no differences relevant to which course of action is appropriate), and that we should not be held back from doing what reason commands by conventional ideas about what is shameful.

I will proceed as follows. After (section 1) a brief sketch of scholarly views on the disturbing theses, I offer (2 and 3) translations of and commentary on the key texts in which they have been transmitted. This prompts a closer look at (4 and 5) the Sceptic arguments that frame the lists of Stoic claims. Finally, (6) I discuss how the disturbing theses might be designed so as to highlight the revisionary nature of Stoic ethics, and (7) I offer a reassessment of the role of the disturbing theses in Stoic philosophy.

1. The Disturbing Theses and the Reception of Early Stoic Political Philosophy

Let me begin with a cursory summary of the claims I call the disturbing theses: temples, gymnasia, and courthouses need not be built; coinage is unnecessary; only the virtuous are citizens, friends, relatives, and free—everyone else is at war with each other, an enemy, alienated, and a slave; Zeno holds the doctrine of the so-called community of women; men and women are to wear the same dress; no part of the body is to be fully covered; nothing is shameful about incest and other conventionally abhorred sexual actions; if an amputated limb is useful for food, we should eat it; the traditional educational curriculum is useless; no special effort is to be made for one's parents' (or any other) funerals; coinage need not be introduced; it is a matter of discussion how the sage makes his living.[7] These ideas have survived in four lists, two in Diogenes Laertius, the other two in Sextus Empiricus (DL 7.32–34, DL 7.187–189, SE PH

---

[7]This list is not complete, insofar as we know of different versions of some of the theses (especially on sexual matters).

3.245–249, SE M 11.189–196), and some of the material is discussed by Philodemus.[8] Furthermore, a few similar theses are scattered through a variety of works, often in polemical contexts.

The thesis that only the virtuous are citizens, friends, relatives, and free while those who are commonly thought to be citizens, friends, relatives, and free are public and private enemies, alienated, and slaves is notably different from the other claims. It does not address a specific sphere of life or type of action. Rather, it is a typical Stoic paradox, a thesis that seems implausible on the surface and needs to be interpreted as part of the Stoic conception of wisdom. Nevertheless, it is obvious why the thesis fits into the conspectus—it is as scandalous as the other ideas. Any ancient reader would assume that, while not being virtuous and wise, he can be a citizen, a friend, a relative, and free. It is highly offensive to tell 'real-life' fellow-citizens that in fact they are enemies, enslaved, and so on.

While some scholars (perhaps most clearly Paul Vander Waerdt) approach early Stoic political philosophy almost exclusively by focusing on its conceptions of the cosmic city and the common law, the disturbing theses have shaped the reception of early Stoic political philosophy enormously. Basically, we can either adopt the view that these claims make up an important portion of the core of Stoic thought in this field, or we can attempt to marginalize them. Both of these approaches have their difficulties. If we take the disturbing theses at face value as they are reported, we must explain why the Stoics shifted, in this field, into a mode of discussion that is very different from their mode of discussion in all other fields: concrete and specific rather than abstract and general. We must further explain the gap between the very concreteness of the disturbing theses and the abstract theses on law, reason, nature, and the cosmos, which clearly also belong to the core of early Stoic political philosophy. If, on the

---

[8]The text of *De Stoiciis* is transmitted in two papyri: *PHerc.* 155 and *PHerc.* 339, which are edited by T. Dorandi: "Filodemo. Gli Stoici (*PHerc.* 155 e 339)," *Cronache Ercolanesi* 12 (1982): 91–133. This edition comes with an Italian translation and commentary. A French translation and a discussion of Diogenes of Sinope's *Republic* is presented in "La Politeia de Diogène de Sinope et quelques remarques sur sa pensée politique," in *Le Cynisme ancien et ses prolongements*, ed. M.-O. Goulet-Cazé and R. Goulet (Paris: Presses universitaires de France, 1993), 57–68. All passages relating to Diogenes' and Zeno's *Republic* are also presented, in Greek and French, in Goulet-Cazé, *Les Kynica*.

other hand, we marginalize the disturbing theses, we must offer a convincing argument for why this is justified. Traditionally, this approach has been pursued through two ideas (or a mix thereof). First, it has been suggested that these claims derive from Zeno's earliest work and go back, as it were, to his pre-Stoic philosophizing. Second, closely related to the first idea, we might think that these claims reflect an early, *Cynic* period in Zeno's thought.[9]

Let us briefly consider why these suggestions are implausible. Zeno is said to have read books about Socrates before his arrival in Athens, and when he came to Athens, he studied with Crates (DL 7.31–32). According to an anecdote reported by Diogenes, Zeno read through book 2 of Xenophon's *Memorabilia* in a bookstore in Athens; he asked the proprietor where such a man as Socrates could be found and was directed to Crates (DL 7.2–3).[10] Zeno became a student of Crates, and it thus appears possible that, in an early work, he is writing under Crates' influence. Zeno's *Republic* may seem to be such an early treatise, and the theses from the *Republic* that are reported in DL 7.32–34 might betray the Cynic influence. Whatever Zeno's claims precisely mean, they recall ideas we associate with Cynic philosophy.[11] Even though it is arguable whether each of the

---

[9] For testimony on Zeno's *Republic*, see SVF 1.259–271 and Philodemus, *De Stoiciis*, ed. T. Dorandi. See also H. C. Baldry, "Zeno's Ideal State," *Journal of Hellenic Studies* 79 (1959): 3–15, for a list of relevant passages. For an excellent collection of texts relevant to the disturbing theses, see Goulet-Cazé, *Les Kynica*; see also Francesca Alesse, "La *Repubblica* di Zenone di Cizio e la letteratura socratica," *Studi italiani di filologia classica*, 3rd ser., 16.1 (1998): 17–38. I am not offering my own collection of fragments relevant to Zeno's political philosophy, or early Stoic political philosophy in general. As will become clear throughout the book, I regard early Stoic political thought as deeply integrated with major theories in Stoic philosophy, both in ethics and in physics. While I argue that the Stoics engage in genuinely political questions, I do not think that their views in political philosophy are clearly to be separated from many of their views in ethics and physics.

[10] This story is tied to the further anecdote that Zeno was too decent to assimilate himself to Cynic shamelessness (DL 7.3). Interestingly, this report does not fit in well with the idea that Zeno had something like a thoroughly 'Cynic phase' at an early stage of his career. For what it is worth, it contradicts the assumption that Zeno's shameless views arise from a temporary adoption of the general shamelessness of Cynic thinking and attitudes to life.

[11] J. Mansfeld has argued for this claim in an influential article, "Diogenes Laertius on Stoic Philosophy," *Elenchos* 7 (1986): 297–382, 344 and 346; M. I. Finley also emphasizes the closeness to Cynic antinomianism, "Utopianism Ancient and

theses corresponds in detail to ideas we know independently from the Cynics, it seems sufficiently clear that someone could *present* them as propagating a version of antinomianism (abolition of political institutions, traditional customs, cultural institutions, etc.) and thus as similar to Cynic teachings. This similarity, however, may have irritated later Stoics. As Francesca Alesse has argued, we have to assume lively Stoic debate about the history of the school and its Socratic ancestry.[12] The Stoics understand themselves as the true heirs of Socrates. One might assume that this provides them with a good reason to emphasize Zeno's time as Crates' student, but in fact, as Alesse convincingly shows, it does not. Quite to the contrary, the Stoics begin early on to minimize Crates' influence on Zeno, in favor of a much more direct association with Socrates. At best, Crates is allowed to be a link in the chain that connects the Stoics with Socrates, not a philosophical influence on Zeno in his own right. Thus there may have been Stoics who tried to isolate everything that could give the impression that there was a Cynic influence on Zeno, and by doing so provided lists of claims that were then picked up by doxography.[13]

Philodemus's discussion adds to the association of Zenonian and Cynic teachings. Largely due to Philodemus (*De Stoiciis*, col. 15.1–4), Zeno's *Republic* has traditionally been considered a youthful and perhaps foolish work, written under the influence of Cynic philosophy. Philodemus writes in the first century BCE (and thus significantly earlier than both Sextus and Diogenes Laertius, but also significantly later than either Zeno or Diogenes of Sinope), and he may have had copies of both Zeno's *Republic* and Diogenes' *Republic*.[14] But he gives a highly selective, polemical picture of both

---

Modern," in *The Use and Abuse of History* (London: Hogarth, 1975), 188; see also *Sextus Empiricus: Against the Ethicists*, translated with an introduction by Richard Bett (Oxford: Clarendon Press, 2000), 208; all subsequent citations are to this edition. Schofield, *The Stoic Idea*, 10–13, offers a detailed discussion of the individual claims and their relationship to Cynic teachings.

[12]Francesca Alesse, *La Stoa e la Tradizione Socratica* (Naples: Bibliopolis, 2000).

[13]Goulet-Cazé details a number of related, but different, critical Stoic stances toward Zeno's *Republic*. They are concerned, in one way or another, either with minimizing the work's importance or with disputing its authenticity (*Les Kynica*, 15–19).

[14]According to Schofield, there is no evidence that Philodemus had seen Diogenes' *Republic* himself. Schofield suggests that it is likely that Philodemus was drawing only

philosophers.[15] His treatise *On the Stoics* is partly concerned with the refutation of Stoic attempts to explain away the Cynic beginnings of Zeno—Philodemus aligns Zeno and Diogenes, and thus counteracts the Stoic attempts to disassociate Zeno from his Cynic beginnings. He argues that Zeno's *Republic* is genuinely a work by Zeno, and Diogenes' *Republic* by Diogenes, and then goes on to discuss what he ironically calls the 'noble doctrines' of both philosophers.[16]

Does his testimony tell us that Zeno and Diogenes the Cynic share philosophical views? Whatever similarity there is between some Zenonian claims from the *Republic* and Cynic doctrine, even the same wording of some theses would not mean that the rationale Zeno offered for these claims was the same rationale a Cynic would give (witness the so-called community of women—that both Zeno and Plato argue for it by no means makes Zeno a follower of Plato). Thus it is one thing to agree with Mansfeld that a certain closeness to Cynic philosophy is a common denominator of the theses attributed to Zeno in Diogenes Laertius 7.32–34 and quite another to suppose that Zeno and Diogenes share the ideas I am calling the disturbing theses. Later Stoics may well have been irritated at what *appeared* to be close to Cynicism, even though it was a consistent part of Zeno's philosophy if fully understood. Stoic debate over how to present the history of Stoicism is not the same as Stoic debate over

---

on Zeno's *Republic*, while claiming that the material could be found in both books (*The Stoic Idea*, 143–144). Cf. Dirk Obbink, "The Stoic Sage in the Cosmic City," in *Topics in Stoic Philosophy*, ed. Katerina Ierodiakonou (Oxford: Oxford University Press, 2001), 178–195, 183. Goulet-Cazé argues that Philodemus probably had copies of both books; but in her view, this does not make Philodemus a reliable source (*Les Kynica*, 11–27). Much of her study is concerned with pointing out in what ways Philodemus may be tendentious, reporting Stoic and Cynic doctrine deliberately in a highly selective fashion, which is, consequently, distorting.

[15]See Goulet-Cazé, *Les Kynica*.

[16]Philodemus's testimony is, on the whole, primarily useful for questions about the relationship between Zenonian and Cynic philosophy and intra-Stoic debate on Zeno. For the actual reconstruction of the disturbing theses, we need to turn to other sources. Philodemus sets out with a specific aim: to prove that Zeno had a distinctively Cynic phase. Given intra-Stoic debate on the history of the school, this is an effective anti-Stoic move. Philodemus's report on Zeno's *Republic* is highly selective. Philodemus ascribes only one of the disturbing theses directly to Zeno, namely (and without detail), that he discusses sexual activities (*De Stoiciis*, col. 11, p. 100, Dorandi).

a philosophical question. The former debate may be less concerned with truth than with how to present the school within the range of competing philosophical doctrines.

Furthermore, we cannot dismiss the disturbing theses by attributing them to a young man who was yet to develop into the Zeno we are interested in. The easiest way to discard this line of thinking is to draw attention to the fact that only some of the disturbing theses are said to come from Zeno's *Republic*. Others have been taken from later works by him, and still others from a range of treatises by Chrysippus. What is more, doubts can be raised as to whether we should rely on Philodemus's suggestion that the author of the *Republic* was still a foolish youth. As Alesse points out, the relative chronology of Zeno's works that has come down to us may already be a consequence of the Stoic attempt to marginalize anything that reminded readers of Zeno's time as Crates' student.[17] Thus, we cannot even be sure that Zeno's *Republic* is his earliest treatise. So there is clearly no easy way to dismiss the claims about incest, the eating of human flesh, and so on. We have to assume that Zeno and Chrysippus held theories of the cosmic city that, at least under some circumstances, recommended these and other 'shameful' types of action.

Schofield points out that the disturbing theses are mostly preserved by Sceptics. While this is not his proclaimed intention, he thus, as I will argue, identifies a third way that we can rearrange our

---

[17]Alesse, *La Stoa*, 27–36. Andrew Erskine argues that both passages on which the assumption that the *Republic* is a very early work is based (Philodemus, *De Stoiciis*, col. 9, 1–15, and DL 7.4) can be read in the context of the disturbing theses and, thus, do not constitute valid historical evidence; *The Hellenistic Stoa: Political Thought and Action* (Ithaca, N.Y.: Cornell University Press, 1990), 9–15. For a critical discussion of Erskine's argument see Paul Vander Waerdt, "Politics and Philosophy in Stoicism," review of *The Hellenistic Stoa* by Andrew Erskine, *Oxford Studies in Ancient Philosophy* 9 (1991): 185–211, 193–194; compare also Schofield, *The Stoic Idea*, 25.

A further aspect needs to be kept in mind when we consider the association and dissociation of Cynics and Stoics: while later Stoics seem to have had an interest in marginalizing Zeno's time with Crates, critics of the Stoics align Stoics and Cynics. This does not just result in misleading evidence on the Stoics; it may also generate a Stoicized account of the Cynics. For a discussion of such effects see John Moles, "The Cynics and Politics," in *Justice and Generosity: Studies in Hellenistic Social and Political Philosophy*, ed. André Laks and Malcolm Schofield (Cambridge: Cambridge University Press, 1995), 129–158.

picture of early Stoic political philosophy, pushing the disturbing theses away from its theoretical core. Schofield's study opens the path for a reading that ascribes the prominence of these claims to an intense Sceptic interest in them, rather than to a faithful rendering of their status in early Stoic political philosophy. It is this line of thought that I will develop further.

2. The Lists of Disturbing Theses: Diogenes Laertius

We should first note that the disturbing theses differ in their degrees of concreteness and abstraction. Zeno's thesis that only the virtuous are citizens, friends, relatives, and free, which will be central to my discussion in the following chapters, is far more abstract than other claims that are transmitted along with it. It is concerned with the fundamental questions of what citizenship, friendship, being a relative, and freedom *are*. With respect to the rest of the disturbing theses, we might want to distinguish between theses that address institutions and theses that address, broadly speaking, ways of acting.[18] The theses on institutions—temples, courthouses, education, gymnasia—might derive from discussions about piety, the law, virtue, and knowledge, and ultimately the Stoic ideal of wisdom. Hence, they might be closely related to the thesis that only the virtuous (i.e., the sages) are citizens, friends, relatives, and free and might be explicable along similar lines. The theses on ways of acting, however, do not seem to be concerned with wisdom in the same way. The briefest way to describe what is common to them might be this: they claim that conventional judgments on what is scandalous and impious should not hold us back from doing what is appropriate.

It is time to look at the lists of disturbing theses. Two of these lists are transmitted in Diogenes Laertius (one on Zeno, one on Chrysippus), and two in Sextus Empiricus. As a first step, I offer translations and some preliminary commentary.[19]

[18]I am deliberately using this very loose notion so as to avoid talking either of particular actions or of types of action. In chapter 4, I shall discuss in detail whether the Stoics are concerned with particular actions or with types of action.

[19]I am providing here, as in the following three lists, my own translations. These are, however, much indebted to R. H. Hicks's translation for the Loeb Classical

But there are some, and among them Cassius the Sceptic and his followers, who attack Zeno on many points. First they say[20] that in the beginning of his *Republic* he declared general education useless [*achrêston*]; second, that he says that all who are not virtuous are personal and political enemies, slaves, and alienated from one another, including parents from children, brothers from brothers, relatives from relatives. They criticize him again for presenting, in the *Republic*, only those who are virtuous as citizens, friends, relatives, and free (and accordingly, in the view of the Stoics, parents and children are enemies, for they are not wise);[21] that he holds the doctrine [*dogmatizein*], again in the *Republic*, of the community of women, and (in the 200s) that neither temples, lawcourts, nor gymnasia [need to be][22] built in cities;[23] that on coinage he writes as follows, that "it must not be thought that coinage need be introduced for purposes of exchange or for traveling abroad." Further, he commands [*keleuei*] that both men and women wear the same dress and keep no part of the body entirely covered. That the *Republic* is the work of Zeno is attested by Chrysippus in his *On the Republic*. And he has discussed erotic topics in the beginning of that book of his that is entitled *The Art of Love*, but also writes much the same in his *Conversations*. These are the sorts of things to be found in Cassius, but also in Isidorus of Pergamum, the rhetorician, who adds that the passages disapproved by the Stoics were cut out of the books by Athenodorus the Stoic, who was in charge of the Pergamene library; and that afterward, when Athenodorus was detected and compromised, they were put in opposition [or: replaced].[24] So much for the passages in his writings that are regarded as spurious. (DL 7.32–34)

Library (LCL) edition, as well as to Schofield's translation in *The Stoic Idea* and his extensive footnotes on the texts. Diogenes Laertius, *Lives of the Eminent Philosophers*, vol. 2, tr. R. D. Hicks (Cambridge, Mass.: Harvard University Press, 1991).

[20]Reiske suggests *legousin* for the MSS' *legonta*; like Hicks, Schofield, and others, I follow this emendation.

[21]I am here following Schofield's reading of the punctuation (*The Stoic Idea*, 3), which had also been proposed by H. C. Baldry, "Zeno's Ideal State," 4.

[22]See interpretation 3 hereafter.

[23]Note the plural—Zeno does not talk of *one* city. As I shall argue, it is not likely that Zeno discusses a city of sages while Chrysippus discusses a cosmic city, as some scholars think (see chapter 2).

[24]I will discuss this alternative in detail later.

In Diogenes Laertius 7.32–34 we learn about *two* critical stances. (1) Later Stoics disapprove of the Zenonian theses. The Stoic Athenodorus goes so far as to cut out the theses from the manuscripts. (2) Cassius and other Sceptics, who are his students or are in some other sense associated with him, attack Zeno's claims.[25] Obviously, Stoic and Sceptic critiques must differ significantly. If later Stoics disapprove of Zeno's ideas, they adopt a 'dogmatic' perspective, that is, a perspective that goes along with positive claims and assertions. In the case of the Stoic Athenodorus, disapproval is most probably (as Mansfeld argues) based on the apparent closeness of Zeno's theses to Cynic teachings.[26] Given what we know about the Stoic wish to derive their philosophical ancestry directly from Socrates, such censorship seems possible. But the Sceptic critique cannot be thought of as disapproval or dismissal; it must have a specifically Sceptic structure.

The second passage in Diogenes Laertius comes from the report on Chrysippus. It does not seem that the author of the list is primarily concerned with Chrysippus's political philosophy. Rather, he seems to put together anything in Chrysippus that may be considered scandalous. Wachsmuth has suggested that the passage derives from the same source as Diogenes Laertius 7.32–34; Mansfeld has put forward the same thesis, and Schofield adopts it.[27] The most obvious link between both passages consists of the line references (e.g. 'in the 200s'), which are unusual for Diogenes Laertius.

There are those who run down Chrysippus as having written much that is disgusting and unspeakable. For in his work *On the Ancient Natural Philosophers* he puts together a disgusting story about Hera and Zeus, saying in the 600s things that no one would soil his lips by repeating. For they say he makes up this most disgusting story, and

---

[25]This latter attack is tied to a critique the rhetorician Isodorus voiced. Finally, we learn that some regarded the theses as spurious, possibly as a result of such activities as Athenodorus's censorship. This, however, cannot be convincing. It is well attested that Zeno held the claims listed in DL 7.32–34, or similar ones.

[26]J. Mansfeld, "Diogenes Laertius on Stoic Philosophy," *Elenchos* 7 (1986): 344 and 346.

[27]C. Wachsmuth, "Stichometrisches und Bibliothekarisches," *Rheinisches Museum* 34 (1879): 38–51, see 39–42; Mansfeld, "Diogenes Laertius," 344–346; Schofield, *The Stoic Idea*, 5–7.

even if he praises it as a piece of physics, it is more appropriate to
prostitutes than to gods—when it is not even recorded by those who
have written on pictures. It is not to be found in Polemo or Hypsi-
crates, and not even in Antigonus. It is invented by him. Again, in *On
the Republic* he says to have sexual intercourse with mothers and
daughters and sons;[28] and he says the same things also in *On Things
Not to be Chosen for Their Own Sakes*, right at the beginning. In the
third book of his *On Justice* in the 1000s, he commands [*keleuôn*] the
eating of the dead. And in the second book of his *On Life and Making a
Living* he says we should consider how the wise man is to make his living.
And yet for what purpose should he make a living? If it were for the sake
of life, life is indifferent; if for pleasure, that too is indifferent; if for
virtue, that is sufficient in itself for happiness. The ways of making a
living are also ludicrous: for example, being maintained by a king, since
he will have to defer to him; or by a friend, since friendship will then be
bought for gain; or living by his wisdom, for wisdom will then become
mercenary. These are the objections that are made. (DL 7.187–189)

The text can be divided into two parts: a list of disturbing theses
and the discussion of the sage's income. For the latter, we do not get
a line reference. The text enters into substantial discussion that refers
to fundamental Stoic teachings about virtue and the theory of
indifferents. This kind of engagement with arguments, however, is
absent from the rest of the report. Further, the idea that the wise
man must make a living is not contrary to custom in the way, for
example, anthropophagy is. The final section of the text is in fact
highly reminiscent of the discussions Plutarch offers on this issue.
For Plutarch, Chrysippus's ideas on the sage's income are in conflict
with the Stoic theory of indifferents.[29] It thus seems possible that
Diogenes Laertius 7.187–189 ultimately derives from two sources
that adopt different styles of critical examination. The final section
on the sage's income does not seem to belong to the core of the
disturbing theses. It does not address a scandalous Stoic idea; rather,
it aims to point to an inconsistency in Chrysippus's philosophy.

---

[28]I am following Schofield's literal translation: "he says to have sexual intercourse
with." Hicks translates "he permits"; such translations give the misleading impression
that the Stoics formulate rules that prescribe, permit, or prohibit types of action.

[29]See *On Stoic Self-Contradictions* 1043C–1044A and 1047F. In 1043E, Plutarch
names the same three ways of making a living as are reported in DL.

The reports in Sextus Empiricus contain more direct citations and allow us to get a better sense of Zeno's and Chrysippus's theses. But we might pause and ask whether the disturbing theses, as they are attributed to Zeno and Chrysippus in Diogenes Laertius, seem to lay out the institutions for an ideal city and whether they seem to formulate rules of conduct. It might be a natural assumption that at least the latter is the case. However, as we shall see, each of the theses allows for several significantly different interpretations, as follows.

(1) Zeno holds the doctrine of the community of women. It is far from clear what this means. It is unlikely that Zeno endorses a major institution of the ideal city as conceived in Plato's *Republic*, or at least, it is unlikely that he endorses it for the reasons Plato's Socrates adduces. Any Zenonian claim on how sexual relations among un-married partners are not shameful could be reported by claiming that Zeno endorses the community of women (see section 7). (2) Temples, etc., [need not] be built in cities. Where I translate "[need not] be built," we have to supply our own sense to the passive verb. Zeno's claim might originally be a general instruction not to be build temples; this is the reading that assumes that the disturbing theses lay out the institutions and laws of an ideal city.[30] But the claim also might be part of a conditional (e.g., 'if people were genuinely pious, there would be no need to build temples') or of the thesis that temples, *as we know them*, are useless. (3) I have tried to offer a comparatively vague translation of Chrysippus's claims on incest ('says to have sexual intercourse with . . .'). This rendering leaves it open whether Chrysippus generally recommends (or permits) incest, or whether he says that incest can be appropriate.[31] (4) There is only one direct quotation in the lists in Diogenes Laertius: Zeno is reported to say that 'it must not be thought that coinage has to be introduced for purposes of exchange or for traveling abroad.' This thesis is different from, for example, 'there should be no coinage.' Zeno seems to respond to the presumption that, for certain

---

[30]Hicks translates 'prohibits the building of.' Translations of this kind contribute to the impression that we are dealing with a list of rules or laws.

[31]Another view is that incest and anthropophagy are 'recommended,' insofar as the *sage* might rightfully perform these actions. See section 7 and chapter 4 for a detailed discussion of this line of interpretation.

purposes, coinage is necessary, apparently claiming that this is a prejudice. (5) Zeno is said to 'command' that men and women wear the same dress and not keep any part of the body entirely covered. We should note that verbs like 'command' might well be part of the doxographical conventions in reporting political views; they need not go back to the actual wordings of the philosopher's theses.[32] Perhaps Zeno is setting up the rule that men and women *should* wear the same dress. But he might also say that there is no reason for men and women not to wear the same dress. With respect to covering one's body, Zeno might propose a general rule to the effect that one should never cover any part of the body completely (however implausible this may seem). But he might also say something like 'there is no need to keep any part of the body entirely covered.' (6) Similar considerations apply to Chrysippus's 'command' to eat the dead. This might be the general instruction to eat dead human bodies, but it might also, and perhaps much more plausibly, be the instruction to do so in a case where it is appropriate.

3. The Lists of Disturbing Theses: Sextus Empiricus

Let us turn to the relevant passages in Sextus Empiricus.

> Another argument is this. Every art appears to be apprehended through its own, specific products[33] [*erga*] which emerge from it, but there is no specific product of the art of living. . . .
>
> There remains the suggestion that the art of living is apprehended by means of those products which they describe in their books; given that these are many and much alike, I will extract a few of them by way of example. Thus, for instance, Zeno, the founder of their school, says among many other similar things the following about the guidance of

---

[32]For related points compare Goulet-Cazé, *Les Kynica*, 63–65. See also Erskine, *Hellenistic Stoa*, 22 with n. 32, and Dirk Obbink, "The Stoic Sage," 178–195, 182.

[33]The translation of *ergon* is difficult. What is at issue is the activities that go along with each art, but also, in some sense, these activities insofar as they are the products of these arts. For example, if, say, the art of living says one should pray every morning, and people who master the art pray every morning, then praying every morning counts as an *ergon* of the art of living.

children in his *Discourses*[34]: "Have intercourse with one's boy-friend no more and no less than with one who is not one's boy-friend, nor with females [more or less] than with males; for it is not different things, but the same things, that are fitting and appropriate to boy-friend and non-boy-friend, and to females and males." And as concerns piety towards parents, the same man says, with reference to Jocasta and Oedipus, that it was not an awful thing [*deinon*] for him to rub his mother: "If she had been ailing in another part of her body and he had helped her by rubbing it with his hands, there would have been nothing shameful [*aischron*]; if, then, he cheered her up and stopped her suffering by rubbing other parts, and created children that were noble on their mother's side, was that shameful?" And with this also Chrysippus agrees. At least he says in his *Republic*: "I also approve of [*dokei moi*] arranging these matters as is the custom even now among many people, and no bad thing [*ou kakôs*], so that the mother has children with the son and the father with the daughter and the brother with the sister born of the same mother." And he proceeds, in the same treatise, to introduce cannibalism to us. At any rate he says: "and if from a living body a part be cut off that can be used as food, do not bury it or otherwise dispose of it, but consume it, so that from our own parts another part may come into being." And in his book *On What Is Appropriate* he says on the burial of parents in these very words: "When our parents die, we are to use the simplest forms of burial, as though the body—like the nails or teeth or hair—were nothing to us, and we had no need to give any care or attention to a thing like it. Hence, also, when the flesh is useful they will make use of it as food, just as, if one of their own parts were useful, such as an amputated foot, it would be proper for them to use it and similar parts like this; but when the flesh is useless, they will bury it and leave it, or burn it up and leave the ashes, or dispose of them in a more distant spot and pay no more attention to them, like nails or hair."

Of such a kind are most of the things the philosophers say; but they would not dare to put them into practice unless they lived under the laws of the Cyclopses or Laestrygonians. But if they are totally incapable of acting thus, and their actual conduct is common to the laymen, there is no product peculiar to those who are suspected of possessing the art of living. So then, if the arts must certainly be apprehended by means of their specific works, and no work is observed that is specific to the

---

[34]This translation has been suggested by Bett (*Against the Ethicists*, 205) for the parallel passage in M 11 (see hereafter). As Bett points out, this is a work by Zeno (see DL 7.34).

so-called art of living, this art is not apprehended. Therefore, no one can positively say about it that it really exists. (SE PH 3.243–249)[35]

Moreover, every existing art and science is apprehended from the skillful and scientific actions which it gives rise to—medicine, for example, from what is done in medicine, lyre-playing from what is done by the lyre-player, and also painting and sculpture and all similar arts.[36] But the art that is supposedly about living has no actions resulting from it, as we will establish; therefore there is no art of living. Thus, since much is said by the Stoics about the education of children and about honoring one's parents and also piety towards the departed, we will select a few cases from each category for the sake of example and put them forward with a view to constructing our argument.

Well then, about the guidance of children, Zeno, the founder of the school, covers some such points as these in his *Discourses*: "Have intercourse with one's boy-friend no more and no less than with one who is not one's boy-friend, nor with females [more or less] than with males; for it is not different things, but the same things, that are fitting and appropriate to boy-friend and non-boy-friend, and to females and males." And again: "Have you had intercourse with your beloved? I have not. Did you not desire to have intercourse with him? Yes indeed. But though desiring to get him for yourself, were you afraid to ask him? God, no! But did you ask him? Yes indeed. But he didn't submit to you? No, he didn't." And about honoring one's parents, one could cite their blather about sex with one's mother. At any rate Zeno, having put down the things which are recorded about Jocasta and Oedipus, says that it was not an awful thing [*deinon*] for him to rub his mother. "If he had helped her by rubbing her body with his hands when she was sick, there would have been nothing shameful [*aischron*]; if, then, he stopped her suffering and cheered her up by rubbing her with another part, and creating children that were noble on their mother's side, what was shameful in that?" And Chrysippus in his *Republic* says, word for word: "I also approve of [*dokei moi*]

[35]For my translations of both passages in Sextus Empiricus, I have consulted R.G. Bury (LCL), Julia Annas and Jonathan Barnes, *Outlines of Scepticism* (Cambridge: Cambridge University Press, 1994), and Bett, *Against the Ethicists*, and adopted various expressions from each of them. The translation of the passage in PH 3 draws most significantly on Bury, the translation of the passage in M 11 on Bett.

[36]It is striking that both lyre-playing and sculpture, Aristotle's examples in *Nichomachean Ethics* 1.7, are mentioned.

arranging these matters as is the custom even now among many people, and no bad thing [*ou kakôs*], so that the mother has children with the son and the father with the daughter and the brother with the sister born of the same mother." And an example of their piety towards the departed would be their recommendations about cannibalism, for they approve not only of eating the dead, but also their own flesh, if some part of their body should happen to be cut off. And the following is said by Chrysippus in his *On Justice*: "And if some part of our limbs is cut off which is useful for food, do not bury it or otherwise dispose of it, but consume it, so that from our own parts another part may come into being." And in his *On What Is Appropriate*, in discussing the burial of one's parents, he says explicitly: "When our parents die, we are to use the simplest forms of burial, consistently with the body's being nothing to us, like nails or hair, and with our not needing to give it any such care and attention. Hence, also, when the flesh is useful they will make use of it as food, just as, if one of their own parts were useful, such as an amputated foot, it would be proper for them to use it and similar parts like this; but when the flesh is useless, they will bury it and place the monument upon them, or burn it up and leave the ashes, or dispose of them in a more distant spot and pay no more attention to them, like nails or hair."

Thus say the Stoics; but we must bring against them the next point in our argument. Either they recommend doing these things with the idea that young people will put them into practice, or with the idea that they will not put them into practice. But certainly not with the idea that they will put them into practice; for the laws forbid them, unless one has to live with the Laestrygonians and Cyclopses, among whom it is lawful "to eat human flesh and then to drink pure milk." But if it is with the idea that they will not put them into practice, the art of life becomes redundant, since the practice of it is impossible. (SE M 11.188–196, tr. Bett with changes)

Other than in Diogenes Laertius, we can here see how the lists of Stoic claims are framed by *Sceptic arguments*.[37] Further, the focus here is on *types of actions*, not on institutions like temples or courthouses. Before turning to the analysis of the Sceptic arguments, we should

[37]If we compare the material on Pyrrhonism in Diogenes with Sextus's writings, it seems overall more likely that Diogenes, who postdates Sextus, has not used Sextus as his source but relies on one or several other authors. For a more detailed account of the relationship between Sextus and Diogenes, see Bett, *Against the Ethicists*, xxvi–xxvii.

pursue further the question whether the early Stoics formulate rules of conduct. In Sextus, we here have a number of direct citations on problematic types of action, and we might thus be able to draw somewhat firmer conclusions than in the case of Diogenes Laertius.

1. When Zeno says "have intercourse with one's boy-friend no more and no less than with one who is not one's boy-friend," he does not talk about having *as much* intercourse with someone who is one's boyfriend as with someone who is not, etc. Rather, he talks about the idea that it is no more and no less fitting to have intercourse with the one than with the other. The reasoning he offers thus refers to *differences* that we conventionally think are relevant to how one should act but that, according to Zeno, are not. This suggests that we should study his thesis in the context of the theory of appropriate action. The same applies to Zeno's reflections on Jocasta and Oedipus.

2. Chrysippus says he "approves of" incest. But he does not say that everyone *should* practice incest. Rather, he seems to infer from the observation that incest is not a bad thing when practiced by other cultures that this practice is not in itself despicable.

3. On the eating of human flesh, we should note that the slander about Stoic cannibalism that is attested in various places in ancient writings might go back to the much more confined claim that we should eat *amputated* limbs *if they are useful* for food. This claim might be best understood as the thesis that there are occasions when it is appropriate to cut off one of our limbs, and when, *if* this limb should be useful for food, we should eat it. This thesis need not translate into a general rule. It may only say that, in the unlikely case that our amputated limb seems like the best thing we can eat, then we should eat it. This kind of instruction is not a rule that prescribes a type of action. It is a mere illustration of the claim that one should regard that action as appropriate and perform it that, according to perfect deliberation, turns out to be appropriate, even if this means doing something that is conventionally considered scandalous.

4. On Stoic premises, there are no occasions where dead human bodies or amputated limbs have *any value*.[38] While one normally has a

---

[38] The Stoic views on funerals are, in effect, less in conflict with ancient legal thought than the rest of the disturbing theses. E.g., in Plutarch's *Lycurgus* 27 we read that Lycurgus made laws about burial that were supposed to counteract superstition and superfluous luxury. Cicero praises the ancestral Roman laws for limiting expenditure in burial, so that differences in wealth would be eliminated (*De leg.* 2.22; cf. 2.61–62).

healthier alternative to eating one's cut-off leg (so that it will rarely be appropriate to eat it), usually nothing speaks in favor of a grand funeral. Dead bodies should not mean anything to us. However we bury our parents, our mode of burial should reflect this. Again, this instruction need not be interpreted as a rule. Rather, Chrysippus is alerting us to the consequences of recognizing that certain things *do not even have* value (i.e., not only are they not *good*; what is more, they are not even *valuable*). Whatever we end up doing, we should not consider things that are completely irrelevant to action (such as amputated limbs, dead bodies, cut-off hair, etc.) as valuable. Chrysippus is not prescribing types of action; he is explaining how some things we tend to be attached to really have no value, and thus do not provide relevant considerations for action.

5. The point of several of the Stoic theses seems to be that a certain course of action that is conventionally regarded as despicable is not bad, shameful, or awful. We may speculate that Zeno and Chrysippus are addressing what they conceive to be prejudices—that certain types of action cannot, whatever the circumstances, be appropriate, because they are shameful. At *Outlines of Scepticism* 3.207, Sextus reports a related piece of Stoic doctrine that contains a telling phrase that might be understood along similar lines. According to the Stoics, it is not 'out of place' (*ouk atopon*) to eat human flesh. I shall return to this phrase at the end of the chapter. At this point, we should note that, given doxographical conventions and the polemical spirit of some authors, a change from 'it is not out of place to φ' or 'it is not shameful to φ' to 'the Stoics say one should φ' might easily occur or even be made deliberately. But it creates the impression that the Stoics prescribe a type of action, an impression that may be misrepresentative.

We thus arrive at the following picture. The four lists of disturbing theses do not necessitate, and what is more, do not speak in favor of an interpretation according to which Zeno and Chrysippus formulate *rules of conduct* by 'recommending' incest, anthropophagy, and so on. The careful formulations of the Stoics according to which something is 'no more and no less' to be done or 'not a bad thing' indicate that the Stoic theses have a different structure. The Sceptic lists create two misleading impressions: that the Stoics formulate general rules of conduct, and that they wrote treatises in which the disturbing theses made up a *continuous text* on the art of life. Once we pay attention to the fact that the claims come from a wide variety of writings, it is obvious that the latter is as misrepresentative as the former.

4. The Stoic 'Art of Life'

Both passages in Sextus come from chapters in which Sextus discusses whether there is an art of life (PH 3.239–249, M 11.168–215). This question is at the heart of Pyrrhonism. The Sceptic, as Sextus describes him at the beginning of the *Outlines*, begins to philosophize in order to determine which impressions are true and which are false and to thus gain quietude (*ataraxia*). Whoever holds views on what is good and bad is in a state of inner turmoil. If he does not have what he considers good, he takes himself to suffer from the lack of it, and tries to obtain that which he deems good. If he has what he considers good, he is disturbed because he fears losing it. But he who suspends judgment is quiet (PH 1.26–27). The Sceptic's 'conversion' is initiated and brought about by philosophical investigation. Among the questions the Sceptic investigates, questions about what is good and what is bad are particularly disruptive. Knowing what is good and what is bad is a precondition for successfully securing the good and avoiding the bad. Disturbance is partly due to the fact that it may not be easy to do so. It becomes worse once we realize that we are not even sure what to strive for and what to keep away from. If we worry about having and not having the good *and* about whether we know what the good is in the first place, we are in the state from which the Sceptic escapes. This picture of dogmatic affliction and Sceptic tranquility is a key starting point of Pyrrhonism.

Ideally, one knows what is good and bad, succeeds in securing and avoiding it, and thus possesses the tranquility of the good life. If different views on the good and bad appear equally (un)compelling, as they do to the Sceptic, one may at least produce the tranquility of suspended judgment through discussion of these views. Everything else appears worse (with a view to tranquility and thus the good life): to worry about what is good and bad, or to be unable to secure the good and avoid the bad. But suppose one knew what is good and bad. Even if the chase after goods might seem unappealing (simply because one would be *chasing* them, running after them, as it were, and maybe not getting them), it would be dogmatic not to engage in it.[39] Sceptic tranquility rests on arguments that produce a balance between different views on what the good is; if the arguments indeed showed that such-and-such *is* the good, suspension of judgment would be an arbitrary and an ultimately dogmatic stance. The Sceptic would have to give up suspension of judgment and strive for what has been shown to be the good. For these reasons, Sextus's chapters on whether there is an art of life (*technê peri ton bion*) are a key part of Pyrrhonism.[40]

But how could one call into question that there is an art of life? Both lists of Stoic claims in Sextus are presented within arguments that discuss the existence of the art of living by asking for its *products*, that is, the real-life performance of the actions that the theory describes. Clearly, almost all philosophers make a visible effort to do the things they recommend in their theories. Consider Epicureans, who—in agreement with their claim that doing philosophy is pleasurable—spend their life doing philosophy. But Sextus (or his source) seeks out dogmatic teachings on how to live that do not have the slightest repercussions in the lives of those who propose them. The existence of an art, Sextus says, is apprehended by the specific actions or products resulting from it. The art of life, however, that is represented through the disturbing theses of the Stoics does not have any manifestations in the lives of those who possess it—the Stoics. But if the art of life has no specific actions or products resulting from it, it is not apprehended, and we cannot firmly say that it really exists. This is the structure of the argument in *Outlines*

---

[39]For a discussion of this kind of happiness see Gisela Striker, "Ataraxia: Happiness as Tranquillity," *Monist* 73 (1990): 97–110.

[40]Bett translates 'skill relating to life' (*Against the Ethicists*). This clearly is more literal. Still, it seems that the traditional translation as 'art of life' is so entrenched in the discussion of ancient philosophy that the notion of an 'art' (instead of 'skill') does not really seem to be misleading.

In this context, knowledge of what is good and bad is considered to be both *theoretical* and *practical* knowledge. Whoever has this knowledge masters the art of life. See Gisela Striker, "Following Nature: A Study in Stoic Ethics," *Oxford Studies in Ancient Philosophy* 9 (1991): 1–73, sec. 3; and A. Long, "Socrates in Hellenistic Philosophy," *Classical Quarterly* 38 (1988): 150–171. Zeno defines *technê* as a systematic set of cognitions (*katalêpseis*) that is unified in practice and directed toward a *telos* that is beneficial for life (Olympiodorus, *On Plato's Gorgias* 12.1, LS 42A). Sextus reports that the Stoics define knowledge (*epistêmê*) of what is good, bad, and neither good nor bad as the *technê peri ton bion* (M 11.170).

of Scepticism 3.243–249, the first of Sextus's lists of disturbing theses quoted earlier.

The Stoic claims about incest, one's parents' funerals, and so on are *uniquely* fitted to a Sceptic argument of this type. No matter how revisionist philosophical teachings may be, their proponents usually make some effort to actually follow them (witness the Cynics). The Stoic claims cited earlier seem to be a striking exception. We do not have the least bit of testimony on Zeno or Chrysippus engaging in any unconventional sexual relationships, eating human flesh, despising a conventional education (consider Chrysippus's many references to mythical stories, which testify to his study of the poets), or any other behaviour that would remind us of these claims. Thus for a Sceptic who wants to argue that the art of living may not exist by presenting a theory of the good life and pointing to the complete absence of any products of this theory, hardly anything could be better suited than the disturbing theses. Sextus suggests that the Stoic claims are examples representing many more claims of this kind. However, the fact that Sextus chooses the *same* ideas in *Against the Mathematicians* 11.188–196 and in *Outlines of Scepticism* 3.243–249 makes it unlikely that much can be found that will serve the Sceptic as effectively as the Stoic ideas on incest, burial, and the eating of human flesh.

The aim of *Outlines of Scepticism* 3.243–249 is surely not to give a summary of early Stoic political philosophy—the author does not seem to be concerned with a specific field in Stoicism. Rather, it seems obvious that the Sceptic author is presenting a collection of Stoic claims whose common denominator is that not even those who propose them would ever dare to put any of them into practice. Sextus writes for an audience for whom the Cyclopses and the Laestrygonians are proverbial beings *without law*. To say that the Stoics would only dare to put these things into practice if living under the law of the Cyclopses and Laestrygonians is to say that they would only put it into practice if living under *no* law. Both are cannibals of some sort (Homer presents them as eating Odysseus's companions).[41] Stoic claims, so the suggestion goes, are as outland-

---

[41] For the Cyclopses see *Od.* 9.112–115, 215; for the Laestrygonians see *Od.* 10.106–132. The Cyclops Polyphemus is presented not only as lawless and uncivilized but also as scorning all the gods (9.274–76) and Zeus (277).

ish as to remind us of a mythopoeic world of uncivilized monsters, not of any human community.

It is interesting that the Sceptics do not fall into the trap of associating the Stoics with the Cynics. It seems highly likely that they would have been familiar with discussions that see 'shamelessness' as the common factor in Stoic and Cynic philosophy (with respect to the Cynics, complaints about their shamelessness are commonplace). However, for the purposes of the kind of argument Sextus presents in *Outlines of Scepticism* 3.243–249 and *Against the Mathematicians* 11.188–196, this association would ruin everything. If the Sceptic idea were just to enumerate extreme and revisionist ideas on how to live, the Cynics would offer perfect material. But since the Sceptic arguments draw on the fact that there are claims about the good life that do not have the slightest manifestations in the real lives of their proponents, the Cynics were the worst choice.

Surely, the Stoics have much more to say on how we should live than what Sextus cares to report. Sextus's portrait of Stoic recommendations for the good life is extremely one-sided; even in Sextus himself we find a lot of material that paints a different picture. The Sceptic project of presenting the Stoic art of life by extracting and compiling the most extreme comments on particular types of action from a wide variety of Stoic writings is almost ironically daring and misrepresentative.

It is part of the project of presenting Zeno's and Chrysippus's theses on incest, and so on, as their art of life that each of these claims must look like an *instruction* on how to live. The Sceptics thus have a vital interest in *phrasing* whatever scandalous detail of Stoic doctrine they can find as if it were a generally recommended course of action. Once we see that even this aspect of the testimony may be filtered through the Sceptics' argumentative goals (not merely through the accidents of doxographical transmission), we should be very hesitant to accept it at face value. I have already suggested that the verbatim citations of the disturbing theses indicate that Zeno's and Chrysippus's theses do not have the form 'one should' (or 'it is permitted to,' 'it is forbidden to'). When we recognize the Sceptic interest in making it seem as if the Stoic views on incest, and so on, belong to their account of an *art of life*, it seems even more unlikely that Zeno and Chrysippus put forward rules of this kind.

The argument in *Outlines of Scepticism* 3.243–249 is based on the dogmatic assumption that every art goes along with its specific products or actions.[42] This claim can be traced back to Aristotle's famous function argument in *Nicomachean Ethics* 1.7.[43] At the very beginning of the argument, Aristotle says that the flute-player—and the sculptor and every artist—has his *ergon* and his *praxis* (NE 1.7, 1097b24–1098a18). From the idea that each artist has a specific function, or specific product, it is—at least for the purposes of the Sceptic—just one step to the assumption that every art has its specific product. Given the prominence of the function argument in Aristotle's ethics, we may imagine that this claim is a readily available dogmatic assumption. And Sextus probably trusts that many dogmatists share some version of it. Sextus presents a Hellenistic variant: he says that every art is *apprehended* (*katalambanesthai*) by its specific *erga*, thus making use of a verb that has become a technical term through the Stoic theory of knowledge.

Unlike the argument in *Outlines of Scepticism* 3.243–249, Sextus's argument in *Against the Mathematicians* 11.188–196 does not lead to suspension of judgment on whether or not an art of life really exists. In *Against the Mathematicians* 11, Sextus ends up not making dialectical use of the premise that every art has its product.[44] He concludes with the claim that an art that is not put into practice is

[42]It can thus be characterized as a dialectical argument. This notion of a dialectical argument, understood as a Sceptical argument based on the assumptions of a dogmatic opponent, was first suggested by P. Couissin, "Le stoicisme de la nouvelle Académie," *Revue d'histoire de la Philosophie* 36 (1929): 241–276. See A. M. Ioppolo, *Opinione e Scienza: Il dibattito tra Stoizi e Accademici nel III e nel II a.C.* (Naples: Bibliopolis, 1986), 57; and K. Vogt, *Skepsis und Lebenspraxis: Das pyrrhonische Leben ohne Meinungen* (Freiburg: Alber Verlag, 1998), 36.

[43]Standard English translations render *ergon* as 'function,' and thus this argument has become known as the function argument. Even though the notion of a function may capture much of what is at issue in Aristotle's ethics (and has been integral to interpretations of Aristotle's notion of excellence), it seems important not to forget the literal meaning of *ergon*: work. When Aristotle leads into his argument, he pairs *ergon* with *praxis* (1097b26). We start out from the idea that each artist has *his* work; the things he does are specific to his art. It is not clear that this would be adequately captured by saying that each artist has a function. It is not the function of the flute-player to play the flute, but it is what he, specifically, does.

[44]Cf. Bett, *Against the Ethicists*, 206–208.

redundant. For present purposes, we need not compare the strength of both arguments and raise questions about their provenance.[45] Rather, it is important to note that we find two *different* arguments on whether there is an art of life in Sextus's writings, both of which make use of the disturbing theses. What is more, these arguments do not just vary in emphasis or detail. They seem to derive from different Sceptic outlooks (or different phases in Sextus's Sceptic thought): the argument in *Against the Mathematicians* 11 is, in a way we need not discuss here in any detail, less concerned with the avoidance of drawing a conclusion that sounds like a view one comes to adopt (that might be in conflict with Sceptic suspension of judgment) than the argument in *Outlines of Scepticism* 3.

5. Variants of Sceptic Argument

It is the merit of Schofield's study to have first emphasized the significance of the fact that Diogenes Laertius 7.32–24, Diogenes Laertius 7.187–189, *Outlines of Scepticism* 3.243–249, and *Against the Mathematicians* 11.188–196 derive from Pyrrhonian texts. However, we should not (as Schofield does) assume that they all go back to *one* Pyrrhonian collection of Stoic claims.[46] The fact that even the two arguments in Sextus derive from *different* variants of Scepticism (or different phases of Sextus's thinking) indicates that there is not *one* text in the background of the four lists. And while the passages in Diogenes Laertius *may* go back to one of the initial sources of Sextus,

---

[45]The relative chronology of Sextus's works has been studied in detail by Karl Janaçek, *Prolegomena to Sextus Empiricus* (Olomouc: N.p., 1948), and "Skeptische Zweitropenlehre und Sextus Empiricus," *Eirene* 8 (1970): 47–55. Janaçek's philological data speak in favor of considering *Adversus Mathematicos* as the later work. Emidio Spinelli argues in a number of publications that we should not be tempted to overthrow this relative chronology; see, e.g., *Sesto Empirico: Contro gli Etici*, ed. and tr. Spinelli (Naples: Bibliopolis, 1995). Bett introduces his translation and commentary of M 11 with a detailed discussion of the relative chronology of Sextus's writings. Against the traditional view, he makes a case for the claim that M 7–11 are earlier than PH 1–3 (*Against the Ethicists*, 26).

[46]Schofield, *The Stoic Idea*, 14–18; see Paul Vander Waerdt, "Zeno's Republic and the Origins of Natural Law," in *The Socratic Movement*, ed. Vander Waerdt (Ithaca, N.Y.: Cornell University Press, 1994), 272–308, 286.

they may also go back to another author.[47] These observations suggest the following. The disturbing theses are stock material for Sceptic arguments, and they have been variously utilized at different points in the history of Scepticism.[48]

For Schofield, it is essential that the four passages go back to one text. This assumption helps him make sense of a difficult verb in the framework story in Diogenes Laertius 7.32–34: "the passages of which the Stoics disapproved were cut out of the books by Athenodorus the Stoic, who was in charge of the Pergamene library; and . . . afterwards, when Athenodorus was detected and compromised, they were put into opposition [or: replaced] [*antitethênai*]" (DL 7.34).

The Greek manuscripts say *antitethênai*: the theses have been put into opposition. But the text does not give any indication of what the Stoic claims have been put into opposition *to*; the sentence is incomplete if we read *antitethênai*. If we follow some translators and render the text as saying that the theses have been 'replaced' (which has the advantage of generating a plausible sequence of the theses being cut out first and replaced later), we need to emend the text.[49] One of the central ideas in Schofield's interpretation is that *antitethênai* can be made sense of if we recognize that it is a technical

---

[47]Schofield (*The Stoic Idea*, 3–21 argues that DL 7.32–34 and 7.187–189 both go back to the Sceptic Cassius. This view was first put forward by C. Wachsmuth, "Stichometrisches und Bibliothekarisches," *Rheinisches Museum* 34 (1879): 38–51; see also Mansfeld, "Diogenes Laertius," 344–346. Schofield adds the passages in Sextus to Cassius's heritage, mostly on the ground that the passages seem, in his view, atypical for Sextus. However, it is not easy to see what would count as atypical for Sextus (in a sense, nothing could be more typical for Sextus than a text that makes use of older Sceptic material). The general claim that both passages in Sextus would be atypical for him seems difficult to defend, especially when we consider that both passages are significantly *different from each other*. That both passages in Diogenes go back to Cassius is plausible, but not certain.

[48]I prefer to refer to these arguments as Sceptic rather than Pyrrhonian because it seems conceivable to me that they have a history within both Sceptic schools, or at least that the material Sextus makes use of has also been utilized in Academic Scepticism.

[49]R. D. Hicks translates 'replace,' Marcello Gigante 'inseriti' (*Diogene Laerzio: Vite dei Filosofi*, Bari: Laterza, 1987). Schofield draws attention to the fact that both Hicks and Gigante translate as if they emended the text, while in fact they retain the MSS text (*The Stoic Idea*, 4).

term in Scepticism. To put things into opposition is what Pyrrhonian Sceptics do.[50] Schofield proceeds by working out a complete list of all the claims found in the four passages, and then argues that the way to make sense of the end of Diogenes Laertius 7.34 is to assume that *all* those claims that are attributed to Zeno's *Republic* have been put into opposition with other Stoic claims on the same subjects.[51] Thus, the Sceptic author would have put each thesis from the *Republic* into opposition with a further Stoic claim on the same matter.[52] He would not only have generated pairs of conflicting theses, but more specifically he would have shown that Zeno's *Republic* is, as a whole, in conflict with theses Zeno proposes elsewhere and with Chrysippean ideas.[53] However, as Paul Vander Waerdt remarks (without much ado in a footnote), the oppositions Schofield puts together are less clear than one might wish.[54] The disturbing theses are difficult to understand, but the difficulty is not that they would stand pair-wise in opposition to one another. Rather, Sextus treats the disturbing theses as *all of the same kind*, and so does the report in Diogenes Laertius 7.187–189. This suggests that the disturbing theses are seen as homogeneous within the Sceptic arguments. Since Schofield's other assumption, namely, that the four reports go back to *one* Sceptic, is also problematic, I will not pursue the details of his proposal further.

But we should note that taking *antitethênai* seriously as a technical term of the Sceptics does not necessarily mean that we should

---

[50] *The Stoic Idea*, 8.

[51] Schofield does not offer specific argument for why we should suppose the Stoic theses have been put into opposition with other Stoic theses instead of something else. He says that this is "natural to assume" (*The Stoic Idea*, 8).

[52] For the details on which thesis is, according to Schofield, opposed to which thesis, see *The Stoic Idea*, 15–20.

[53] Schofield's interpretation goes even one step further: Cassius's strategy, he argues, "consists in portraying the *Republic* as morally elevated in comparison to the unrestrained self-indulgence and moral banality exemplified in other Stoic texts" (*The Stoic Idea*, 17). A common feature within the pairs of opposition would be that the claims from the *Republic* propose high ethical and religious standards, while the opposing claims have a base and vulgar ring to them.

[54] See Paul Vander Waerdt ("Zeno's Republic," 286) and Brad Inwood, review of *The Stoic Idea* by Malcolm Schofield, *Bryn Mawr Classical Review*, http://ccat.sas.upenn.edu/bmcr/1992/03.03.13.html.

expect the Sceptics to collect *opposing theses*.[55] Sextus defines Scepticism as an ability to put appearances (*phainomena*) and thoughts (*nooumena*) into opposition (*dunamis antithetikê*): *nooumena* are put into opposition with *nooumena, phainomena* with *phainomena,* and *nooumena* with *phainomena* (PH 1.8). This definition indicates that *antitethênai* does not refer solely to the opposition of thoughts with thoughts—it also refers to the opposition of thoughts with appearances and appearances with appearances. What is more, the fact that this is how Sextus *defines* Scepticism suggests that he extends the boundaries of what 'putting into opposition' *literally* means. According to Sextus, it refers to *all* of the Sceptic's argumentative abilities.[56]

If we consider Sextus's use of the term as the technical, Sceptic use of *antitethênai*, the interpretation of the passage in Diogenes Laertius does *not depend* on how we understand the difficult verb. Assuming that *antitethênai* covers a range of Sceptic argumentative techniques, the text says that the Sceptics investigated the Stoic theses in their specific Sceptic way. That this is what the Sceptics do is already clear from the beginning of the passage, which says that Cassius the Sceptic and those around him have subjected the Stoic theses to their criticism. If we think the text needs to be emended, we

---

[55]In "Gibt es eine Lebenskunst?" I discuss in more detail why we should not assume that Sceptical argument is restricted to putting dogmatic claims in opposition.

[56]While I cannot argue for this claim here, it seems to me that the term *antitethênai* is part of Sextus's (or some other relatively late Sceptic's) attempt to integrate various versions of Pyrrhonism into one philosophy. Sextus uses the notion of putting things into opposition several times when he explains Sceptic argument generally. But the term is notably absent when he presents the different sets of Modes, presumably making use of older Sceptic material. The first time we encounter the expression is when Sextus explains the Tenth Mode. While the first nine of the Ten Modes—the various conflicts between appearances—might seem to lend themselves perfectly to a description according to which the Sceptic puts appearances into opposition with each other, the modes are in fact described repeatedly as arguing from differences (*diaphora*). The Sceptic's activity is presented as *comparing* (*sunkrinein*) these different appearances, and thus arguing from the *divergency in things* (*anômalia pragmatôn*) (PH 1.163). The Ten Modes are transmitted in three versions: In Sextus's *Outlines,* in Diogenes' report on Pyrrhonism, and in Philo of Alexandria (for a discussion of the differences see J. Annas and J. Barnes, *The Modes of Scepticism* (Cambridge: Cambridge University Press, 1985). Neither in Diogenes nor in Philo does *antithetênai* play any role in the presentation of this mode. The expression is used only in Sextus's presentation of the Tenth Mode.

can still gather from it that Sceptics subjected the Stoic claims to their argumentative strategies. One way or another, the text is fully compatible with what I suggest: that Sceptics have used the Stoic theses in a *variety* of similar arguments.

This view is further confirmed if we include *Outlines of Scepticism* 3.198–234 in our discussion. This section precedes the chapter on whether there is an art of life. At *Outlines of Scepticism* 3.198, Sextus remarks that it might be worthwhile to go into some detail on the shameful and not shameful, holy and unholy, laws and customs, piety toward the gods, respect for the deceased, and similar matters, since a huge variety of views are to be found on these matters. He then provides a long list of forms of life, covering customs of different peoples and deeds of Cronos, Zeus, Hermes, and the Amazons, as well as a number of Stoic theses that are very similar to the claims we find in the lists, and a few revisionary ideas by other philosophers (PH 3.198–234).[57]

From the long commentaries by Sextus on Aenesidemus' modes of argument, it becomes clear that collecting monstrosities, unusual experiences, and foreign customs is a general Sceptic preoccupation. We can see the Sceptic, as it were, in the midst of manuscripts with texts by Hesiod, Homer, Herodotus, and those philosophers who have ventured into revisionist ideas on the good life. Among these, the Stoics were ultimately the most rewarding source for the Sceptic: the prime audience of the Sceptic consisted of other philosophers. These other philosophers may disregard much the Sceptic finds in Hesiod, Homer, or Herodotus as myth and badly researched, outdated historiography. The more material the Sceptic can find that stems from philosophers, the more forceful his argument will be *for its dogmatic addressees*. And while some other philosophers may also have 'strange' ideas to offer, the Stoics are—unlike, for example, Heraclitus—direct opponents of the Sceptics.

The argumentative structure of *Outlines of Scepticism* 3.198–234 is slightly mixed: Sextus says he will show the discrepancy (*anômalia*)

---

[57]For the Stoic claims see: PH 3.200, 201, 205, 206, 207. Heraclitus, Epicurus, the Cynics, and the Cyrenaics are mentioned; Plato's community of women is cited; Aristotle is mentioned once—but only in a brief introduction to the discussion of different religious rites and forms of sacrifice (PH 3.218). The text reads largely as if Hesiod and Herodotus were the sources. In 3.231, Sextus explicitly refers to Herodotus.

in what people think about how one should live, and he ends by referring to the disagreement (*diaphônia*) he has presented. But while he moves from one strange custom to the next, he often contrasts it not only with other customs but also with 'how things are with us [*par' hêmin*]' and how 'our' law is. The passage thus indicates that on the one hand the disturbing theses lend themselves to Sceptic arguments that rely on the diversity of different ways of life and beliefs about how to live. On the other hand, the Stoic theses can be contrasted with 'normal life,' with life as 'we' know it and with the customs or laws that 'we' know. But how do these kinds of contrast make up Sceptic arguments?

The Tenth Mode, on Sextus's account, argues from forms of life, customs and laws, mythical belief, and dogmatic claims (PH 1.37). Forms of life, customs, and laws (and, insofar as they are reflected in practices, mythical beliefs) are, within the Sceptic framework, *appearances*.[58] One of Sextus's examples for the Tenth Mode is the conflict between Epicurus's claim that the gods do not pay any attention to us and the general practice of prayer (PH 1.155). Epicurus's claim is obviously a *thesis* and thus a *nooumenon*. But the general practice of prayer is not. In order to make sense of the argument, we must assume that Sextus does not understand the term *phainomena* as exclusively relating to perceptual appearances (even though this is how he explains it in PH 1.9). Rather, he seems to rely on an understanding of the term that he develops in his account of appearances as the Sceptic criterion. The Sceptic follows appearances in a very wide sense of the term, a sense that includes common practices and traditions (PH 1.21–24). The common practice of prayer can thus be considered an *appearance*. The contrast between Epicurus's theological view and the practice of prayer offers an example for a variant of the Tenth Mode that opposes appearances and thoughts by putting dogmatic claims

---

[58] A custom is a common way of doing something (PH 1.146). A way of life (*agôgê*) can be adopted by one or several persons—it is understood as the choice of how to live or act (PH 1.145). Once we tie in these explanations with Sextus's general account of the Sceptic life, it becomes clear that customs and ways of life count as *phainomena* in his presentation of Scepticism. The Sceptic *agôgê* itself consists in an undogmatic acceptance of what others do, what has come down by tradition and is part of the education the Sceptic happens to have received—all these count as appearances (PH 1.23–24; PH 1.17). For a different view see Annas and Barnes, *Modes*, 160.

about how to live in opposition with the normal ways of life. And this seems to be part of the structure of the argument in *Outlines of Scepticism* 3.198–234: the disturbing theses are contrasted with 'our' normal life and our laws.[59] They thus lend themselves to a third variant of Sceptic argument, different from the arguments in *Outlines of Scepticism* 3.243–249 and *Against the Mathematicians* 11.188–196.

Once we understand the Pyrrhonian background to the texts that are traditionally regarded as key testimony of early Stoic political philosophy, our picture of this part of Stoic philosophy is seriously challenged. The Stoic claims lend themselves quite uniquely to an important field of Sceptic argument—questions about whether there is anything good or bad and whether there is an art of life. Within the exposition of Pyrrhonian philosophy, these questions are about as important as whether there is a criterion of truth, or whether there is proof—they are among the key questions on which the Sceptic aims to induce suspension of judgment. It is not surprising that dogmatic theses that are of great help in inducing suspension of judgment on such questions are transmitted at various places and in different versions. If we read the disturbing theses in light of these considerations about Pyrrhonian philosophy, we see that the Stoic claims may very well have gained their status as, comparatively, very well-attested Stoic doctrine because they were of great importance for the Sceptics, *not* because they were at the core of early Stoic political philosophy.

6. Stoic Revisionism

But what, we may ask, originally gave the disturbing theses their fame, if not a prominent role within the *Stoic* texts? The thesis that only the virtuous are citizens, relatives, friends, and free certainly looks like a core thesis of Zeno's political philosophy. It explores the

---

[59] Another example Sextus gives while explaining the Tenth Mode testifies to this type of argument with respect to the disturbing theses: Chrysippus says incest is indifferent, and we oppose this with the law (again, understood as a practice and thus an appearance) (PH 1.160). For a more detailed discussion of how this kind of conflict generates suspension of judgment, see my "Gibt es eine Lebenskunst," 12–17.

notion of wisdom as related to important political conceptions. Some of the theses on institutions (temples, courthouses, gymnasia, education) may also be set in this context, and they may have a similarly paradoxical structure (see section 7). But what about incest, anthropophagy, and so on? The Stoic theses on how these types of action are not shameful might be best interpreted as *examples* that the Stoics employed in order to explain the full implications of their thought about appropriate action.

At this point, it is worthwhile to briefly consider some characteristics of how the Stoics present their views in ethics. The Stoics are aware that readers of their works may say that, after all, their theory is ultimately just another way of framing a Platonic or Peripatetic theory. Platonic and Peripatetic philosophers give prominence to virtue, and, in one way or another, less importance to things like wealth and health. The difference between their theories and the Stoic claim that only virtue is good, while other things have value or disvalue, could seem to be merely terminological; the implications of the Stoic ideas would thus be seriously underestimated.[60] In the face of such possible responses, examples that emphasize the revisionist nature of one's theory rather than its plausibility or closeness to intuitions seem to make a lot of sense. These examples would have stood out within the works from which they were taken, without necessarily being their main tenets.

We may also consider whether the Stoic use of examples is rooted in a tradition that extends back to Socrates' way of being, through his own life, some kind of exemplum for revisionist ideas of the good life. As I argued, it does not seem that Zeno 'converted' to a Cynic lifestyle at any point, but he certainly gave much thought to the

---

[60]It is not clear to what extent the Stoics were acquainted with Aristotle's philosophy. Alesse offers a detailed argument on why we might think the Stoics knew Aristotle (*La Stoa*, 233–262). Cf. F. H. Sandbach, "Aristotle's Legacy to Stoic Ethics," *Bulletin of the London University Institute of Classical Studies* 15 (1968): 72–85. Matters are further complicated by the ways Stoic ethics *influences* Hellenistic Aristotelian ethics, which may appear to bring the different theories closer together. While this cannot account for the initial formulation of claims by Zeno, it might explain some of the insistence of later, but still relatively early, Stoics on extreme examples. For discussion of the influence of Stoic ethics on Hellenistic debates see William W. Fortenbaugh, ed., *Stoic and Peripatetic Ethics: The Work of Arius Didymus* (New Brunswick, N. J.: Transaction Books, 1983); see also Julia Annas, "Aristotelian Political Theory in the Hellenistic Period," in Laks and Schofield, *Justice and Generosity*, 74–94.

structure of Cynic philosophizing. While I cannot defend my claims on Cynic philosophy in any detail, I would like to suggest that Cynic methodology had some influence on Stoic forms of exposition. The Cynics aim to bring out quite fundamental, theoretical claims by specific 'shocking' actions of their own; they thus, in a way, teach by example.[61] Their examples, of course, are enacted exempla, and this is not at all the case for the Stoics. But it still seems that this method of conveying philosophical theory may have had some influence on the Stoics. While the Stoics do not *do* shocking things, their use of examples may similarly shock and disturb *intentionally*. Let us assume (see section 7) that the claim that it is unproblematic to eat one's amputated leg serves to illustrate how even types of action that are conventionally considered shameful can be appropriate. We can imagine that Zeno and Chrysippus are well aware of how revolting the idea of eating one's own amputated leg is, and that they use it exactly for this reason. The example seems to say: do not misunderstand our theory as somehow talking about abstract ideas, tacitly assuming that the ideal Stoic agent will end up performing the same actions as the ideal agent of less revisionary theories.

The Sceptics are not the only ones to pick up on passages in Stoic philosophy that seem inconsistent with the way the Stoic philosophers themselves apparently live. Plutarch is reported to have written eight anti-Stoic works and one further treatise critiquing both the Stoics and the Epicureans. Two of Plutarch's critical works (and a conspectus of a third) are preserved: *De Stoicorum Repugnantiis* (*On Stoic Self-Contradictions*) and *De Communibus Notitiis Adversus Stoicos* (*On Common Conceptions*).[62] The former engages with a point similar to that of Sextus. the Stoics do not seem to do any of the things they propose in their account of the good life

---

[61]This suggestion is controversial for the following reason. Scholars disagree on whether the Cynics put forward anything like a theory (which my claim implies) or whether their stance is entirely negative. I am following the reconstruction of Moles, "The Cynics and Politics." In my view, the main argument in favor of this line of interpretation is that some of the claims attributed to Diogenes exhibit subtle compositional and terminological refinement, which seems to indicate conceptual theorizing on the relevant questions (see DL 6.72).

[62]All three texts are in Plutarch, *Moralia* 13, pt. 2, LCL. See Harold Cherniss, introduction to Plutarch, *On Stoic Self-Contradictions* (*De Stoicorum Repugnantiis*), LCL, 369–411.

(see 1033A–B). However, Plutarch does not discuss the disturbing theses.[63] For him, much more basic points of Stoic doctrine seem to conflict with the life of the Stoic philosophers. Think, for example, of the Stoic doctrine that only virtue is good, and that things like health and life merely have value. It is apparent how it might seem to someone who sets out to expose the weaknesses of Stoicism that this doctrine does not have manifestations in the lives of those who propose it. Like adherents of Platonic or Aristotelian theories, they may seem to value virtue *more* than health—as seen from the outside, the actions of someone who thinks that virtue is good and that health has value might seem to be just the same as those of someone who thinks that virtue is the highest good and health a lower level good, at least for the most part. The Stoics need to explain how their theory does not collapse into a more traditional ethical theory. In Plutarch's eyes, the lives of the Stoics themselves show that this is exactly what happens: the Stoics live more in accordance with the teachings of other philosophers than with their own (1033C).

Once we include such treatises in our study, the history of the disturbing theses appears to be an *exemplary*, and particularly crass, case of what is characteristic of significant portions of our testimony on early Stoic philosophy. Stoic philosophy offers potential critics (and even those who, like Plutarch, consider it very seriously) every chance to latch onto its counterintuitive aspects. Plutarch cites Chrysippus, who says that it is due to the exceeding greatness and beauty of the Stoic teachings that they seem like fiction and not on the level of humans and human nature (*On Stoic Self-Contradictions* 1041F). Plutarch makes it seem as if Chrysippus says this in response to the charge that Stoic ethics is completely removed from human life, a perspective he apparently does not deny but rather endorses.

The proposed line of interpreting the disturbing theses recalls what are known as Stoic paradoxes, the Stoics' most strikingly counterintuitive theses.[64] As we shall see in much detail in the follow-

---

[63] As we will see in chapter 2, Plutarch's discussion of Zeno's *Republic* is generally respectful. He takes it to be a serious work, apart from the discussion of sexual matters. This indicates that in his view (and it is likely that he had access to the treatise) discussion of sexual matters is a comparatively minor part—important enough to be mentioned, but not sufficiently important as to spoil the seriousness of the work for him.

[64] Cf. Bett, *Against the Ethicists*, 187.

ing chapters, the paradoxical thesis that only sages are citizens, friends, relatives, and free is centrally concerned with the *reinterpretation* of key philosophical notions, while the claims on incest and anthropophagy are not. If the claims on temples, education, etc., were related to the thesis that only the sages are citizens, friends, relatives, and free, they, too, might be comprehensible in terms of how the Stoics reinterpret core philosophical notions. But even with respect to the theses on incest, anthropophagy, etc., which have a different structure from the Stoic paradoxes, we should note an important feature they share with them: the Stoics emphasize rather than downplay the *revisionary* nature of their theories.

The characterization of some Stoic tenets as paradoxical apparently goes back to the Stoics themselves.[65] Cicero describes the paradoxical tenets as *admirabilia contraque opinionem omnium*, which brings out how the notion of a paradox is understood in this context: *paradoxa* are, quite literally, contrary to (*para*) belief (*doxa*), and they are perplexing. Famous examples are 'Everyone who is not wise is a fool' or 'The sage has no affections,' claims that are stark and extreme. They look as if they are intended to make us ask how anyone can possibly hold these beliefs, leading us to reconsider the key notions that are at issue and to want to know more about the theoretical context of these claims.

In order to understand the Stoic conception of a paradox, we need to keep in mind what the Stoics think about *doxai*, beliefs or opinions: they are held by fools, and they are generated by weak assent, a kind of assent the sage never gives. The sage has no opinions. The opinions people hold are thus by no means a starting point for Stoic thought, and it does not count against a theory if it is in conflict with opinions. However, the Stoics claim that their theories are in agreement with so-called preconceptions, that is, with naturally acquired notions of how things are.[66] Ultimately, they need to show that however revisionary their doctrines look at

---

[65]For Zeno, see Gnomolog. Monac. 196 (= SVF 1.281), for Cleanthes Arrianus Epict. diss. IV 1,173 (= SVF 1.619); Cicero attributes this terminology to the Stoics themselves, *Paradoxa Stoicorum* 4.

[66]On preconceptions, consensus, and beliefs, see Charles Brittain, "Common Sense: Concepts, Definition and Meaning in and out of the Stoa," in *Language and Learning. Philosophy of Language in the Hellenistic Age: Proceedings of the Ninth Symposium Hellenisticum*, ed. Dorothea Frede and Brad Inwood (Cambridge: Cambridge University Press, 2005), 164–209.

first glance, once we think our way through all the difficult issues involved, these doctrines are actually in agreement with very basic assumptions we already make. If the disturbing theses are shocking in a manner that is comparable to the paradoxes, that is, if they intentionally emphasize the revisionary nature of Stoic thought, something like this must be true for them as well. Once we think our way through the complicated questions concerning appropriate action, we realize that no matter how awful the ideas of eating one's leg or making nothing of one's father's funeral sound, they really are not awful at all.

7. *Ways of Making Sense of the Disturbing Theses*

While, according to my interpretation, the disturbing theses are not at the core of early Stoic political philosophy, at least some of them are part of it. Others derive from treatises on physics, appropriate action, and so on, but they seem similar enough to those that come from treatises on political philosophy. Even if we should not think that the city that Stoic political thought envisages is generally characterized by the eating of amputated limbs and marriage within one's family, we need to say something about the context in which Zeno and Chrysippus may have adduced the theses that have gained such prominence. I shall not go through each of the claims individually.[67] Ultimately, I do not think we can fully clarify the context and function of each of them—they are transmitted in a vocabulary that is highly contingent on the doxographic tradition. But it seems fitting to present at least a sketch of how we can think about the role of the disturbing theses in Stoic philosophy at the end of this chapter.

Traditionally, scholars have primarily pursued three ways of providing an explanatory context for the disturbing theses (if they do not ascribe the claims to a 'Cynic phase' of Zeno). First, the disturbing theses might be interpreted as focusing on a core notion of *concord*.

---

[67] In particular, I have no suggestion for how we should understand Zeno's claim on coinage other than the weak claim mentioned earlier: that he seems to dispute what he considers a false judgment—that coinage needs to be introduced for certain purposes (rather than presenting a specific policy on coinage of his own).

Second, the city the Stoics envisage might seem to be a *city of sages*. If so, then much of what is needed in a mundane city of fools might be unnecessary.[68] Third, the Stoics famously declare that things that conventionally count as *goods*—health, life, wealth, and so on—are mere *indifferents*. Some of the disturbing theses seem to point out how things we tend to care about are not really good, and thus not worthy objects of our pursuit. As I will argue, none of these approaches is convincing. Ultimately, as I suggest, we need to explore the Stoic notion of wisdom and theory of appropriate action if we wish to gain a better understanding of the disturbing theses—the former in relation to the claims about institutions, the latter in relation to claims about ways of acting that are traditionally regarded as shameful.

The so-called community of women has seemed to scholars to confirm the view that the Stoic laws are designed so as to enhance *unity*.[69] Presumably, Zeno values unity as highly as Plato and 'accepts' some institutions, like the community of women, from Plato, adding, in a similar spirit, others like the uniform dress code for women and men. However, the community of women is perhaps the thesis most difficult to assess. The expression 'community of women' might stand for a variety of different theses.[70] We have no evidence to illuminate what exactly Zeno discusses in this regard. The claim that he 'teaches' the community of women might be derived from, for instance, a thesis to the effect that it is no more and no less appropriate to have intercourse with one woman than with another (so that the institution of marriage apparently becomes obsolete) or something along these lines. It does not seem that Zeno or Chrysippus are suggesting, like Plato in the *Republic*, that people (or a certain class) should not be living in families and should not

---

[68] Baldry ("Zeno's Ideal State") proposes a reading that integrates the first and the second approach to the disturbing theses: the community Zeno discusses in his *Republic* is a community of sages, *and* only sages can live harmoniously together. Concord (*homonoia*) and friendship thus appear to be key notions of Zeno's political philosophy. Baldry's picture has been influential, and both Erskine and Schofield present versions of it.

[69] See Erskine, *Hellenistic Stoa*, 24–26, and Schofield, *The Stoic Idea*, chap. 2.

[70] The phrase 'community of women' appears to be a doxographical expression that is used for a range of views. Diogenes Laertius's more detailed testimony on this issue is highly confusing and seems to present a mix of Stoic, Cynic, and Platonic ideas (7.131).

consider their natural parents as their parents and their natural siblings as their siblings. Even though the Stoics also use a more ambitious sense of 'being a relative' (see chapter 2), one is to take into account whether someone is one's father, one's sister, and so on, in order to act appropriately. But if it seems doubtful whether the term 'community of women' refers to a similar train of thought as it does in Plato, then it is by no means clear that it has anything to do with enhancing unity. And if we admit that the notion of a community of women need not go back to the discussion of unity in a city, the disturbing theses, in general, offer very little reason to think that Zeno and Chrysippus are concerned with a political ideal of unity.

But what about the second idea, that certain institutions are useless *in a city of sages*? This idea plays out differently with respect to the theses on institutions and the theses on ways of acting. First, in a city of sages, courthouses might be unnecessary because all citizens abide by the law anyway, education useless because all citizens already have knowledge, etc.[71] Second, no type of action needs to be prohibited in a city of sages, since the sage, based on her perfect judgment, is going to choose the right course of action. General prohibitions are for fools, who are well served by guidelines. But such general rules are not perfect—while they are adequate for the most part, they are unable to account for very exceptional situations. The sage, able to rely fully on his knowledge, can determine whether a situation is the exceptional one in which it is appropriate to eat his arm or marry his mother.[72]

Our assessment of this approach depends on the stance we take with respect to a core question in the interpretation of early Stoic political philosophy—whether the ideal city of the Stoics is a city of sages or, rather, a cosmic city of all human beings.[73] In the disturbing theses themselves, neither Zeno nor Chrysippus seem to refer to any city at all. But we can get some indication of their context by considering the fact that they are *prescriptive* and *address agents*. This, it may seem, is

---

[71] Vander Waerdt argues that the disturbing theses are plausible once we recognize that the Stoic city is a city of sages ("Zeno's Republic," 286–288).

[72] This reading can go along with the thesis that the Stoics propose rules: if the Stoics formulate *exceptions* for the sage, then these might be exceptions *to rules*.

[73] I discuss the question whether Zeno conceives of a city of sages and Chrysippus of a cosmic city in chapter 2.

in itself a powerful argument against the second approach (however, these matters deserve more detailed argument, which I shall turn to in chapter 4). It is a fundamental misunderstanding of Stoic philosophy to assume that Zeno and Chrysippus would formulate views on what the sages *should* do (it is by considering what sages do that we understand what *we should* do). If the disturbing theses derived from an account of a city of sages, the disturbing theses should read like factual statements—there *are* no temples, there *is* no education, the eating of amputated limbs is not considered impious, and so on. But this is not the way the theses have come down to us. Quite to the contrary, the theses address progressors, telling them that there need not be temples or that they should not think that a certain type of action is 'out of place.'

Let us turn to the third approach. It might seem that the Stoics call certain institutions—gymnasia, education, courthouses, temples, etc.—useless because these are places whose importance is, conventionally, overestimated. In actual cities, courthouses and temples are to be held in honor, but in fact, one might think that, according to Stoic ethics, they are not good and thus do not deserve this respect. Perhaps the Stoics discuss temples, courthouses, gymnasia, and education when they discuss the difference between the good and the indifferent.[74] Perhaps temples, courthouses, gymnasia, and education are examples of things we take to be good, while in fact they are merely valuable. And a similar account may help with the theses on types of action. Amputated legs, dead bodies, and so on are really no good at all, and we tend to be unduly attached to them. Why should we not eat the leg, or why should we make a big affair of our dead parents' bodies? But this line of thought is misleading, or at least, it deserves significant clarification. Consider first the Stoic theses on institutions. Temples, courthouses, etc., are not straightforward candidates for indifferents in the technical sense of the Stoics. Indifferents are indifferent to happiness, but not to action; they are preferred or dispreferred and have value or disvalue. A courthouse might be a preferred indifferent, insofar as it is a

---

[74]I discuss this distinction in detail in chapter 4. For now, it is enough if we remind ourselves of its most basic assumptions: only virtue is good; all other things that are traditionally regarded as good are indifferent. But indifferent things have value and disvalue, i.e., are preferred and dispreferred.

building; insofar as a building is a possession, it might be considered something that contributes to someone's wealth. But this is not what a courthouse stands for—a courthouse is considered a place of law and justice. Similarly, temples are buildings and thus a form of property. But temples are primarily viewed as places of worship, places that are sacred. When the Stoics say that there need be neither temples nor courthouses, they do not seem to be saying that buildings should be considered as contributing to the preferred indifferent 'wealth,' as opposed to what we mistakenly consider the good of wealth. And insofar as temples or courthouses are buildings and thus have value, the Stoics would *not* suggest that we should do without them. The Stoics do not recommend abolishing things of value (life, health, wealth, etc.), and they certainly do not suggest that things of value have no use.[75] Consider next the claims regarding types of action. It is clearly the case that attachment to an amputated arm or dead human body is, from the Stoic point of view, irrational. And to some extent, this explains why the Stoics suggest that one should neither invest in grand funerals nor be held back from eating one's amputated leg by conventional ideas. But again, the rationale for these claims is not that legs or dead bodies only have *value*, and are not good. Rather, dead bodies and amputated limbs *do not have value*. They are *not* examples of indifferents.

Alternatively, let me propose two other lines of thought. First, while the disturbing theses do not describe life in a city of sages, in some sense they take the perspective of the sage. The Stoic theses on institutions assert how things are *strictly speaking*, if we fully understand their role in human life. We have testimony explaining the Stoic stance on temples as going back to the idea that temples are not worth much. Temples are to be rejected because, as mere products of human building, they are not worth much and thus not sacred.[76] But, as we saw, the point of this claim cannot be that temples are merely valuable and should therefore be abolished; the Stoics do not consider valuable things useless. A second report on temples helps to clarify what the core of the Stoic argument very likely is: there is no need for temples if

---

[75]See Erskine, *Hellenistic Stoa*, 24.
[76]Plutarch, *On Stoic Self-Contradictions* 1034B.

people have—as they should—the divine in their minds.[77] Suppose the Stoic thesis that temples are not worth much derives from a context in which the shortcomings of conventional piety are discussed. The Stoics might well go as far as to *dismiss* traditional religious practices. If *real* piety is having one's soul in a divine condition, then anyone who is not a sage is very far from being pious. If temples are the place where people worship in their foolish way, they are, in a sense, places of *impiety*. Real piety is wisdom, and the religious practices of fools are so far removed from wisdom that we can easily envisage a context in which the Stoics would call them *impious*, just as they call anyone who is not wise a fool. What the sage understands about temples, courthouses, gymnasia, and education is that these are not really places of piety, law, and education. The claim that temples are *not worth much* is tied to the idea that they are *not sacred*. It says that actual temples lack the very property that should define them. And thus an actual temple, in a sense, is no temple. What the sage understands about courthouses, temples, gymnasia and education is that they are really not what they are usually taken to be.

If this leads to the correct interpretation of some of the disturbing theses, it accords extraordinarily well with Stoic ideas that are better attested. The Stoics are famous for radically reinterpreting notions. As we shall see in detail in chapter 3, they offer revised notions of many fields of expertise according to which each of these fields *really* is an aspect of wisdom. To be a judge in the true sense is to be wise, to be a priest in the true sense is to be wise, and so on. Judges, as we usually encounter them, actually *are no* judges, and priests as we know them *are no* priests. To *be* either of these persons *is to be wise*. It is in the context of these ideas that the claims about institutions being useless make a lot of sense. If temples as we know them are not temples, courthouses not courthouses, etc., then we can do without them. On this interpretation, the theses about temples, courthouses, gymnasia, etc., turn out to be very abstract considerations, concerned with explicating the notion of wisdom.

But how could such abstract discussions be transmitted in the form of theses that apparently instruct us to abolish the core institutions of the cities we live in? Suppose a Sceptic reads Stoic treatises on the law or doxography on the Stoic conception of law. With only

---

[77]Epiphanius reports the following reasoning for Zeno: temples should not be built, but men should have the divine in their minds (*Adv. Haeres.* 3.2,9 = SVF 1.146).

a few moves, he can turn the view that only the law that pervades the cosmos *is law* into the claim that the Stoics abolish courthouses. If only this 'cosmic law' (as we might call it in a provisional way) is law, the legal practices in courthouses may be said to be *unlawful*. And any such phrase in the Stoic treatises could be reflected in doxography as the claim that, according to the Stoics, there should be no courthouses. Similar trains of thought can easily be constructed for temples and educational institutions.

Thus we can save a version of the second approach to the disturbing theses—the approach that explains them, most broadly speaking, by reference to the Stoic notion of wisdom. But only some of them can be explained in this way. What about those that recommend courses of action (those on dress codes, burial, and anthropophagy and some of the claims about incest and other forms of sexual conduct, perhaps including the community of women)? In order to interpret them, we must turn to Stoic thought about appropriate action.

Kathêkonta—appropriate activities—involve the consideration of indifferents. If an agent acts appropriately, she 'selects' indifferents (things of value and disvalue) so as to decide what she should be doing. (The interpretation of this theory is, in many respects, controversial; at this point, I am assuming some of the claims that I will defend in chapter 4.) The Stoics seem to have written extensive treatises on what is appropriate for agents in *all kinds of situations*, depending on their roles and stations in life, with whom they interact, and what exactly the circumstances are. As we saw, several of the disturbing theses are not attributed to treatises on political philosophy but to Chrysippus's *On What Is Appropriate* and his *On Things Not to be Chosen for Their Own Sakes*. In these works, Chrysippus may have discussed a broad variety of different situations, suggesting an appropriate course of action for each one.

What is particularly prominent in the direct quotations of disturbing theses is the idea that one should not be held back from certain types of action by conventional ideas. This line of thought is partly presented with a view to *presumed distinctions*. Zeno seems to discuss sexual actions that are conventionally deemed forbidden by referring to the distinctions that inform customs—distinctions between male and female, this or that part of the body, and so on. These distinctions do not hold up to Stoic scrutiny. When we consider the spectrum of indifferents (and thus of things we must consider in deliberation)—health, illness, life, death, etc.—it does not seem to give us the tools to regard traditional distinctions like that between girlfriend and boyfriend as relevant to the appropriateness of actions.

SE PH 3.207 suggests that the clause '*ouk atopon einai*' might be an expression the Stoics used: a certain activity is 'not out of place.' In his book *Exhortations*, Chrysippus says that "cohabitation with mothers and daughters and sisters, eating certain things, and going directly from childbed or deathbed to a holy place have been condemned without reason [*alogôs diabeblêtai*]" (Plutarch, *On Stoic Self-Contradictions* 1044F–1045A, tr. Cherniss). The point of this statement does not seem to be that cohabitation with mothers, daughters, sisters, the eating of certain things, etc., are generally permissible or even prescribed. Rather, the point is that there is *no reason* to think that these types of action are *generally forbidden*—that is, those who condemn these actions have no compelling arguments to offer.

Consider the case of eating an amputated limb. Chrysippus's claim on this issue seems to discuss the rare case where one amputates a limb that is healthy and thus not dangerous to eat, *and* where it is useful to eat this limb (rather than something else, we might add). In such a case, he seems to be saying, it is appropriate to eat one's amputated limb. A claim like this does not generate a rule, for example, that people should eat human flesh. Rather, it seems to highlight the fact that custom and tradition should not matter to deliberation. If we happen to be in a situation where we need to amputate a healthy limb (rare enough!) and this limb is useful to eat (even rarer!), then we should not be held back from eating it by conventional ideas. Those of the Stoic claims that tell us to not regard certain courses of action as shameful or 'out of place' seem to illustrate that some kinds of things do not even have value and are thus not relevant to action. Things of value, that is, preferred and dispreferred indifferents, are relevant to action—they are the things we should perfectly select and deselect. But they do not give us reason to back up many conventional ideas on what kinds of differences matter or what is a scandalous act. As I suggest, this type of thesis thus addresses a specific aspect of Stoic thought about appropriate action: that, in addition to understanding how health, wealth, and so on are merely valuable and not good, we need also to understand that some other things *do not even have value* (and that some distinctions imply a difference in value that does not truly exist).[78]

At this point, I have not yet argued for many of the assumptions I am making—the details of Stoic thought about the city, wisdom, law, and appropriate action will be the subject of the following chapters. Whether my sketch of how we might explain the disturbing theses is convincing depends to a large extent on ideas I have yet to present. But at this point, we can already see that the disturbing theses can plausibly be understood as illustrating abstract points in a deliberately 'shocking' way. Further, we can already draw some provisional conclusions with respect to the question of whether the disturbing theses provide evidence for the view that the Stoic law consists of *rules*. As I suggest, they do not. The testimony is fully compatible with the assumption that the Stoics 'command' specific courses of action only insofar as they argue that, in a case where reasoning about appropriateness says that we should eat an amputated limb or marry our mother, the fact that these things are traditionally considered scandalous should not stop us. If reason prescribes doing something, we should not be held back by convention.

[78]Note that this reading of how the disturbing theses relate to Stoic thought about appropriate action does not make use of a notion of 'exceptional circumstances.' Rather, it sketches a way we can think about these claims without appealing to *exceptions*. As I shall argue in detail in chapter 4, the Stoics do not work with such a notion, contrary to how their doctrine has often been reconstructed. It is quite customary in the literature to rephrase the Stoic theses by adding the predicate 'exceptional' or 'special.' See, e.g., Obbink: "It has been suggested that some of the objectionable features were offered as examples of indifferents; others, like cannibalism *in extremis*, as examples of what the wise might justly do in special circumstances, *kata peristasin*" ("The Stoic Sage," 182). While Vander Waerdt explains all other disturbing theses by reference to perfect reason, he argues that the claims about anthropophagy must be understood as referring to *special* situations. The sage will eat human flesh, as Vander Waerdt says, "under the stress of circumstances"—*kata peristasin* ("The Stoic Sage" 194, 300). I will discuss the notion *kata peristasin* in chapter 4.

2

The Community of All Human Beings

A fundamental question to ask about early Stoic political philosophy is what kind of city the Stoics discuss. Given that both Zeno and Chrysippus write treatises on the *politeia*, it seems likely that they, like Plato, discuss an *ideal* city. But, as I shall argue, they do not. Rather, the early Stoics discuss a city that is *real*. The city discussed by the early Stoics—and as I shall argue, already by Zeno—*is the cosmos.*

In what sense, we may ask, is the cosmos a city? As I shall argue, the Stoics capture a range of ideas by comparing the cosmos to a city: most important, the cosmos is a city insofar as it is regulated by *law*.[1] Second, it 'consists of' its citizens; the cosmos is sustained by those of its parts that have perfect reason, and is in this sense a city of sages and gods. Third, it is a habitation—it is the place in

---

[1] The Stoics define the city as "a group of people living in the same place and administered by law" (Dio Chrysostom 36.20 = SVF 3.329 = LS 67J). A distinction between two senses of 'city' is preserved at Clem. *Strom.* 4.26 (= SVF 3.327). The Stoics say that the universe (*ouranos*) is a city in the proper sense, but that those here on earth are not—they are called cities but are really not. For a city or a people is something good, an organization (*sustêma*) or group (*plêthos*) of men administered by law that exhibits refinement. A similar picture is evoked by Seneca (*De Ot.* 4), who asks us to envisage two states, one "great and truly common," the other that in which we happen to be born. The great and common city includes both gods and men. Cleanthes formulates a famous argument on what the city is: "If a city is a habitable structure, in which people who take refuge have access to the dispensation of justice (*dikê*), a city is surely something civilized (*asteion*); but a city is this sort of habitation; therefore a city is something civilized" (Stobaeus 2.103,14–17 = SVF 1.587 part = LS 67I). Cleanthes' argument is directed against an argument by the Cynic Diogenes (DL 6.72). Cleanthes elevates the notion of a city as something fine or excellent in

which all human beings jointly live. And fourth, it exhibits the characteristic structure of a city: there are rulers and ruled, gods and human beings.

While the Stoics discuss a city that is real rather than ideal, their notion of the city is still *normative*. Even though the comparison of cosmos and city partly relies on the everyday assumption that cities are places of law, the kind of law we find in ordinary cities is not law in the technical sense of the Stoics. The law of ordinary cities is not the common law, which is identical with reason and Zeus. A place needs to be governed by law in this technical—that is normative—sense in order to truly be a city. For this reason, the cosmos is *the only city*.

The Stoic theory thus differs significantly from the type of theory we are most familiar with in the context of ancient philosophy; Plato's *Republic* presents an ideal city that *could* and *should* be established.[2] Given this familiarity, one is easily misled into thinking that the ancient discussion of ideal cities is generally concerned with a conception of a city as it should be, a city we should strive to bring about. Plato's *Republic* looms large in the background of Hellenistic discussions (and in the minds of modern scholars), and it is almost inevitable that one tries to understand the cosmic city by comparing it with Plato's ideal city. Plato's city *could* come into being, but, once it existed, it would inevitably start to deteriorate. Socrates and his interlocutors in the *Republic* call it a 'city founded in speech.' It is a theoretical construct, generated in philosophical discussion. Once it became real, it would enter the realm of things that 'become,' in the technical sense of Plato's metaphysics in the *Republic*. The ideal and the real city of Plato's *Republic* thus differ ontologically (which explains why the real city would deteriorate). As firm opponents of Platonic metaphysics, however, the Stoics could not conceive of

---

the sense of civilized (*asteion*). On the controversy about Diogenes' argument see Moles, "The Cynics," in *The Cambridge History of Greek and Roman Thought*, ed. Christopher Rowe and Malcolm Schofield (Cambridge: Cambridge University Press, 2000), 415–434. Cleanthes' argument seems to be ad hominem, and we have difficulties understanding Diogenes' position (let alone what Cleanthes takes it to be). We have no direct quotations on how Zeno or Chrysippus *defines* the city.

[2]The details of such a reading are controversial. See André Laks, "Legislation and Demiurgy: On the Relationship between Plato's *Republic* and *Laws*," *Classical Antiquity* 9 (1990): 209–229.

ideal and real cities along these lines. They do not name conditions (like Plato's 'three waves') under which an ideal city could become a reality.[3] Unlike Plato, the Stoics describe a city *that already exists*. The cosmos *as a city* exists, will not deteriorate, and could not be instituted through any human effort. The cosmos is the common 'home' to all its inhabitants, and it is regulated by the law. Since no city other than the cosmos is regulated by the *common* law—or, as we might say, the only law the Stoics acknowledge to be a law—the cosmos is the *only* city.

These brief remarks expose a methodological problem that is best dealt with explicitly at the outset of a discussion on the theory of the cosmic city. Plutarch says that Zeno wrote his *Republic* in response to Plato's *Republic* (*On Stoic Self-Contradictions* 1034F), and it is quite obvious that Zeno himself makes and invites the comparison between his theory and Plato's conception of the ideal city. It is evident from many aspects of his philosophy that Zeno thought in detail about Plato's dialogues.[4] Insofar as early Stoicism sides with Socrates and against Plato, Plato (and the Platonic Socrates) is an important point of reference.[5] However, it is sometimes assumed that Plato's *Republic* is the main point of reference for Zeno, to the

[3]As is well known, whether Plato's ideal city comes into being depends, most important, on whether philosophers rule (the 'third wave'), i.e., whether someone with the necessary talents can be found and can be brought up without being corrupted in his or her youth.

[4]As Francesca Alesse convincingly points out, Zeno's time as a student in the Academy (starting in 314 BCE) was probably much longer than was often thought. Quite possibly Zeno was still a student at the Academy when he started teaching himself; *La Stoa e la Tradizione Socratica* (Naples: Bibliopolis, 2000), 79–104, esp. 104).

[5]The Stoics seem to draw on different sources in their perception of Socrates: Plato's dialogues are of course highly important, but Aristotle's discussions of Socratic ideas might also figure in their picture of Socrates. And of course there are the works of other Socratics, first and foremost Xenophon. While I cannot argue for this claim, it seems to me that the Stoics were highly sophisticated interpreters of Plato—interpreters who engaged with theoretical options that Plato sometimes only alludes to or implies, and who were aware of the difficulties in tracing what is Socratic vs. Platonic, and so on. On the extent to which the Stoics were familiar with Aristotle's thought see Alesse (*La Stoa*, 233) and F. H. Sandbach, "Aristotle's Legacy to Stoic Ethics," *Bulletin of the London University Institute of Classical Studies* 15 (1968): 72–85. Cf. also Stephen Menn, "Physics as Virtue," *Proceedings of the Boston Area Colloquium in Ancient Philosophy* 11, ed. John J. Clearly and William C. Wians (1995): 1–34, and Nussbaum, "Commentary on Menn (Stephen Menn, 'Physics as Virtue')," in the same volume, 35–45.

extent that he is writing something like a 'counter-*Republic*' to Plato's *Republic*.[6] This seems to me to push matters too far.[7] Early Stoic political thought reflects engagement with a wide range of earlier thought. It has long been acknowledged that the early Stoics seem to have studied Heraclitus.[8] Further, consider the longstanding (partly sophistic) discussion of the relationship of nature and law, as well as the tradition of writings about the constitution (*politeia*).[9] Note further that, by claiming that 'law is king,' Chrysippus makes a reference to a famous idea of Pindar, an idea whose repercussions can be found in numerous ancient texts. Chrysippus is famous for his engagement with the poets, and it seems more than likely that he invested much thought into the interpretation of poetry. Plato's *Republic* is an important point of reference, but it is far from being the only one.[10]

[6]Paul Vander Waerdt argues that Zeno's *Republic* is an answer to the "conventionalist challenge" that Glaucon and Adeimantus put forward in *Republic* 2—it serves to show that justice is "naturally choiceworthy"; "Zeno's Republic and the Origins of Natural Law," in *The Socratic Movement*, ed. Vander Waerdt (Ithaca, N.Y.: Cornell University Press, 1994), 277.

[7]Malcolm Schofield argues that anyone writing a *Republic* will be inviting comparison with Plato's *Republic*, and that Zeno "may be presumed to have been attempting, like Plato, to show how a *polis*—on the ordinary understanding of *polis*—can be reformed or reconstructed to satisfy some cherished goal or goals"; *The Stoic Idea of the City* (Chicago: University of Chicago Press, 1999), 25.

[8]Even though Schofield thinks that Plato's *Republic* is Zeno's major point of reference in writing his own *Republic*, he discusses a number of ways the early Stoics seem to have engaged with Heraclitus (*The Stoic Idea*).

[9]For a detailed discussion of the latter tradition see Stephen Menn, "On Plato's *Politeia*," *Proceedings of the Boston Area Colloquium* 21, ed. John J. Cleary and Gary M. Gurtler (2005): 1–55. I am grateful to Stephen Menn for discussion of these matters and for making available to me the article prior to its publication.

[10]Even within Plato, the *Republic* is not the only relevant point of reference. Ultimately, many more questions concerning Plato's philosophy have some bearing on the interpretation of early Stoic political philosophy: how we interpret the development of Plato's political thought; whether some aspects of the *Republic* were considered 'Socratic' as opposed to 'Platonic' (either in the Academy or by the Stoics); whether the *Statesman* was mostly read for the method of division or for its political thought; whether the *Laws* was considered to express Plato's ultimate stance, which could make the *Republic* appear as transitional and still partly 'Socratic'; and whether the *Timaeus* and perhaps even *Philebus* 28d–30b were interpreted as directly relevant to political philosophy. Similarly, one might speculate on whether the Stoics, when

My references to Plato, as well as to earlier philosophers, will be scarce. A study that explores how Zeno, Cleanthes, and Chrysippus engage with earlier political thought would have to be considerably longer and would have to engage with a wide range of material. Rather than pursue this path, I shall focus on the evidence we have for the early Stoic views, trying to interpret it, as far as possible, without relying on particular interpretations of Plato, the Cynics, sophistic debates about law and nature, Greek poets, Heraclitus, and others. Insofar as I refer to Plato—as I did in introducing the Stoic project of discussing a cosmic city—my goals are mostly expository. Since we are so much more familiar with Plato's *Republic* than with any Stoic theory, reference to this text can help us understand different theoretical options. But none of my claims about the early Stoics depends on a specific reading of Plato's dialogues.

My brief excursus on the various theories, authors, and debates the early Stoics might refer to in their political thought also relates to another important point. In our assessment of early Stoic political philosophy and of whether what the Stoics do deserves to be called political philosophy, we should not limit ourselves to a specific

---

studying the *Gorgias* next to the *Republic*, believed that the Socrates of the *Gorgias* focuses on the true subject matter of political philosophy—the relationship of law and nature—while Plato loses sight of this question in the *Republic*. Interpretations of Zeno's *Republic* that make extensive use of the relationship to Plato's *Republic* have the further strategic disadvantage that any claim about the Stoic theory will depend on a specific reading of the *Republic*. Schofield writes: "my argument will make frequent recourse to antecedents of Zeno's ideas in Plato's work, especially the *Republic*. Several of the provisions itemized in DL 7.32–33, of course, are naturally interpreted as repeating elements of Plato's communist program or as pushing further than Plato himself had done" (*The Stoic Idea*, 25). Paul Vander Waerdt describes the key question of Plato's political philosophy as dealing with "natural justice." The "conventionalist challenge" posed by Glaucon and Adeimantus in *Republic* 2 is, according to Vander Waerdt, at the center of what Plato engages with. Vander Waerdt takes Zeno to side with Plato, but as offering a rival account of how justice is natural ("Zeno's Republic," 277). Very briefly put, the difficulty with this approach seems to be the following. Like Schofield, Vander Waerdt begins from a claim about Plato's *Republic*. Scholars will not only disagree on whether the so-called conventionalist challenge or Thrasymachus's 'amoralist' challenge are at the heart of what Plato wants to refute in the *Republic*. It is also not clear whether the 'conventionalist challenge' engages with *natural* justice—whether this is even a notion that Plato pursues in the *Republic*.

picture of political philosophy. It is not the case that the Stoics engage in political philosophy if they, like Plato in the *Republic*, address the question 'what is justice?'[11] More generally, the Stoics need not discuss the best constitution, different types of constitutions, the laws of the best city, and justice in the best city in order to engage in political philosophy.

Recent scholarship sometimes suggests that we are confined to two options: that the early Stoics *either* do political philosophy in the sense of conceiving of an ideal city and discussing its laws and institutions *or* discuss the virtue of an individual agent.[12] I think that neither Zeno nor Chrysippus engages in proposing laws and institutions for an ideal city, be it a city of sages or a worldwide state yet to be established. But I do not think that we must confine the task of political philosophy to this kind of project. By instructing us on how we should *view all other human beings* and how we should *relate to them*, the early Stoics engage in very vital political questions—questions about the scope of our political concern. All human beings concern us in a sense that goes beyond recognizing that the 'most distant Mysian' is also a human being, a sense that includes taking *his* life, health, and so on to be relevant to our actions.

By thinking of the world as a city, the early Stoics side with a conception of political philosophy that focuses on the relationship

[11]One way of thinking that the Stoics do not engage in political philosophy proper is to observe that they do not seem to focus specifically on questions of *justice*, and indeed Annas remarks on this fact: "the Stoics have no systematic answer to the question, how justice as a virtue of the individual agent relates to justice as a virtue of the institutions"; *The Morality of Happiness* (New York: Oxford University Press, 1995), 311. However, it is not clear to me why we should limit our conception of what counts as political philosophy to the discussion of justice.

[12]Julia Annas argues that the Stoics take what she refers to as a "depoliticized outlook." On her reading, "the idealized political community, being a simply moral one, is not a political notion at all, and the very fact that the Stoics say that actual cities are not really cities suggests that they reject specifically political discussion in favour of a redefinition of political terms which uses them in a context where political issues do not arise" (*Morality of Happiness*, 302–311, 306). In her "Aristotelian Political Theory," in *Justice and Generosity: Studies in Hellenistic Social and Political Philosophy*, ed. A. Laks and M. Schofield (Cambridge: Cambridge University Press, 1995), Annas employs the notion of a "robust political philosophy" (74–77). If we follow Annas and take a political philosophy to be robust only if it engages with the analysis of the *polis* as 'we' (i.e., the Greeks at the time) know it, then the Stoic theory may not be political philosophy.

between law and nature. Their theory of the cosmic city thus takes up questions that, within ancient discussions, are traditionally considered to be deeply political—questions about the status of the actual laws within cities as we know them. The Stoics regard the cosmic city as the only real city, and the law that pervades the cosmos as the only real law. Nature is the place of law, and it is so *insofar* as it (or: the universe) is a city. *Actual* (in the sense of: ordinary) cities and their laws are dismissed. But the idea is not that we should leave these cities and live as expatriate-cosmopolitanists. Rather, the idea is to recognize that actual cities do not ultimately 'live up' to being cities; actual laws are not real laws, and actual cities are not real cities.

This chapter will be devoted to a detailed analysis of the testimony on citizenship in the cosmos. The sources offer four different theses on who is, or should be seen as, a citizen: the sages (S); all human beings (H); human beings and the gods (HG); the sages and the gods (SG) (section 1). I will be defending the view that none of these claims needs to be discarded as spurious. Two theses are central to this interpretation: First, (S) does not commit us to envisaging a 'city of sages' (section 2). Second, we should not give up on the evidence that ascribes (H), the claim about all human beings as fellow-citizens, to Zeno's *Republic* (sections 3–5). Since the general tendency in recent scholarship is to dismiss this passage, I will spend considerable time arguing against this view.[13] Once we admit the relevant testimony, we can see a very important link between the Stoic theory of *oikeiôsis*, a cornerstone of Stoic ethics, and political philosophy. The Stoics ask us to see all human beings as 'belonging to us' in a political sense—a sense that explains the kinship of all human beings as a relationship of being each other's fellow-inhabitants in *one polis*, the cosmos. The theory of the cosmic city has, surprisingly, not yet been interpreted as closely connected to the theory of *oikeiôsis*. The connection has, of course, been seen, but it has been spelled out mostly by those who are interested in understanding the theory of *oikeiôsis*, not by those who reconstruct early Stoic political philosophy. Discussions of *oikeiôsis* standardly

---

[13]After detailed discussion by Schofield, Vander Waerdt, and others, Dirk Obbink does not engage in detail with this passage in his discussion of the testimony on Zeno's *Republic*; "The Stoic Sage in the Cosmic City," in *Topics in Stoic Philosophy*, ed. Katerina Ierodiakonou (Oxford: Oxford University Press, 2001), 180–184.

emphasize its so-called *social* dimensions. In such contexts, the idea of a kinship of all human beings (the 'social' side of *oikeiôsis*) is often said to have a political dimension. However, these views about the theory of *oikeiôsis* are *not brought to bear on the interpretation of the sources* concerning the cosmic city and the question of who its citizens are. I will argue that the relevant ideas are so deeply related that we should make the connection, and that we can find additional justification for doing so by considering the way ancient authors present both topics in unison. Once we do, we can see that, in an important way, early Stoic political philosophy goes beyond envisaging the ideal of an individual living perfectly in the cosmos. The early Stoics argue that a perfect life is a life that recognizes the concerns of all human beings as relevant to one's own actions.[14] Most important, I argue that we should discuss the Stoic conception of the cosmic city and its inhabitants in unison with the theory of *oikeiôsis*. In this chapter, I thus focus on what the early Stoics have to say about the community of *all human beings*, that is, on (H) and (HG). I will discuss (S) and (SG) in more detail in chapter 3.

1. Four Theses on Citizenship

Stoic philosophy is sometimes advertised as discussing what we might today call 'global justice' or cosmopolitanism.[15] If the cosmic perspective in some sense encompasses *all human beings*, it seems that the Stoics leave behind the limitations of political theories that focus on one state, unrelated to others, in favor of a worldwide perspective. Readers of Plato's *Republic* have often found it unsatisfactory that we do not hear much about the way Plato's city relates

---

[14]Rachel Barney calls the question of how the concerns of others figure in the sage's deliberation a "puzzle in Stoic ethics." Seemingly, the perfect agent is concerned about *her* health, wealth, life, and so on, but not about that of others. "A Puzzle in Stoic Ethics," *Oxford Studies in Ancient Philosophy* 24 (2003): 303–340. I am much indebted to this article, which seems to me to point out a major difficulty in the interpretation of Stoic ethics. As I shall argue, the Stoic ideal of considering all human beings as fellow-citizens implies that we come to regard their concerns as our concerns, i.e., as relevant to our deliberation.

[15]For a discussion of the history of 'cosmopolitanism' see P. Coulmas, *Les citoyens du monde: Histoire du Cosmopolitanisme* (Paris: Albin Michel, 1995).

to other cities or whether its justice includes dealings with other political communities.[16] If the early Stoics thought that political philosophy should have a significantly wider scope—the scope of the whole world—this would be highly interesting. If they did, then (H), the idea that in some sense all human beings are citizens, should be a core aspect of early Stoic political philosophy. It would appear to open the path to a political perspective that encompasses all human beings and to key ideas of the later conception of natural law.

Nussbaum draws attention to similar issues in her foreword to the second edition of Schofield's monograph *The Stoic Idea of the City*. According to Nussbaum, Stoic political philosophy refers in an important sense to all human beings, and this is part of its attraction.[17] However, the few scholars who have recently engaged in detailed and comprehensive studies of this field agree that the one source that reports Zeno as talking about all human beings is misleading. Schofield, Vander Waerdt, and Obbink all think that Zeno discusses a *city of sages*. On this picture, the conception of the cosmic city is later than Zeno, and perhaps even later than Chrysippus.[18] Chrysippus does not seem to differ with Zeno in his conception of the sages as the only human beings who are able to lead lawful lives. But at the same time, it is Chrysippus who compares the cosmos to a city. Is Stoic cosmopolitanism thus a later development, a development that involves a significant departure from the early theory?[19]

---

[16]Judging from the analogy with the soul, it would seem that it does. But this is not an explicit concern of the *Republic*, and we would probably have to include interpretation of the *Timaeus* and *Critias* to discuss Plato's views on these matters.

[17]Nussbaum in Schofield (*The Stoic Idea*, xii).

[18]Obbink writes that the notion of the universe as a city "develops over time through a succession of thinkers, from Zeno's exclusive city of the wise and Chrysippus's conception of the cosmos as a polity of gods and wise men, to Cicero and the later view that all men live (or ought to live) under the same canons of natural law" ("The Stoic Sage," 178; cf. Vander Waerdt, "Zeno's Republic," 276 n. 18). But even though Obbink holds the foregoing view, he thinks that Chrysippus sees himself as spelling out Zeno's ideas (184).

[19]It has often been observed that Stoic ethics starts out with a stark emphasis on the sage and later on becomes more interested in the ethical life of ordinary people. We could speculate about whether reference to all human beings coincides with a growing interest in the average human being. For a recent exposition of this view see Anne Banateanu, *La théorie stoïcienne de l'amitié. Essai de reconstruction*

However, the four theses on citizenship—(S), (SG), (H), and (HG)—are all ascribed to the *early* Stoics (or, at least, they purport to portray orthodox—that is, early—Stoic thought). Perhaps, we may conjecture, there is already a relevant shift from Zeno to Chrysippus. In this case, the four theses would seem to be explicable in developmental terms: (S), the thesis that only the sages are citizens, and possibly (SG), the thesis that only sages and gods are citizens, would belong to the earlier picture of a city of sages (in a sense, gods *are* sages). Theses (H), that we should view all other human beings as fellow-citizens, and (HG), that human beings and gods together live in the cosmos, would make up the Chrysippean (or at any rate post-Zenonian) theory of a cosmic city. However, as I shall argue, the evidence does not support the assumption that, in comparing the cosmos to a city, Chrysippus takes himself to move away from Zeno. Further, and this will be central to my argument, it is Zeno himself who advises us to regard all human beings as fellow-citizens, and this claim is integral to the conception of a cosmic city. Most plausibly, the theory of the cosmic city encompasses different theoretical perspectives, a perspective on how the cosmos *is* home to all rational beings who live in it (human beings and gods) and a perspective on how it is an *ideal* to live *lawfully* in this cosmic city as a sage and citizen. Both Zeno and Chrysippus seem to envisage a worldwide community of all human beings, but they also explore the ideal of being a perfectly wise part of the world.

I shall thus argue that (S), (SG), (H), and (HG) are part of one complex theory. My argument for this thesis will run through all of this chapter, but we may note the most important points of disagreement at the outset. Three considerations may seem to speak in favor of the view I contest—the view that Zeno conceives of a city of sages and later Stoics of a worldwide city: (1) Zeno does not mention a cosmic city; (2) Zeno says that only the sages are citizens; and

(Fribourg: Editions Universitaires Fribourg Suisse, 2001), 145. But this suggestion is not plausible. Obbink calls into question whether, if the early Stoics were exclusively talking about a city of the wise, later Stoics would indeed have gone so far as to compromise this doctrine in such a significant way as to make a directly opposing claim on citizenship ("The Stoic Sage," 181). Here Obbink rightly demands caution: if later Stoic authors focus on how all human beings are related through one law, it is likely that they understand themselves as engaged in the further development of ideas that are already present in the early doctrine.

(3) the report that ascribes a version of (H) to Zeno may appear to be untrustworthy. However, (1) Zeno also does not mention a city of sages, and even in Chrysippus we seem to be dealing with a *comparison of cosmos and city*, so that the notion of a cosmic city is shorthand for something that is in fact more complicated; (2) the claim that only the sages are citizens is more plausibly interpreted as referring to the *special status* of wise beings in the cosmos; and (3) the report that ascribes a version of (H) to Zeno seems, as I shall argue, as trustworthy as the report according to which he holds that only sages are citizens.[20]

One discrepancy among the views that Zeno, Cleanthes, and Chrysippus hold in political philosophy might lie in the importance that is given to discussion of the gods and, perhaps even more generally, to physics.[21] The sources on Zeno's *Republic* not only do not mention the cosmos as city but also do not refer to the gods as citizens. Cleanthes seems to have been the early Stoic with the most pronounced interest in theology, and Chrysippus is famous for explaining how a sage is no different from a god.[22] Both of them may have shifted the emphasis within the discussion of citizenship, so that greater attention was given to the role of the gods in the cosmos. However, if we look at the physical doctrines ascribed to Zeno, it is clear that the theological ideas that are central to the conception of gods as 'citizens' are not new in Cleanthes or Chrysippus.[23] There may be a shift in emphasis, so that the theory from Cleanthes or Chrysippus onward talks more directly about the gods. But, as I shall argue in chapter 3, being a citizen amounts most importantly to being a part of the universe that has perfect reason,

---

[20]We might further remind ourselves of the disturbing theses. Chrysippus holds, it seems, virtually the same views as Zeno on the kinds of issues that are discussed there.

[21]Keimpe Algra discusses an impression we may get from the sources: that Zeno, while writing on physics, does not delve into physics to the same extent as into ethics ("Zeno of Citium and Stoic Cosmology," *Elenchos* 24 (2003): 9–32). If this impression is accurate, as to some extent it appears to be, Zeno's views in political philosophy might be tied up with cosmology in a general rather than a detailed manner.

[22]I shall discuss the relevant passages in chapter 3.

[23]As I will discuss in detail in chapter 3, one plausible way of understanding the notion of citizen-gods is to think of them as the planets. The relevant physical claims for this are ascribed to Zeno: The planets are "intelligent and prudent and have the fieriness of designing fire."

and it would seem that Zeno shares the core premises for making this claim about the gods.

2. *"Only the Sages are Citizens"*

Let me begin with (S), the thesis that only the sages are citizens, or rather, that only the sages are citizens, friends, relatives, and free:[24]

> All who are not virtuous are personal and public enemies, slaves, and alienated from one another, including parents from children, brothers from brothers, relatives from relatives. They criticize him again for presenting . . . only virtuous people in the *Republic* as citizens, friends, relatives, and free. (DL 7.32–33; tr. LS with changes)[25]

What Zeno says is that only the virtuous, that is, the sages, are citizens. But the passage has traditionally been given a stronger reading. The claim that only the sages are citizens has been taken to mean that Zeno envisages a *city of sages*, a city that is entirely populated by sages. This reading, however, fails to appreciate that the inhabitants of a polis do not all have the same status. Some are its full citizens, and others are not. Further, those who have the status of citizens might plausibly be said to constitute the city, and there is perhaps even a sense in which the city consists of them. As we shall see, this is analogous to the Stoic picture. Insofar as only the sages are citizens, they in some sense constitute the cosmic city; but all other human beings live in it too.[26]

---

[24]Throughout this book, I shall sometimes, when the context makes this clear, refer to the more confined thesis—that only the sages are citizens—as (S). But for the most part, (S) stands for the fourfold thesis that only the sages are citizens, friends, relatives, and free.

[25]In order to see why the passage is taken as evidence for the claim that only sages are citizens, we need to replace 'virtuous' with 'wise.' In Stoic ethics, to be wise and to be virtuous amount to the same thing. The two dichotomous distinctions between fools and sages, and between vice and virtue, can be used quite interchangeably.

[26]When Cicero reports how, according to the Stoics, only the sages are citizens, he goes on to say: "and there aren't any cities or citizen-bodies except those of the wise" (*Academica* 2.136). As we shall see, there is a sense in which the cosmos is constituted, sustained, and governed by the wise. But at the same time it is the home of all human beings.

Zeno uses terms in both a technical sense (political enemies, personal enemies, slaves, alienated, citizen, friend, free, relative) and an everyday one (parents, children, brothers, relatives). It is well attested that the Stoics consciously go back and forth between technical and everyday uses of words. The famous paradoxes partly rely on the fact that the reader is acquainted with the Stoic, technical sense of a notion but still finds the nontechnical, everyday sense more natural. Thus, a statement like 'Everything bad is common to the fool' makes sense (at least to the degree to which the Stoic theory convinces us) once we remind ourselves that really only vice is bad. The paradoxical impression derives from the fact that we cannot fully forget the way words are used in everyday speech. Chrysippus remarks that if someone understands what preferred and dispreferred indifferents are, but wishes to refer to them as good and bad things, then insofar as he is correct with respect to the 'significates,' that may be accepted, since he would be aiming at the ordinary use of the words (Plutarch, *On Stoic Self-Contradictions* 1048A = SVF 3.137 = LS 58H). However revisionary their theories may be, the Stoics do not focus on drastic reformations of our *ways of speaking* about the good, relatives, friendship, and so on—rather, they put their own technical language next to the everyday use of words, thus emphasizing the difference between the views implied in everyday ways of speaking and the views proposed in their theories.

Thesis (S) is quite typical of early Stoic philosophy, and it lends itself to the label 'paradoxical.' The idea that only the virtuous are relatives and that brothers are alienated is incomprehensible if we do not understand that each of the terms involved—being a relative, being alienated—is a technical term, a term that is highly revisionary compared to conventional notions. Just as 'being a relative' can still be used in an ordinary sense, so can the words 'citizen,' 'friend,' and 'free.' Friends in a conventional sense are enemies in a technical sense, free people in a conventional sense are slaves in a technical sense, and citizens in a conventional sense are political enemies in the Stoic, technical sense. In each case, the technical sense is a *normative* sense: someone can only count as a friend, a relative, a free human being, and a citizen if she meets certain standards. As we shall see in chapter 3, (S) conforms to a *type* of thesis that is central to early Stoic philosophy: 'Only the sage is X.' Only the sage is a priest, a judge, a soothsayer, and so on. Once we acknowledge the implications of this (and

I am postponing detailed discussion of these matters to chapter 3), it seems very unlikely that Zeno is concerned with a city of sages (just as he is not concerned with actual temples in which sages are instituted as priests when he claims that only the sages are priests).[27] Like other theses of the form 'Only the sage is X,' (S) is concerned with explicating the notion of wisdom.

Further, if we were to take the first part of (S), on which I shall focus in this chapter, to describe a city of sages (as I suggest we should not), we would lose sight of the fact that (S) is *as much about fools* as about sages. All nonsages are *at war with each other*.[28] That (S) has these two sides should alert us to the fact that it is, as it were, a 'typical' Stoic claim about the stark contrast between wisdom and foolishness. Both sides of the claim seem to relate to the same state of affairs. If we assume that Zeno is, like Chrysippus, concerned with human life in the cosmos, this makes perfect sense: only sages are citizens of *this* world, and all others in this world are at war with each other.

In conventional poleis, those who are not citizens divide up into several groups: most important, slaves and resident aliens.[29] Those

---

[27] If we think that the thesis 'only the sages are priests' has practical implications, these are certainly not that we should get rid of the existing priests and give their positions to sages—Zeno does not write under the assumption that sages will be available for the job. The practical implications might rather be that in the way we lay out the religious institutions of the city, we should emphasize the philosophical education of priests.

[28] The fact that the claim is part of the Sceptic lists (see chapter 1) seems to owe more to its negative side: While not everybody will share the view that only the virtuous are citizens, some citizens may well think of themselves as rather virtuous, and the citizenship of the virtuous is not too far from the traditional idea that the *kaloi k'agathoi* (the excellent) are those who have the highest political status. Only by the added negative side to the claim, that those who fall short of the rigorous Stoic ideal of virtue are in fact enemies, does the Stoic thesis become scandalous and apparently enter into direct conflict with reality.

[29] We might also think of women (who are traditionally not considered a separate group of people in the city, but who are at the same time also not considered citizens). The Stoics do not speak of female sages, and they do not argue for the claim that wisdom is equally attainable for women and men. However, nothing in the conception of the sage refers to anything but the state of a human being's rational soul. Throughout my discussion, I will usually fall in with the language of the sources, simply because it seems artificial to move from a quote where a sage is referred to as a man directly into paraphrase where the sage is a woman. At other points, I speak of agents and sages as women—I do not think that anything in Stoic philosophy speaks against the idea that a sage can be a woman. This results in a slightly odd mix, but it seems, all things considered, sufficiently faithful to the Stoic doctrine.

who are full citizens are tied together by a kind of civic friendship. Only those who live in other cities will be regarded as enemies and as potential opponents in war. Thesis (S) is partly so offensive because it does away with such conventional distinctions. According to (S), those who are not wise *all fall into the same class*, regardless of their social status and regardless of where they live. We *all* are slaves, and aliens, and enemies.

But what about the fact that Zeno does not mention a cosmic city? Admittedly, he does not, and he does not seem to frame (S) as a claim about human life in the *cosmos*. Like any other claim of the form 'Only the sages are X,' the thesis seems to apply generally to all human beings. The precise formulation of the comparison between cosmos and city may postdate Zeno—we cannot clarify this point on the basis of the testimony. But there is no fundamental difference between discussion of how sages and all other human beings relate to each other *in the cosmos* and how they relate to each other quite generally. The general perspective is a perspective on human life in nature or the world. Even Chrysippus only *compares* the universe to a city—talk about the cosmic city is shorthand for this comparison. So, although the notion of the cosmic city is somewhat better supported in Chrysippus than in Zeno, the basic picture of a better or worse human life in the world seems to be one that they both share.[30]

We should also note that Zeno does not speak of *any* city; whatever notion of a city we ascribe to him, we must supply it through interpretation of the texts. Zeno talks of citizens without referring to a city. While this may be attributed to the scarcity of the sources, it is more likely part of the point Zeno is making. A notion of citizenship that does not refer to a specific place closely resembles

---

[30]We might compare this kind of development within early Stoic thought to the famous difference between different early *telos*-formulae. Zeno defines the goal as 'life in agreement,' and he seemingly did not see the need to offer a complete phrase that elucidates what one's life should be in agreement with. The brief formula 'life in agreement' probably implicitly refers to life in agreement with nature, but it may also refer to some kind of internal consistency of the virtuous agent. Scholars largely agree that the fact that Zeno does not add 'with nature' does not mean that he would not accept the implications of this addition. Zeno's political views might be formulated in a similarly dense way.

the Stoic notion of law. If Stoic claims about the law were not so famous and so fundamental to our picture of Stoic philosophy, we might feel just as strong an urge to ask 'a law of which city?' as to ask 'a citizen of which city?' In the everyday sense, a law or a custom is a law or custom of a specific place at a specific time. The idea that there is a law *independent* of any city is difficult to understand if we are not already thinking in terms of the natural law tradition.[31] (However, once we begin to think of the cosmos *as a city*, the common law is in some sense the law of a specific place—the cosmos. The cosmos is regulated by the law, thus we can describe it as a city.) The notion of citizenship might be explicable along lines similar to that of the law: sages are citizens in the same ambitious sense in which the law is the law, not of a particular place, but with a view to a fundamental analysis of human life in nature. Thus we can identify the city whose citizens are the sages: the cosmos is this city. But there are many others who live in the cosmos. The cosmic city is not a city of sages.

Before we turn to (H), let me add some more general considerations regarding Stoic talk about the sage. Stoic ethics famously centers around such claims as 'the sage does not have any affections [*pathê*],' 'whoever is not wise is a fool,' and so on. The emphasis on these claims can lead first-time readers of the Stoic texts to the impression that the Stoics actually *address* the sage instead of envisaging real-life persons. The ordinary progressor may appear to be an afterthought, and the Stoic thesis that there are no degrees of virtue or vice but only (in the rare cases of someone becoming a sage) instantaneous transitions adds to the impression that the Stoics are not concerned with the imperfect virtue of normal human beings. Given that most students of their philosophy will not see themselves as perfectly virtuous, the focus on the sage may seem to make Stoic ethics quite uninteresting. Further, the rigid distinction between fools and sages may evoke the impression that the Stoics develop two separate ethics: one for ordinary human beings, the other

---

[31] When Cicero lists a number of paradoxical claims, including the thesis that only the wise are citizens and free, he says that, according to the Stoics, the writings of Lycurgus and Solon and the Twelve Tables are not laws (*Academica* 2.136). Stoic views about the law imply that no actual laws really are laws. The Stoic notion of the law, like the notion of citizenship, does not refer to any specific time and place.

for sages.[32] But it would of course be foolish to assume that the Stoics wrote for a (nonexistent) audience of sages. The focus on the sage needs to be understood differently. Even though this is quite obvious, there is very little *explicit* discussion in the literature on Stoic ethics about how we are to understand the role of the sage. Scholars of Stoic philosophy seem to fall in with how the Stoics talk about the sage as a tool for sorting out the details of the theories; in scholarly commentary, the sage starts his own theoretical life very much as in the Stoic texts themselves. But in what sense is the sage a tool for developing theories? Is the sage a theoretical construct, like Plato's 'city founded in speech'? Or is the sage a human being with whom we may meet, even if up until now we have not?

For most areas in Stoic ethics, it may not really matter whether we assume that, according to the Stoics, there are a few sages or none at all. But for the conception of citizenship, the question seems to make a difference: if, according to the Stoics, it is plausible to assume that at any given moment there are a few sages, the *community* among these sages may figure importantly into early Stoic political philosophy. But if it seems likely that, at many times during the history of humankind, there is only one sage or even none at all, this is less plausible. (To this one might object that, at any given point in time, there are many sages, since the gods are sages. But even though it is in some sense true that the gods are sages, this is not how the Stoics use the term. Note that the claim that the sage is rarer than a phoenix would not make sense if we assumed that the notion of a sage refers equally to human sages and gods.) If it is likely that there is only one sage or that there are none at all at a given time, then (S) must be interpreted in a way that allows it to be true (on Stoic terms) independently of whether there are any human sages at a given time.

Two suggestions have been quite influential in the reception of Stoic philosophy: that the Stoics may have pointed to Socrates and the Cynic Diogenes as examples of sagehood, and that Zeno may initially have been susceptible to some kind of Cynic arrogance that made him

---

[32]Inwood offers a brief overview of those scholarly works that suggested such readings of Stoic ethics, "Rules and Reasoning in Stoic Ethics," in Ierodiakonou, *Topics in Stoic Philosophy*, 95–127. As he remarks, the enormous progress of scholarship on Stoic philosophy has shown that these interpretations are misleading.

prone to see himself as a sage, just as presumably some Cynics saw themselves as sages. According to both suggestions, the Stoics would have considered the sage a rare occurrence, admitting of one or perhaps a few instances within known history. The first suggestion, according to which the Stoics may have cited Socrates as a sage, has, as Long and Sedley remark, become commonplace in the scholarly literature, although its foundations are questionable.[33] As an overall picture of the development of Stoic philosophy, it is less misleading than the second idea; the Stoics certainly do regard Socrates as an exceptional figure. But as Brouwer argues convincingly, Stoic references to Socrates' wisdom are quite tenuous, and are furthermore in line with how Socrates is presented in Plato's *Apology*—seemingly the wisest, but not on account of *being wise*.[34] According to the second idea, which has been presented by Rudolf Hirzel, there was a development from early, early Stoicism to later early Stoicism, during which the Cynic pull toward delusions about one's own status wore off.[35] The early Stoics would have moved from a picture according to which there are a few sages, including the Stoic philosopher himself, to one focusing on the theoretical use of the conception of the sage. However, this idea relies on a picture of Cynic philosophy that, given more recent research, cannot be endorsed.[36] Neither Zeno nor later Stoics seem to consider themselves wise.[37]

A third suggestion might be that the Stoics quite generally *have to* think of themselves as wise if they propose their theories as true. This problem is posed by Sextus Empiricus (M 7.432–435), but it does not

[33]See LS, 2:367. As René Brouwer points out, Odysseus and Heracles are further candidates who may have been cited as sages by the early Stoics; "Sagehood and the Stoics," *Oxford Studies in Ancient Philosophy* 23 (2002): 181–224, 198–199.

[34]See Brouwer, "Sagehood," 196.

[35]R. Hirzel, *Untersuchungen zu Cicero's philosophischen Schriften* Vol. 2, 1, *Die Entwicklung der stoischen Philosophie* (Leipzig, 1882), 271–298.

[36]Important recent studies of Cynicism include Marie-Odile Goulet-Cazé, "La Politeia de Diogène de Sinope et quelques remarques sur sa pensée politique," in *Le cynisme ancien et ses prolongements*, ed. M.-O. Goulet-Cazé and R. Goulet (Paris: Presses universitaires de France, 1993), 57–68. John Moles, "Le cosmopolitisme cynique," in Goulet-Cazé and Goulet, *Le cynisme*, 259–280; Moles, "The Cynics and Politics," in Laks and Schofield, *Justice and Generosity*, 129–158, and "The Cynics."

[37]A thorough discussion of this question, to which I am much indebted, is offered by Brouwer, "Sagehood."

present a serious challenge.[38] One need not be wise in order to have cognition (*katalêpsis*) or in order to assent to true impressions. The Stoics can present true claims without having either knowledge or wisdom. They could even think that their philosophizing would be different if they were wise and had knowledge. It is a mark of the ignorant that assent is *changeable* (M 7.151–157). As long as a philosopher is still going back and forth between different versions of a theory, weighing arguments for various options, she does not have knowledge—she could still revise her judgment on the details of her theory. For the purposes of working with the conception of a perfect person (or soul, or agent) it does not matter that one is not such a person.

Are we left with the impression that, according to the early Stoics, neither they nor anyone else is or was wise? This conclusion needs to be qualified. It is relatively well attested that, according to the Stoics, the sage is rarer than a phoenix.[39] A phoenix is a mythical creature that reportedly comes into being every five hundred years. The comparison seems to highlight that the sage is someone extremely rare, but may now and again come into being. While being able to actually name a sage does not seem to be integral to the theory, it does matter that the sage is not a theoretical construct in the sense of Plato's 'city founded in speech.' The city described in Plato's *Republic* has some kind of theoretical existence. If it came into being, it would be part of the 'realm of becoming.' The sage, however, cannot be thought of along the lines of such metaphysical distinctions. It seems important that at no point is the Stoic 'ideal' conceived of as having some kind of theoretical existence: it is not 'constructed in thought' in the way Plato's city is, and the sage whom we may encounter is exactly the sage whom the theories talk about, in all respects. At every moment, the ideal is considered as a person that might live somewhere, even though we have not happened to meet her. The ambiguity in the sources, which highlight the very ideality of the sage on the one hand but keep talking as if there were a few sages on the other, seems to reflect this metaphysical point. Like the ideal city of the Stoics, their ideal person is not a theoretical entity. Even if, at a given moment, we cannot name a

---

[38]Cf. Brouwer, "Sagehood," 199–201.
[39]For the relevant passages see Brouwer, "Sagehood," 195–198.

single sage, it remains essential to our conception of the sage that there might be one.

The sage must be thought of as a model of perfection, existing as a human being within the world as it is. But since she is rarer than a phoenix, we should probably not assume that *several* sages live at the same time, scattered throughout the world. *If* there are a few sages, they make up a community: together with the gods, they belong to the community of those who have perfect reason. But the role (S) plays in Stoic political philosophy cannot depend on whether this is the case at a given moment. Thesis (S) must be true, even if there is not a single sage. And this means that the core of (S) must be about wisdom, not about a city of sages: (S) must be concerned with spelling out the ideal of wisdom that all human beings should strive to attain.

Zeno is reported to begin the *Republic* by saying that his work applies to the places and times in which he lived.[40] On the suggested reading, we can see how this makes sense. At any given point in time, only the sages are citizens. Zeno can address his own times and places by saying that the citizens of existing cities are in fact *enemies*. His introductory remark seems to be in line with the paradoxical style of (S). As a preface to such claims as (S), Zeno, as it were, says that these are things that he truly means. When he says that all but the wise are slaves, enemies, and so on, he is talking about *us*, his readers. When we come to understand things, we will see how miserable our lives are, and how we are adequately called slaves, enemies, and so on. Zeno's *Republic* thus is certainly applicable to his own times, as it would be to ours.

Before we turn to (H), let us briefly look at (SG), a line from a report on Diogenes of Babylon, head of the school in the mid–second century and student of Chrysippus (we do not have any testimony that ascribes precisely *this* claim to Zeno, Cleanthes, or

---

[40]Philodemus, *De Stoicis*, col. 12, 1–6, p. 100, Dorandi. For a different interpretation see Obbink, "The Stoic Sage," 183. Obbink suggests that this may imply that Zeno's conception "had a less than ideal quality about it." See also Goulet-Cazé, who says that we do not have reason to doubt that Zeno sees himself as presenting a political project that could be brought about in his lifetime and with his contemporaries; *Les Kynica du stoïcisme*, Hermes Einzelschriften vol. 89 (Stuttgart: Franz Steiner Verlag, 2003), 29–30.

Chrysippus): "For among fools there is no city or law, but rather among the organizations [*sustêmatôn*] of gods and sages."[41]

I am referring to this thesis as (SG) because I take it to imply that gods and sages are *citizens*. It is the perfect rationality of the sage that makes her a citizen, and the same should apply to the gods. While this part of my interpretation is relatively uncontroversial, it might seem that this testimony poses a serious threat to my claim that the early Stoics are not concerned with a city of sages. Does (SG) not seem to say that the only real city is a city of sages and gods?

The notion of a city is here used in one of the senses that are central to the Stoic conception of the city: the city is associated with the law; a city is a place that is regulated by the law. Thus the claim that there is no city among fools is directly tied to the claim that, among them, there is no law. What does it mean that there is no law among fools? Fools are not able to live by the law. This, of course, does not make the law a law for gods and sages only—the law pervades the cosmos as a whole. Fools *should* live by the law, which is a common law for all beings with reason. However, as long as they are fools, they do not. As I suggest, we should understand the Stoic notion of a city in a similar manner. The claim that among fools there is no city does not mean that fools do not live in the cosmic city. Rather, it means that they do not live up to being citizens of this city; they do not 'constitute' it by being its citizens. Sages and gods, on the other hand, constitute 'systems' or 'organizations,' an idea we shall explore in more detail in chapter 3. There I shall argue that there is a sense in which the cosmos is *one* through those parts of it that have perfect reason. Sages and gods in some sense *constitute* the cosmos, and thus, the cosmic city. Without them, there is no city. Theses (S) and (SG) leave room for (H) and (HG). The cosmic city only exists because some parts of the cosmos have

[41]For the relatively long passage from which I draw this quotation see ed. S. Sudhaus, *Philodemi volumina rhetorica*, vol. 2 (Leipzig: Teubner, 1896), 212; see also SVF 3, Diogenes fr. 117. I am using Obbink's translation and reconstruction of the text ("The Stoic Sage," 193). SVF reads *politeia* where Obbink reads *polis*; accordingly, the translation would be: "For among fools there is no constitution or law." In this reading, both terms ('constitution' and 'law') might more or less refer to the same thing—there are no legal institutions and no law among fools. Again, the main point would be that fools are not citizens.

perfect reason. But it is also the home and habitation of those who are merely rational.

3. All Human Beings

Thesis (H), the claim that all human beings are to be seen as fellow-citizens, is ascribed to Zeno's *Republic*:[42]

> The much-admired *Republic* of Zeno...is aimed at this one main point, that we should not dwell in cities or peoples,[43] each one marked out by its own notions of what is just [*idiois dikaiois*],[44] but we should regard all human beings as our fellow members of the populace and fellow-citizens, and there should be one way of life and order, like that of a herd grazing together and nurtured by a common law. Zeno wrote this, picturing as it were a dream or image of a philosopher's well-regulated regime. (Plutarch, *De virt. Alex.* 329A–B = SVF 1.262 part = LS 67A)[45]

Much of my argument will depend on whether this testimony is trustworthy. It has been dismissed for a number of reasons, the most important being (1) that it seems to be in disagreement with (S); (2) that it 'sounds Platonic' and therefore not Stoic; and (3) the way Plutarch's text continues (see hereafter). Since opposition to Plutarch's report is—with the important exception of Goulet-Cazé—virtually unanimous, I will devote significant space to establishing its trustworthiness.

As has often been observed, Plutarch's text is full of allusions to Plato. Despite this, the Platonic vocabulary and imagery does not obscure the core of Zeno's ideas. The key clause, "that we should not dwell in cities or peoples, each one marked out by its own

---

[42]I have offered an earlier version of my views on Plutarch's testimony in "Plutarch über Zenons Traum," in *Antike Philosophie Verstehen: Understanding Ancient Philosophy*, ed. Marcel v. Ackeren and Jörn Müller (Darmstadt: WBG, 2006), 196–217.

[43]See Schofield, *The Stoic Idea*, 104 n. 1.

[44]The Greek does not talk of 'notions.' My translation aims at capturing the very broad sense of the Greek. The idea seems to be that, conventionally, each city has its own legal usages, as well as customs that imply claims on what is right and wrong.

[45]Translation adapted from Vander Waerdt and Schofield.

notions of what is just, but we should regard all human beings as our fellow members of the populace and fellow-citizens, and there should be one way of life and order," is free from any Platonic terms and could thus be a quite accurate paraphrase of what Zeno is saying. The following comparison, "like that of a herd grazing together and nurtured by a common law," may, given the Platonic imagery, be Plutarch's own addition. But this addition takes up what is most probably Zenonian—the notion of the common law.[46] Thus, we can admit that the passage is tainted by Platonic vocabulary and still save the key statements—that according to Zeno, we should regard all others as our fellow-citizens, and that all human beings are tied together by a common law. In this chapter, I shall focus on the first of these ideas, Zeno's instruction on how we are to see all other human beings. This part of the report actually sounds thoroughly Stoic: it recalls the core idea of the social dimension of *oikeiôsis*, that we should regard all others as 'belonging to us.'

Plutarch's testimony on Zeno's *Republic* is, on the whole, remarkably respectful, and even though Plutarch wrote several books that discuss Stoic philosophy critically, he seems to think highly of this particular work. His one objection is that the discussion of sexual matters does not belong in an otherwise serious work of philosophy (*Quaestiones Convivales* 3.6,1; 653 E = SVF 1.252). This remark indicates, as Goulet-Cazé argues, that Plutarch knows Zeno's *Republic*, and that the book as a whole seems to him to present matters of philosophical interest.[47] It should count as relevant evidence for the reliability of Plutarch's report that he tells us that this idea is the *key* thesis of the *Republic*.[48] It seems unlikely that a relatively respectful author would intentionally misrepresent what he says is the basic thesis of a work.

---

[46] As it has long been observed, Zeno may be inspired by Heraclitus's notion of a divine law (DK 22 B 114).

[47] Goulet-Cazé, *Les Kynica*, 66. The remark also affirms what I argued for in chapter 1—that the *Republic* is unlikely to consist mostly of lists of the disturbing theses. The fact that Plutarch takes the book largely to be respectable is counter-evidence not only to Philodemus but also to the Sceptic sources. In a book about Alexander's virtue, Plutarch would certainly not associate Zeno's political thought with Alexander's political achievements if he did not take the former to be respectable and even praiseworthy.

[48] Goulet-Cazé, *Les Kynica*, 33.

Both Vander Waerdt and Schofield argue that we have to dismiss the idea that Zeno talks about all human beings; Vander Waerdt because he takes it to be inconsistent with the thesis that only the sages are citizens, Schofield because of the way the passage continues.[49] Both suggest that, *really*, Plutarch means to talk throughout the passage only about the sages: the sages are fellow-citizens, not all human beings. On this reading, however, Zeno would tell *us*, that is, *fools*, to regard *all sages* as fellow-citizens. This is not at all plausible.

In order to discuss Schofield's view, let me present the passage in its context. According to Plutarch, Zeno does not discuss who *is* a citizen at this point in the *Republic*. Rather, Zeno talks about who *should be seen as* a citizen. We have to assume that this perspective also applies to the first part of Zeno's claim, that is, that Zeno does not tell us to literally move out of the actual cities we live in when he tells us not to dwell in cities, but rather to not *consider* ourselves to be citizens of these cities. Plutarch goes on to say that while Zeno had this philosophical dream, Alexander gave effect to the theory. Alexander did not follow the views Plutarch ascribes to Aristotle: ruling differently over Greeks and barbarians, considering the first as friends and the latter as brutes. Rather, he aimed at bringing all under one rule, mixing together their ways of life (*De Alex. virt.* 329 B). Alexander "instructed all to think of the whole inhabited world as their fatherland, his camp as their acropolis and garrison, the good as their kin [*suggeneis*], the bad as strangers [*allophulous*]" (329 C). Alexander's policy is this: rather than considering the barbarians as strangers, people should regard as strangers those who are bad. Greeks and barbarians, Plutarch continues, should, under Alexander's regime, not be distinguished by different dress codes, and so on; the virtuous are the Greeks, and the bad are the barbarians (329 D).

Plutarch presents Alexander as a ruler who applies Stoic principles. This, however, cannot be fully correct. Even though Plutarch's

---

[49]Vander Waerdt argues that Plutarch's " 'all human beings' is best understood to refer to those capable of living according to the common law—that is, to all wise human beings" ("Zeno's Republic," 284). See Schofield, *The Stoic Idea*, 105, Baldry, "Zeno's Ideal State," 12–13, and Andrew Erskine, *The Hellenistic Stoa: Political Thought and Action* (Ithaca, N.Y.: Cornell University Press, 1990), 18–22, on whether the passage is compatible with the claim that only the sages are citizens.

Alexander seems to adopt Zeno's opposition between friends and enemies, and relatives and strangers, he does *not* tell people to see *everyone* as a fellow-citizen (that is what one should do according to Zeno). There will be many who are not virtuous, and if one followed Alexander's instruction, one would consider them as strangers. On Stoic assumptions, in fact, hardly anyone counts as virtuous, and thus Alexander would tell us to regard everyone as strangers, which is quite different from Zeno's claim. Plutarch's Alexander seems to operate on a significantly relaxed notion of virtue. In his instruction, it is assumed that many of his addressees will be virtuous, and that they are well advised in considering all other virtuous people, no matter whether they are Greek or barbarian, as their friends. Zeno, on the other hand, certainly does not assume that he is addressing himself to virtuous or wise people.

It thus does not seem to me that we can push for an interpretation that leaves Alexander and Zeno with exactly the same view. Plutarch's Alexander is certainly deeply inspired by Stoic thought, even suggesting the same way of dressing for everyone. But in saying that only the good are friends, he does not adopt the rigorous Stoic conception of what it takes to be virtuous. Plutarch's account is ultimately about Alexander. This kind of misfit between Stoic views and Alexander's admirable practice may not matter too much to him at this point, and I think that it should not matter to our interpretation of Zeno's thought.

A reading that replaces 'all human beings' with 'the sages' in Zeno's instruction is incomprehensible, and the interpretative goal of crediting Plutarch with a fully correct comparison between Zeno and Alexander should not outweigh this fact. If we replaced 'all human beings' with 'sage,' Zeno would tell ordinary progressors to regard all *sages* as *their* fellow-citizens. Surely, this cannot be what Zeno says. There is also no point in telling the sages to view all other sages as fellow-citizens. It is precisely the figure of the sage that tells us what we should do. To read a Stoic text as telling the sages what to do is to completely misconstrue the role of the sage. Neither Vander Waerdt nor Schofield takes into account that Plutarch does not attribute the claim that all human beings *are* citizens to Zeno but the claim that *we*, that is, ordinary progressors, *should regard* all human beings as fellow-citizens. Once we see this, it is impossible to simply replace 'all human beings' with 'sages.'

The interpretative task is thus to explain how Zeno can ask us to see all others as fellow-citizens, when in fact they are not, at least in some sense, since only the sages are citizens. Does Zeno instruct us to see others as what they are, or as what they are not? While the latter is not an impossible train of thought, it is completely foreign to Stoic philosophy. Within Stoic ethics, surely all our dispositions should be based on knowledge, not on false opinions. Seeing others as fellow-citizens must be based on recognizing that they *are* fellow-citizens. Thus, we are left with the question of how Zeno can on the one hand instruct ordinary progressors to see all others as fellow-citizens, if on the other hand he says that only the sages are citizens.

An obvious way of getting out of the difficulty without discarding Plutarch's testimony is to assume that, within early Stoic thought, different notions of citizenship are at play. But do we have any evidence for this? I think we have, and this evidence is at the heart of early Stoic political philosophy. If we turn to (HG), we hear that both human beings and gods *live* in the cosmos, human beings as subjects of the gods, the gods as their rulers.

4. *Humans and Gods, and Sages and Gods*

While (HG) is often cited, there is virtually no scholarly discussion about the role of the gods in early Stoic political philosophy. Such discussion is much needed, because it would contribute to the debate on the relationship of ethics and physics and, even more basically, because it is difficult to see *who* these gods are (the planets? the Olympians?).[50] But these questions will be postponed to chapter 3; the immediate purpose of this chapter is to show how all four claims on citizenship can be read as presenting one, consistent theory.

Arius Didymus reports (HG); his account refers to the early Stoics, but not specifically to Zeno or Chrysippus:

[50] A recent collection of articles on Hellenistic theology covers key aspects of Stoic theology: *Traditions in Theology: Studies in Hellenistic Theology: Its Background and Aftermath*, papers presented at the Eighth Symposium Hellenisticum, ed. Dorothea Frede and André Laks (Leiden: Brill, 2002). See esp. Dorothea Frede, "Theodicy and Providential Care in Stoicism," 85–117, and David Sedley, "The Origins of Stoic God," 41–83. The Stoics are primarily concerned with god in the singular, and this is what these recent articles are most directly discussing.

The world is said to be an organization [*sustêma*] of heaven and air
and earth and sea and the natures [*phuseôn*] within them. The world is
also called the habitation [*oikêtêrion*][51] of gods and men, [and the
structure consisting of gods and men,] and the things created for their
sake. For just as there are two meanings of city, first as habitation and
second as the structure of its inhabitants along with its citizens, so the
world is like a city consisting of gods and men, with the gods serving
as rulers and men as their subjects. They are members of a community
because of their participation in reason, which is law by nature [*phusei
nomos*];[52] and everything else is created for their sake. In consequence
of which it must be believed that the god who administers the whole
exercises providence for men, being beneficent, kind, well disposed to
men, just and having all the virtues. (Arius Didymus, ap. Eusebius,
Praep. Evang. 15.15.3–5 = SVF 2.528 part = LS 67L)[53]

The cosmos is said to be *like a city,* insofar as it is the habitation
of gods and men, and insofar as gods rule and men are being ruled,
that is, with respect to the social structure among those who live in
it.[54] The comparison of cosmos and city is introduced on the basis of
two explanations of the notion of a city. First, we can think of a city
as a habitation, and insofar as the cosmos is inhabited, it is justly
compared to a city. Second, a city is the structure of its inhabitants
along with its citizens, that is, it is an organization among its partic-
ipants, who can have different roles. The two different kinds of

[51]The word *oikêtêrion* is difficult to interpret. The cosmos as *oikêtêrion* may not just
be a *place* to live in; it may be a 'house' in the sense of an organized habitation. At the
same time, *oikos* is related to *oikeion*, 'familiar' or 'belonging to one,' and may thus
relate to the Stoic notion *oikeiôsis*. A parallel passage is Cicero, *De Natura Deorum*
2.154. According to Cicero's report, the universe was created for the sake of gods and
men, and it is the common home of gods and men, or a city that belongs to both. The
argument that is given for this claim is that humans and gods live "according to law
and justice by the use of reason." See D. Frede on the conception of the cosmos as a
'home' ("Theodicy," 106).

[52]This term is not part of a direct quotation; it may stem from the early Stoics, but
it could also be a later way of expressing what the early Stoics presumably had in mind.

[53]Translation based on LS and Obbink, with modifications.

[54]Diogenes Laertius reports a threefold distinction of what the Stoics take 'cosmos' to mean (DL 7.137 = SVF 2.526 part = LS 44F). According to the second sense,
the cosmos is understood as 'world-order' (*diakosmêsis*). This notion seems to say
more or less the same thing as *sustêma* in the foregoing passage.

members of the cosmos are gods and human beings, and it seems only plausible to assume that these have the status of, respectively, citizens and inhabitants. Gods rule, and as we shall see in chapter 3, only beings with perfect reason rule; to be a ruler and to be a citizen really are two dimensions of wisdom. Thus the cosmos is, second, like a city insofar as it has members of different status, who stand in a relationship of ruling and being ruled to each other. If we construe the text along these lines, (HG) does not amount to the claim that all human beings and the gods *are citizens*. Rather, the gods are citizens, while humans (if they are not sages) have some lower kind of political status.

Thesis (HG) introduces a relevant kinship between all human beings, as well as between human beings and the gods: both gods and humans participate in reason. However, only the gods administer the universe. Even though the passage does not give much detail, it clearly relies on the assumption that human beings and gods participate in reason to different degrees. Human beings are rational. But the gods are "beneficent, kind, well disposed to me, just and having all the virtues"; that is, their souls are in the perfect state of virtue and knowledge—they have perfect reason and are therefore rulers.

While Plutarch reported a Zenonian claim on how we should see others, the passage in Arius Didymus talks about all human beings *as they are*. Gods have perfect reason, while humans (for the most part, we might add) do not, and this accounts for their participation in *reason* and *law*, each in their own way. The distinction between inhabitants and citizens must be deliberate—it cannot be that gods and human beings live according to the law in the same sense, if gods have perfect reason and human beings (excluding sages) do not. The report in Arius Didymus adds to both (S) and (H) by offering a description of the cosmos *as it is*: human beings have reason, but not perfect reason; the world is ruled by the gods, who have perfect reason; there is some community among all who share reason. If we take into account the distinction between reason and perfect reason—or, as I shall also put it, between being rational and being perfectly reasonable—it is clear that, while there is *one* community of all participating in reason, there is also a community of all those who are perfectly reasonable (witness [SG]), and a community of those who are rational. Reason provides the kind of kinship that makes for a community, and reason comes in degrees.[55] Communities, it seems, can also come in degrees.

The passage in Arius provides us with two notions: citizen and inhabitant. Accordingly, we could say that the community of the rational is the community of inhabitants, and the community of the perfectly reasonable that of the citizens. But Arius does not give us a direct quotation, and it is unclear whether the term translated 'inhabitant' is a technical term in Stoic philosophy or whether Arius just mirrors a Stoic point in his own words. In any case, (HG) supplies us with a distinction between being a citizen in a strong sense, which implies that one has perfect reason, and being a citizen in a weaker sense, which implies that one is rational. It is exactly this distinction that we need in order to see how (S) and (H) fit together.

If we take (HG) seriously (as is traditionally done), we really cannot dismiss Plutarch's testimony. If all human beings live, with the gods, in one community, it is clear that, at some level, the theory *is* concerned with all human beings. Once we see that one way or another we will have to accommodate a perspective on all human beings that does not stipulate that they have all become wise, we surely do not have grounds to dismiss the testimony that, according to Zeno, we should see all others as fellow-citizens.

Before I return to the interpretation of (H), a few more comments on (HG). Unlike (S) and (H), Arius Didymus's report seems to take us into physics: Arius Didymus presents a Stoic account of the *cosmos*. Theology is, for the Stoics, part of physics. A theory that explains how the gods or god administers the world is, at least in a very important sense, a theory of physics. Is (HG) testimony for early Stoic political thought, or is it rather a piece of physics?

Traditional interpretations of Stoic philosophy have stressed how closely related core concepts of Stoic philosophy—reason, law, nature, god—are. Through discussion of Stoic statements on how the three disciplines of ethics, physics, and logic relate and make up one whole (compared to a living being, an egg, or a garden— DL 7.39–40), such interpretations have emphasized how deeply

---

[55]Cicero presents a Stoic *scala naturae*, which includes the gods as a highest kind of entity (*De Natura Deorum* 2.33–34). The difference between human beings and gods is, according to this passage, that human beings can *attain* virtue and thus perfect reason, while gods do not need to strive for it, since they already have it.

interwoven Stoic ethics and physics are. Julia Annas has seriously challenged this picture, leading in turn to a much more detailed discussion of its implications.[56] According to Annas, Chrysippus's claim that logic comes first, ethics second, and physics last, with theology as its crowning end (Plutarch, *On Stoic Self-Contradictions* 1035 A–B) can be interpreted as saying that ethics does not build on physics. Stoic ethics, according to this suggestion, may *lead up* to physics but is theoretically independent. Annas draws attention to the fact that those passages where Chrysippus famously says that the key ethical ideas are best approached from the study of nature (see 1035 C) come from works on physics, not ethics.[57] Once one has gotten to physics and theology, the study of the cosmos and god would back up one's insights in ethics. Annas concludes that

> there are two levels on which one studies ethics: first as a subject in its own right, with the proper kind of methodology, in which our intuitions are subjected to reflection and articulation, and theoretical concepts and distinctions are introduced which explain and make sense of our intuitions; and then later (if one advances that far) as a subject within Stoic philosophy as a whole.[58]

[56]Julia Annas, *The Morality of Happiness* (New York: Oxford University Press, 1995), esp. 159–179 and 262–276. Some studies had already been published, and Annas responds to them—most important, Gisela Striker, "Following Nature: A Study in Stoic Ethics," and the articles in *The Norms of Nature*, ed. M. Schofield and G. Striker (Cambridge: Cambridge University Press, 1986). But Annas's work has initiated new interest in the question to what extent physics figures in Stoic ethics: see e.g. Brad Inwood, review of *Morality of Happiness* by J. Annas, *Ancient Philosophy* 15 (1995): 647–666; J. M. Cooper, "Eudaimonism, the Appeal to Nature and 'Moral Duty' in Stoicism," in *Aristotle, Kant, and the Stoics: Rethinking Happiness and Duty*, ed. S. Engstrom and J. Whiting (Cambridge: Cambridge University Press, 1996), 261–284; Cooper, "Eudaimonism and the Appeal to Nature in the Morality of Happiness: Comments on Julia Annas, *The Morality of Happiness*," *Philosophy and Phenomenological Research* 55 (1995): 587–598; J. Annas, "From Nature to Happiness" (review of *Papers in Hellenistic Epistemology and Ethics* by G. Striker), *Apeiron* 31.1 (1998): 59–73; Menn, "Physics as Virtue." For an earlier treatment of these issues see Nicholas White, "The Role of Physics in Stoic Ethics," *Southern Journal of Philosophy* 23, supp. (1985): 57–74.

[57]Annas refers to Brunschwig, who makes the same observation but comes to some different conclusions; J. Brunschwig, "On a Book-Title by Chrysippus: 'On the Fact That the Ancients Admitted Dialectic along with Demonstrations,' " *Oxford Studies in Ancient Philosophy*, supp. (1991): 81–95.

[58]Annas, *Morality of Happiness*, 164.

In a later and briefer presentation of her view, she writes: "Each of the parts [of philosophy] (logic, physics, ethics) is developed separately in the appropriate way and with the appropriate methodology; finally all are grasped together in a holistic way."[59] If we follow Annas's account, we might hope to be able to reconstruct early Stoic political philosophy, which is a part of ethics, without engaging with Stoic physics. Physics may back up the theory, but it might not be integral to understanding its main argument.

Annas's picture of Stoic ethics has been critically examined, and I cannot engage with all the difficult questions involved.[60] Most important, it seems to me that any strict division between the three philosophical disciplines is in conflict with fundamental Stoic assumptions about virtue, knowledge, and the soul. As I will discuss in more detail, a generic distinction of different virtues in Stoic philosophy is a distinction between logic, physics, and ethics *as virtues*.[61] Together, these virtues add up to the knowledge of the sage. Given Stoic assumptions about the unity of the soul, ethics is not concerned with knowledge that matters to practical reasoning, while physics and logic consist of knowledge that matters to theorizing. Rather, the disposition of knowledge is one unified disposition. The Stoics apparently disagreed about what to teach first, and equally about what insights are ultimately 'the highest.' But attempts at answering these questions do not imply that the three disciplines are in any significant way independent from each other. Scholarly literature on the Stoic debates about what subject is to be valued highest, second, and third (or taught first, second, and third) tends to focus on rivaling accounts of the *ordering* of disciplines. But next to the testimony on this controversy we are also told that some Stoics have *not* given precedence to any part over the other.

[59] Annas, "Nature to Happiness," 67.

[60] See note 56. A recent contribution to the debate is Gábor Betegh, "Cosmological Ethics in the Timaeus and Early Stoicism," *Oxford Studies in Ancient Philosophy* 23 (2002): 273–290. Of course, Annas's approach can be seen from two related but different perspectives. As long as we are concerned with exegesis, it will be important to insist on the relevance of physics for ethics (if we disagree with Annas's reading). But, at the same time, it may seem attractive to see how much of Stoic ethics we can reconstruct without making substantial cosmological or theological assumptions. Annas's book has, in part, attracted so much interest because this line of thinking is inspiring to ethicists.

[61] Aetius 1, *Preface* 2 = SVF 2.35 = LS 26A.

Diogenes Laertius remarks that the Stoics used to *present* them in *mixed form* (DL 7.40).[62] It is the latter view that is praised by Cato, the proponent of Stoic doctrine in Cicero's *De Finibus*: he claims to have spoken as long as he did because he was taken with the admirable order and harmony of the components of Stoic philosophy. Every single component of Stoic philosophy is connected with the rest, so that nothing could be relocated to a different place within the whole body of thought (3.74). What he admires is not that three separate disciplines are consistent with each other. Rather, what amazes him is how *all* of Stoic philosophy is one.

Arius Didymus's report seems to present us with precisely this kind of crossdisciplinary reasoning. While Arius Didymus may well only be drawing on works in physics (note that he begins with a distinction between different notions of the cosmos), the arguments he reports are not confined to physics. The passage does not stop at comparing the cosmos to a city. It describes the cosmos as an inhabited place with a political structure, where some rule and others are ruled. Since the Stoics themselves, in the context of discussing the cosmos, apparently *cross the boundaries of the disciplines* in this way, it seems that we are justified in doing the same when we reconstruct their theory.

A last remark on this kind of physico-ethical theorizing. It has been doubted whether the early Stoics actually engage in political philosophy. One way of raising the question whether they do is to ask whether they are, ultimately, proposing a physical rather than an ethical picture of the universe, with all living beings in it as its parts. If we take the passage from Arius as exemplary, it is clear that this worry is misguided. Early Stoic political philosophy certainly is, to some extent, a theory about the political dimensions of life in the cosmos, the latter being a core concept of physics. It is also a theory about living a perfectly reasonable life in the cosmos, which is

---

[62]Some parts of Stoic logic seem quite independent from ethics and physics, and thus it is not surprising that the major disagreement seems to have been on the place of ethics and physics—logic can easily come first, because one probably can understand some of it (even if not such notions as knowledge or reason) before having studied physics and ethics. On Chrysippus's way of beginning ethical treatises with theological claims even though theology supposedly is the 'crowning end' of philosophy, see Schofield, "Two Stoic Approaches to Justice," in Laks and Schofield, *Justice and Generosity*, 191–212, 195 and 210.

pervaded by reason—or Zeus, or the law, depending which Stoic formulation we want to take up. It is by no means unusual for a specific theory within Stoicism to be connected to the rest of Stoic philosophy in such an intricate way; this is what Cato admires. If we presuppose a notion of political philosophy that considers it separate from other fields in philosophy, then of course the Stoics do not engage in it. But this is an absurd premise; it leads to the conclusion that the Stoics do not engage in ethics or epistemology or physics either, since in each case, their theories are deeply tied to the rest of philosophy.

Before we return to (H), let me introduce a further piece of testimony, which *combines* reference to the sages *and* reference to all humans beings and the gods. According to Philodemus, in the third book of *On Nature*, Chrysippus presents the cosmos as "a single entity of the wise [*kosmon hena tôn phronimôn*], he says, jointly lived in as a city [*sunpoleiteuomenon*] by gods and human beings" (*PHerc.* 1428, col. 7,21–26).[63] The passage is very difficult to interpret. First, the term 'the wise' might either govern the second clause, so that Chrysippus says that the cosmos is jointly lived in by gods and human *sages*, or it might not, in which case Chrysippus says that the cosmos is jointly lived in by gods and human beings. I do not think that we can decide this question; both readings are plausible aspects of early Stoic thought. But at this point, it is more important to our interpretation to turn to the beginning of the quotation. What exactly Chrysippus is saying about the sages is difficult to unearth from Philodemus's report; the clause *kosmon hena tôn phronimôn* is quite compressed.[64] Obbink offers two variants in his translation: "the cosmos is a single entity of (or for?) the wise."[65] Both of these variants are consistent with Stoic

---

[63] I am translating Obbink's reconstruction of the text, "The Stoic Sage," 184–186. The text is edited by A. Henrichs, "Die Kritik der stoischen Theologie in *PHerc.* 1428," *Cronache Ercolanesi* 4 (1974): 5–32, 20.

[64] I follow Obbink in assuming that what is at issue is not the idea that the universe is one of the wise (in the sense of: the universe is wise, and therefore is one of the wise entities that there are), as André Laks translates. Laks follows Henrichs's translation: "der Kosmos sei einer der Weisen und gehöre zum Staat der Götter und Menschen." Laks, review of *The Stoic Idea* by Malcolm Schofield, *Ancient Philosophy* 14 (1994): 459–60; see also Schofield, *The Stoic Idea*, 74 and n. 19. Schofield translates: "that the universe of the wise is one, citizenship of it being held by gods and men together."

[65] Obbink, "The Stoic Sage," 185.

doctrine. That the cosmos is one is a core thesis of Stoic physics; to understand that the cosmos is one is a central piece of knowledge. Thus, we can first of all say that the cosmos is a single entity for the sages, insofar as they *view* it as one or understand it to be one.[66] This interpretation is confirmed to some extent by the fact that the Stoics seem to refer to Heraclitus and his ideas about the cosmos being one.[67] Maybe we can express a similar idea by taking the genitive to be possessive: the cosmos is one *of* the wise, insofar as only they inhabit it *as* something that is one. Both thoughts are plausible within Stoic philosophy. But we may also think that there is a sense in which the cosmos, or at least the perfectly reasonable component of the cosmos, *consists* of the sages, or the sages and the gods. The Stoics describe the cosmos as a living being, a whole in the sense in which an organism is a whole.[68] This living being has perfect reason, and is, in some sense, *sustained* by this reason. As I will show in great detail in chapter 3, all individuals with perfect reason in some sense 'belong' to the perfectly reasonable soul of the cosmos. The cosmos is, as it were, sustained *as a unity* by its perfect reason. Thus, there is a sense in which the cosmos *consists* of the sages, and this might be the sense in which the cosmos, while being home to all human beings, is a city of sages. I will come back to this conception in chapter 3. For the moment, we can note that it is consistent with both interpretations of the second phrase ("jointly lived in as a city by gods and human beings"). Either Chrysippus says that the cosmos, which consists of sages (or is sustained by what is wise in it), is inhabited by these sages as its citizens; or he says that the cosmos is the common home of gods and human beings. While it is difficult to determine what Chrysippus refers to at this point, it seems that he actually endorses both of these claims.

[66]If I understand him correctly, this is the reading Obbink proposes. Obbink's commentary is not easy to understand: In his actual translation, he seems to favor 'of' over 'for.' In his commentary he seems to go with 'for': "For those who understand, there exists not the kind of chaotic world of diversity and multiplicity experienced by the *aphrones*, but a single world" ("The Stoic Sage," 186).

[67]Philodemus takes Chrysippus to be following Heraclitus (the passage continues: "and that war and Zeus are the same, as Heraclitus also says; and in the fifth [book, *On Nature*] he puts arguments in connection with the thesis that the universe is an animal and rational and exercises understanding and is a god," cols. 7.26–8.4, translation partly Schofield). Heraclitus says in several ways that the universe is one or common, and that this is not apparent to 'the many'; see DK 22 B2 and B30.

[68]See e.g. SE M 9.104.

5. *Citizenship, Reason, and the Theory of* Oikeiôsis

Let us return to the question of how Zeno can ask us to see all others as fellow-citizens, if indeed they are not sages, and therefore not citizens. The distinction (HG) provides, along with Philodemus's testimony, allows us to assume that we are dealing with a stronger and a weaker notion of citizenship. Human beings are related through being rational, but there is a different way of being related for those who are perfectly reasonable. Accordingly, there seems to be a stronger and a weaker notion of being a citizen, the stronger being tied to perfect reason, the weaker to being rational. The idea that one progresses toward virtue by understanding the kinship of reason with all human beings and, in this sense, understanding that they are all one's fellow-citizens is compatible with admitting that only perfectly reasonable beings are citizens in the stronger sense of citizenship. Thesis (S) is consistent with (H).

What Plutarch says about Zeno may further confirm the suggested distinction between a strong and a weak notion of citizenship. Plutarch does not say that, according to Zeno, we should regard all others as citizens. He says that Zeno wants us to see them as our 'fellow-citizens.' What is standardly translated as 'fellow-citizens' includes two terms: *dêmotai* and *politai*—demesmen (those belonging to the same deme or local political community) and citizens. Plutarch seems to use these two terms because he has just presented Zeno as saying that we should not live in different cities or local political communities or (as I argued) that we should not *see* ourselves as living in an actual city (polis) or as belonging to a particular deme; rather, we should see everyone as fellow polis and deme members. If this is what Zeno is saying, then his claim does not amount to the thesis that all human beings are citizens in a normative sense. Rather, he says that actual cities and peoples should not be our point of reference in how we see ourselves and others, and he tells us to relate to everyone as we do to those who belong to the same city and people.

Once we acknowledge the relevance of the fact that Zeno *addresses individuals on how to change*, Plutarch's report fits strikingly well into Stoic philosophy. Coming to see all others as fellow-citizens clearly is a variant of coming to see all others as belonging to us, as the theory of *oikeiôsis* demands. It is not only the ideas of a community of all human beings and a kinship of reason that link (H) and the theory of *oikeiôsis*. Equally important, it is the mode of address, and the idea that it is important *how we see others*. One of the most deeply interesting aspects of the theory of *oikeiôsis* lies in this last point: becoming virtuous importantly involves a change in how we are disposed toward others, or how we see them as belonging to us. The link between ethics and political philosophy I am proposing is, as we will see, quite pervasive in the ancient sources.[69]

Let me present a summary picture of the theory of *oikeiôsis*.[70] The theory starts with the explanation of an animal's *first* impulse. The Stoics introduce the notions of 'what belongs to us' or is 'familiar' (*oikeion*) and 'appropriation' (*oikeiôsis*) by discussing the primary impulse of human beings.[71] Like other animals, humans have an impulse to preserve themselves. Chrysippus explains this by pointing to the fact that every animal is 'familiar' with its own constitution and its consciousness of this. Nature, from the very beginning, familiarizes the animal with itself.[72] Nature would not make an animal 'alien' to itself; it is through being 'familiar' with itself that the animal avoids what is harmful and accepts what is 'familiar' to it (DL 7.85). This line of thought leads, in the first book of

[69]Gisela Striker finds two roles of the theory of *oikeiôsis* in Stoic ethics: "to support the Stoic conception of the *telos*, the final end" and "*oikeiôsis* is said to be the foundation of justice"; "The Role of *oikeiôsis* in Stoic Ethics," in *Essays in Hellenistic Epistemology and Ethics* (Cambridge: Cambridge University Press, 1996), 281–297, esp. 282 and 293–295.

[70]The theory of *oikeiôsis* cannot be ascribed with any certainty to Zeno. The sources mostly speak of Chrysippus. As with some other aspects of Stoic philosophy, we seem to be dealing with a theory that Chrysippus is highly interested in, and that ends up being associated with him in the doxographical literature. This, of course, does not mean that Zeno did not hold essentially the same ideas. But Chrysippus may have developed them further, and we do not know to how great an extent. If the interpretation of Zeno's political philosophy I am proposing is convincing, it lends support to the thesis that Zeno already did create the framework of the theory of *oikeiôsis*. On this reading, Zeno formulated at least the core thought that we should regard all others as belonging to one community.

[71]*Oikeion* might also be rendered as 'what we identify with'; this is suggested by Malcolm Schofield, "Two Stoic Approaches to Justice," 203.

[72]See Jacques Brunschwig, "The Cradle Argument," in *The Norms of Nature: Studies in Hellenistic Ethics*, ed. M. Schofield and Gisela Striker (Cambridge: Cambridge University Press, 1986), 113–144.

Chrysippus's *On Ends*, to the Stoic *telos*-formula of life in accordance with nature, that, in Chrysippus's more elaborate version, is presented as 'life in accordance with the experience of what happens by nature' (DL 7.87). In a second step, Chrysippus's reasoning leads to discussion of the common law:

> our own natures are parts of the nature of the whole. Therefore, living in agreement with nature comes to be the end, which is in accordance with the nature of oneself and that of the whole, engaging in no activity wont to be forbidden by the common law, which is the right reason pervading everything and identical to Zeus, who is the director of the administration of existing things. (DL 7.87–88)[73]

What matters for my present purposes is that Chrysippus himself relates the concept of appropriation to the discussion of the common law, and thus to a key idea of Stoic political philosophy. Since human beings are familiar with themselves, and are part of nature, being familiar with their own natures can be extended to understanding that one is familiar with, or belongs to, *all of nature*—that, in fact, one is part of a whole, animate entity.[74] Living in agreement with nature is living in agreement with one's own nature *and* with nature as a whole, and these are two separate, but not distinct, things; one's own nature is *a part of nature as a whole*.[75] Understanding this means seeing oneself as part of an animate entity governed by *its* right reason, which pervades everything.

Scholars have sometimes distinguished between personal and social *oikeiôsis*, and the ideas just presented are, given this distinction, to be labeled as personal *oikeiôsis*: the human being is, through

---

[73]Translation mostly LS.

[74]The world is, according to Stoic theory, ensouled (see, e.g., DL 7.143).

[75]This is Chrysippus's view, and Cleanthes disagrees with it. According to Cleanthes, life in agreement with nature should be explained as life in agreement with common nature, not as life in agreement with common nature and human nature (DL 7.89). However, this is a confusing piece of testimony, since it presents Cleanthes as disagreeing with Chrysippus, as if Chrysippus were his predecessor. It is difficult to say whether we should not rather assume that Cleanthes spells out the Stoic account of the end in one way, and Chrysippus adds a further aspect. On the different formulae see Striker, "Antipater, or the Art of Living," in Schofield and Striker, *Norms of Nature*, 185–204, and "The Role of *Oikeiôsis*," as well as Michael Frede, "On the Stoic Conception of the Good," in Ierodiakonou, *Topics in Stoic Philosophy*, 71–94.

nature, familiarized with itself and is thus set on a path of development that can eventually lead to a virtuous life.[76] However, it seems that the theory is from its very beginning concerned with explaining the social nature of human beings, so the distinction should be used with some caution.[77] Plutarch complains that Chrysippus does not tire of telling us that we "have an appropriate disposition relative to ourselves as soon as we are born and to our parts and our offspring" (*On Stoic Self-Contradictions* 1038B = SVF 3.179, 2.724 = LS 57E). Nature makes parents love their children, and this love, which is the affective side of seeing them as belonging to oneself, is the bridge to other human beings. In Cicero's presentation of the doctrine, it is but a second step that "mutual attraction between men is also something natural" (*De fin.* 3.62–63). That all human beings should be regarded as 'familiar' or 'belonging to us' is said to follow directly:

> Consequently, the mere fact that someone is a man makes it incumbent on another man not to regard him as alien. Just as some parts of the body, like the eyes and ears, are created as it were for their own sake while others, such as the legs and the hands, serve the needs of the other parts; so, some large animals are created only for themselves, whereas . . . ants, bees, and storks do certain things for the sake of others as well. Human behaviour in this respect is much more closely bonded. We are therefore by nature suited to form unions, societies, and states. The Stoics hold that the world is governed by divine will: it is as it were a city and state shared by men and gods, and each one of us is a part of this world. (*De fin.* 3.63–64 = LS 57G part)[78]

[76]See Annas, *Morality of Happiness*, esp. 263–265 and 275; Brad Inwood, "Comments on Professor Görgemann's Paper: The Two Forms of *oikeiôsis* in Arius and the Stoa," in *On Stoic and Peripatetic Ethics: The Work of Arius Didymus*, ed. W. W. Fortenbaugh (New Brunswick, N.J.: Rutgers University Press, 1983), 190–201; Christopher Gill, "The Stoic Theory of Ethical Development: In What Sense Is Nature a Norm?" in *Was ist das für den Menschen Gute? Menschliche Natur und Güterlehre*, ed. Jan Szaif (Berlin: de Gruyter, 2004), 101–125.

[77]An argument for giving it up altogether is offered by Keimpe Algra, "The Mechanism of Social Appropriation and Its Role in Hellenistic Ethics," *Oxford Studies in Ancient Philosophy* 25 (2003): 265–296, esp. 285.

[78]Translation LS. Cicero may, at the end of the relevant section in *De fin.* 3.64, introduce a thought that is either later or has, in early Stoic political philosophy, not been proposed within the same context—that we prefer the 'common benefit' to our 'individual benefit' by nature. But the bulk of his report in *De fin.* 3.62–64 seems to refer to the early doctrine.

In this report, the idea that all human beings belong together rests on a picture of nature as a whole with parts, which are like the functioning parts of one organism. Becoming virtuous importantly involves *understanding* nature, so that one can then live in agreement with nature, insofar as one understands it. Thus, seeing that others are, like oneself, part of one whole and belong to oneself in the same deep sense in which parts of one organism belong to each other is integral to becoming virtuous or wise. This is tied to the core political idea of the cosmos as a city: each human being is a part of the cosmos, and this can be explained by thinking of the cosmos as one city with all humans and gods as its inhabitants.

A third key passage on *oikeiôsis* supplements the evidence in Diogenes and Cicero. Stobaeus reports how Hierocles, a Stoic who flourished around 100 CE, explains *oikeiôsis* as involving concentric circles of relative closeness around each person's soul. The agent is at the center; next come family members, more and more distant relatives, local residents, fellow-citizens, people from neighboring towns, fellow-countrymen, and finally the whole human race.

> Once all these have been surveyed, it is the task of a well-tempered man, in his proper treatment of each group, to draw the circles together somehow towards the center, and to keep zealously transferring those from the enclosing circles into the enclosed ones.... It is incumbent on us [*proskeitai*] to esteem [*timêteon*] people from the third circle as if they were those from the second, and again to esteem our other relatives as if they were those from the third circle. For although the greater distance in blood will remove some of the affection, we must still try hard to assimilate them. The right point will be reached if, through our own initiative, we reduce the distance of the relationship with each person. (Stobaeus 4.671,7–673,11 = LS 57G)[79]

Hierocles' report captures an important implication that has not been spelled out in detail in the sources on the earlier theory: that we should gradually come to regard all others, no matter how distant they are, as equally belonging to us. With respect to this aspect of the theory, Annas observes that it calls for something

[79]Translation LS, with some changes.

like impartiality.[80] However, what *oikeiôsis* calls for seems to be in interesting ways different from the modern idea that morality demands an impartial perspective. First, the theory of *oikeiôsis* is concerned with our *affective disposition* toward others. It assumes that, in order to relate correctly toward all, we have to 'love' all. And second, we have to take into account Stoic thought about the emotions (*pathê*). The idea is not to 'love' in a sense in which 'love' is a *pathos*. While the Stoics say that the sage has no *pathê*, they do not ask us to envisage a perfect being without any type of affective disposition toward others. The sage has 'rational feelings,' *eupatheia*, and among these is a friendly disposition toward others, involving kindness, generosity, warmth, and affection (DL 7.116). It is this kind of 'love' that, ideally, we would feel for everyone. Thus, while we may think of paternal affection as the kind of emotion that will involve despair and deep grief if the child dies, this is not the kind of affective disposition that is called for toward everyone. According to Stoic ethics, one should not respond in this ·way to the death of one's child. Thus being disposed toward every- one as 'belonging to oneself' does not involve such violent reactions to whatever may happen to anyone else.

Hierocles, writing a few centuries later than the early Stoics, acknowledges what critics will have been quick to point out: that it is not so easy to feel akin to distant strangers. And he adds a psychological strategy on how to bring this about. However, the early Stoics would, quite consistently, not feel the need for such instruction. If virtue is knowledge, and if the soul is one and is rational, then (at least in the terms of the ancient discussion) know- ing that all are kin is *seeing* them all as kin, and this involves being motivationally disposed toward all as the normal person is only toward her closest friends and family—only better, that is, with the kind of 'friendly love' that counts as a rational feeling.

---

[80]See, e.g., Annas, *Morality of Happiness*, 265. For a brief summary of how Annas understands the notion of impartiality see also Annas, "Aristotelian Political Theo- ry," 78. According to Annas, it is central to impartiality "that the agent (i) not weight her own interests merely because they are her own interests, and (ii) not weight her own particular attachments and commitments merely because they are her own." For critical discussion of the Kantian picture Annas's interpretation suggests see Algra, "Social Appropriation," 289–291.

While it might seem impossible, for instance, to fall into deep grief about a distant child's death, it seems quite possible to extend 'rational feelings' to all human beings. Algra argues that what is called for is a universalized partiality, not impartiality. However, even this needs qualification: the Stoic theory can only allow for the kind of partiality that does not go along with *pathê*. What is called for is an extended sense of what belongs to oneself or concerns oneself in a broad sense, tied to the sage's affective disposition. This is different from an impartial point of view in the (standard) sense of modern ethical theory, insofar as it is an affective disposition. It is at the same time different from 'universalized partiality,' insofar as the emotions that usually go along with partiality are not part of the ideal.

Both in Diogenes Laertius and in Cicero, the theory of *oikeiôsis* is tied to key ideas of Stoic political philosophy. The instruction to regard all others as fellow-citizens adds a political dimension to the demands that the theory of *oikeiôsis* outlines; it emphasizes one aspect of 'being affiliated with others'—to regard them as relating to the *same law*. The ancient texts that make the connection between the theory of *oikeiôsis* and political theory culminate in mentioning the common law: what we understand when we see others as belonging to us is that all human beings, as part of the cosmos, share one common law. The political dimension of 'belonging' would, on this reading, consist in the idea that all human beings are tied to each other through the common law. We can also see this connection in an anonymous commentator on the *Theaetetus*, who complains about how unrealistic the Stoic theory is. According to the Stoics, he says, one should relate to oneself in the same way as to the most distant Mysian. The Stoics, he says, derive justice from appropriation; the right way of seeing oneself and others is thought to preserve justice (Anonymous commentary on Plato's *Theaetetus*, 5.18–6.31 = LS 57H). Again, this confirms that the Stoics themselves see the theory of *oikeiôsis* as directly related to political philosophy.

It is part of understanding how others belong to us to see how all human beings belong to one community. This community is explained, in the foregoing passages, in terms of parts and whole: one is to understand how one is a functioning part of an organism. In other contexts, the Stoics explain the community of humans and gods as one of reason. Gods and men are thought of as one community due to their participation in reason, and the difference between humans and gods is that humans may strive for perfect reason, while the gods have perfect reason. Accordingly, what we would understand when we progress toward seeing others as belonging to us is that all human beings are equally related to us, *since they, like us, participate in reason*. But, as we have seen, the kinship of reason is not emphasized in the context of *oikeiôsis*; in the relevant passages we hear about the kinship of being part of one whole. It is *one* aspect of making progress with respect to *oikeiôsis* to understand that humans all belong to each other as parts of nature. It is a *second* aspect that one is a part of the *universe* as a whole, not (merely) a part of a community of all human beings. And the focus on these ideas is not confined to the early theory. Epictetus says that to be a citizen of the world really is to be a *part of it* (*Discourses* 2.10.5–12 = LS 59Q part). Accordingly, to be the fellow-citizen of all human beings is to be, like them, a *part of the universe*.

To modern commentators, it has often seemed more intuitive and compelling to reconstruct the theory of *oikeiôsis* in terms of a community of reason. The progressing human being, on this account, comes to understand how virtue *as reason* is the only good, and comes to see how she is tied to everyone else because all human beings have *reason*. Doing what is appropriate is, again, doing what is justifiable by *reason*, and as one progresses, one is more and more able to consistently choose in such a *reasonable* way. This summary is deliberately one-sided, but it brings out how the Stoic theory can be presented by continued reference to reason, and without reference to nature as a whole with parts. While this account is one-sided and does not reflect the emphasis of the key texts on *oikeiôsis*, none of its individual claims is foreign to Stoic ethics. It also accords well with how Cicero begins his treatise *De Officiis*: he gives an account of first impulse, love for one's offspring, that is designed to lead into discussion of *officia* or *kathêkonta*, appropriate action. Since appropriate action is action that can be accounted for by reason, it is quite fitting to continually stress the role of reason. And this is how Cicero presents the bond between human beings, as a bond of reason (1.11–12).[81] Thus, the

---

[81]Schofield remarks with respect to *De Officiis* 1.11–12 that the bond between all human beings does not, on the Stoic picture, exist on account of their 'humanity' ("Two Stoic Approaches," 203). He stresses that the bond is explained by reference to reason.

reason-based account of *oikeiôsis* may not strain the boundaries of scholarly interpretation too much.[82]

As we can see from passages in other contexts, the Stoics do think that all human beings have reason, and that they are connected by having reason. Further, they hold that those with perfect reason are, again, accordingly connected to each other, and that reason as the soul of the cosmos connects *everything* that is rational, whether perfectly or imperfectly.[83] But the kinship of reason is not what we are primarily to understand when we are becoming progressively 'affiliated' or 'belonging' to the rest of the cosmos. What we are to understand first and foremost is that we indeed belong to the cosmos in a very literal sense, because we are its part, and that the same is the case for all other human beings. If we neglect this aspect of the theory of *oikeiôsis*, we are in danger of seeing the Stoic theory in too Kantian a light or too much as a theory that is independent from theses about the nature of the universe. Ultimately, the two ways of reconstructing *oikeiôsis* converge. Most important, we are part of the cosmos insofar as the *pneuma* of our souls is part of the soul of the cosmos, which is itself *pneuma*. The soul of the cosmos *is* its reason. Thus, understanding how one is a part of the whole *is* understanding how one's own reason should be 'in tune' with the reason of the cosmos. In this way, we reach the foregoing reason-based reconstruction of *oikeiôsis*. But by now it is clear that the notion of reason is, to an important extent, a *physical* notion.

If we bring into focus the picture of human beings as parts of a whole, we can see an element of the Stoic theory that is difficult to see in any other context: the Stoic account of how we relate to others and of how we should see ourselves as relating to others. To regard all others as belonging to us means to regard them as *ourselves*, similarly to the way a father may see his child as a part of himself

---

[82]Gisela Striker says very frankly that, while it seems sufficiently clear to us that the 'consistent life' must be a life of reason, she has not found this argument spelled out in the sources ("The Role of *Oikeiôsis*," 287). Striker mentions that a passage in Epictetus may come close to this thought (*Discourses* 1.6.16–21). This, however, will clearly not count as evidence for the early theory. Striker's discussion of *oikeiôsis* is all the more helpful for her focus both on what seems most plausible to us as modern readers of the texts on *oikeiôsis* and on what can and cannot be sustained by the precise wording of the sources.

[83]See, e.g., Cicero, *De leg.* 1.23 = SVF 3.339.

in an extended sense. This extended sense in which one regards one's children as oneself has something to do with how one sees their concerns. If someone is harming this father's child, he feels as if this person is directly harming him. He is *directly* concerned with this: he perceives the harm that is done to his child as *relevant to himself.*

Understanding how one belongs together with all other human beings has deep implications for ethics and political philosophy. Most fundamentally, it tells us that the concerns of all others *are our concerns.* 'Our concerns,' that is, the things we should take account of in deliberation, are values and disvalues—health, illness, wealth, poverty, and so on. These are the things the Stoics call indifferents. They are neither good nor bad and are thus 'indifferent' with a view to happiness. But they are not indifferent in the usual sense of the term: they bear on action. Appropriate action is action that arises from a fully adequate weighing of all indifferents relevant to a situation. The health or illness, wealth or poverty, life or death, strength or weakness, and so on of others *are our concerns.* If an agent sees all human beings as *belonging to her*, the concerns of all human beings are literally *her concerns.*

The Stoics do not propose a 'theory of justice' that would explore how we are to interact with others and what we owe to them. But this is not because they do not engage with these questions. The Stoics locate these (or similar) questions in the framework of a theory about the shared life of human beings in their only real home, the cosmos. Even though we can only offer a rough sketch of them, these aspects of the Stoic theory become more apparent once we focus on the conception of human beings as parts of the larger living being, the cosmos. A conception of a community of reason that does *not* integrate this picture runs the risk of not finding a place for commitments to others in Stoic ethics. A community of reason might, without this physical side of the theory, be something quite different from a community of 'belonging to all others' in the Stoic sense.

Uncovering the connection between early Stoic political philosophy and the theory of *oikeiôsis* lends very good sense to Plutarch's report that Zeno, in his *Republic*, is instructing ordinary progressors on how to *see* others. Coming to see all others as fellow-citizens is quite distinct from striving to build a political community in which all others will be one's fellow-citizens. The community according to which all others *are* fellow-citizens is already there; it is the cosmos, the whole of which each human being is a part. The Stoics do not envisage a worldwide community that should be established. Rather, they tell us that such a community exists, should be understood, and should transform how we relate to others.

Further, this interpretation enables us to shed some light on why Zeno makes 'being a relative' a core notion of political philosophy. Thesis (S) has four components: only the sages are citizens, friends, relatives, and free. Citizenship and freedom may be quite obvious topics in political philosophy, and in ancient debates, the same is probably true for friendship. But why does Zeno make 'being a relative' into a central conception of his political thought? Part of the answer may be that any kind of community is an adequate topic of political philosophy. But we may also think that, for the early Stoics, the relationship of belonging is indeed a very central philosophical conception, and that it is this conception of 'belonging' that stands behind the term 'being a relative.' In (S), Zeno makes use of vocabulary that becomes a *technical* vocabulary in the theory of *oikeiôsis*:[84] he uses '*oikeion*' to refer both to those who are relatives in a strict sense and to those who are conventionally seen as relatives. But the latter he also calls, together with all who are not virtuous, 'alienated' (*allotrion*) from each other. The fact that Zeno describes the opposite of being a relative in these terms indicates that he is, at this point, using much more technical language than is usually supposed. In ordinary language, there is no expression for the *opposite* of being related—one would simply distinguish between being related or not related. That Zeno uses *allotrion* places his claim within the technical framework of the theory of *oikeiôsis* and confirms the thesis that this theory needs to be seen as closely related to political philosophy.[85]

---

[84]While the Sceptic lists of Stoic theses are misleading as to the general format and substance of early Stoic political philosophy, this passage seems to directly cite Zeno's claim.

[85]As Algra ("Social Appropriation") argues, the kind of vocabulary that is important for the theory of *oikeiôsis* has been used already by Plato and Aristotle. Thus we should not suppose that, if Zeno or Chrysippus develop the theory, they are concerned with questions that have not been part of ancient ethics before. Algra offers a broad analysis of different terms which relate to these questions. As a counterterm for

The technical notions of enmity and being alienated correspond to the notions of citizenship and being a relative and are equally strong. Thus, those who belong to each other in the analogously weak sense of citizenship and kinship can consistently be said to be enemies and alienated. This thesis is paradoxical in quite standard Stoic fashion. It derives its sense from the dichotomies of wisdom and foolishness, virtue and vice, knowledge and ignorance. Whoever is not wise is a fool, and accordingly, whoever is not a citizen in the strong sense is the opposite of being a citizen, an enemy. Whoever is not related in the strong sense is the opposite of it, alienated. But enemies and those who are alienated in this technical sense—that is, all the fools—are at the same time rational, and related to each other as parts of one whole.

'belonging together,' *allophulon* seems to have been most important. Within the Stoic theory, *allotrion* becomes the key technical notion. If Zeno uses this term in the *Republic*, this suggests that he is already conceiving of these matters within the framework of the theory of *oikeiôsis*.

3

Wisdom: Sages and Gods

The community of all human beings, as we have seen, is not an ideal—it is real. The cosmos is home to all human beings, and together with the gods, all human beings live in the cosmic city. However, human beings need to *understand* that this is how they should see themselves—as parts of the cosmos, which is home to a community of all rational beings. And coming to see oneself in this way involves a lot. Ultimately, only the sage understands everything that pertains to this view of oneself—this view presupposes a deep understanding of the cosmos, nature, law, and so on. And it is by gaining this understanding that one becomes a citizen, friend, relative in the strict sense, and a free person. This ideal of living in the cosmos as its citizen, as a friend, relative, and free person is the subject of this chapter. We have seen that all human beings *are* parts of the cosmos, and *are* part of one community, whether or not they see themselves as such. But the technical notions of citizenship, friendship, being a relative, and freedom, set up an ideal of being a part of the cosmic city *in a better way*.

As I hope to show, this ideal is partly developed through the *political dimensions of wisdom*, and partly through the conception of *citizen-gods*. Many of the well-known Stoic claims about the sage's expertise are to be located, at least to some extent, in political philosophy. The sage, presumably, holds all kinds of offices and performs various public functions—he is a priest, a soothsayer, a judge, and so on. Thesis (S), the thesis that only the sage is a citizen, friend, relative, and free person, has the same structure as these claims: 'Only the sage is X.' In order to gain a better understanding of (S), we must first engage with the structure of these claims, and their role in Stoic discussions of wisdom. As I shall argue, these claims do not tell us that the sage lives a life filled with many tasks and occupations.

Rather, they redefine X as an achievement of reason, or, as we might say, a dimension of wisdom. Much of this chapter is devoted to questions about wisdom and knowledge, which, I hope to show, bear importantly on our interpretation of Zeno's claims about citizenship, friendship, being a relative, and being a free person.

Both the sages and the gods are wise, and thus our study of the Stoic conception of wisdom must extend to the gods. Up to now, I have proceeded on the basis of a preliminary notion of gods as perfectly reasonable living beings in the cosmos. But it is far from clear how we should understand the claim that the gods are citizens—and presumably also friends, relatives, and free. The conception of citizen-gods has not yet received much scholarly attention; it is no doubt the element of early Stoic political philosophy that is most alien to modern debates about law and cosmopolitanism. We may also speculate that a basic tenet of Stoic theology has made this idea unappealing, long before contemporary scholarship discovered the Stoics as some kind of cosmopolitanists: Stoic gods are *corporeal*. Whatever elements of early Stoic thought survived in the Christian natural law tradition, this idea has certainly dropped out. For the early Stoics, both sages and gods are physical beings in the cosmos. And there is a second problem: Philodemus complains that the Stoics are deceiving us when they create the impression that there is room for several gods within their theology. Talk of several gods, on his view, cannot be taken seriously. We need not share Philodemus's uncharitable attitude in order to see the problem. Stoic theology centers around a physical notion of god as one of the two basic principles of physics, and it is not clear whether, within this framework, a plural conception of gods can be, or should be given anything more than a metaphorical sense.[1]

Even with respect to the sage it is somewhat surprising to find a plural notion. In the central areas of Stoic ethics, discussion of the sage can be translated into discussion of wisdom, and thus a

---

[1] While important progress on Stoic theology has been made through a recent collection of papers—Dorothea Frede and André Laks, eds., *Traditions in Theology: Studies in Hellenistic Theology: Its Background and Aftermath*, papers presented at the Eighth Symposium Hellenisticum (Leiden: Brill, 2002)—the focus of research on Stoic theology is not on the conception of a plurality of gods. Michael Frede discusses the Stoic claim that god is corporeal, and the question of how divine beings are created by god, in "La Théologie Stoïcienne," in *Les Stoïciens*, directed by Gilbert Romeyer Dherbey and edited by Jean-Baptiste Gourinat (Paris: Librairie Philosophique J. Vrin, 2005), 213–232.

condition of the soul. As I shall argue, this does not really change once the Stoics come to political philosophy. Thesis (S), the claim that only *the sages* are citizens, friends, relatives, and free, can be adequately rephrased as the claim that only *the sage* is a citizen, friend, relative, and free. And (S) must be true (on Stoic assumptions) independently of whether there is, at any given time, any sage at all. If there is one sage, she must be a citizen, friend, relative, and free, with no other sage existing who is, like her, a citizen, relative, friend, or free human being. The sage, as I shall argue, is a citizen of the cosmos insofar as she is able to live by perfect reason or the law. She is a relative insofar as she fully belongs to the cosmos or to what is perfectly reasonable in the cosmos. She is free insofar as nothing about her own condition obstructs her life according to reason. She is a friend insofar as any two perfectly reasonable beings in the cosmos (e.g., a sage and a god) benefit each other. None of these notions implies that there must be several sages. Indeed, if there were no sages at all, we could still think that this is how the gods live in the cosmos.

A chapter on sages and gods must begin by pointing out why these are best discussed together. With respect to virtue, a sage and a god are the same (section 1). However, as physical beings, they are not. It is the aim of this chapter to elucidate the first three components of (S): that only the sages are citizens, friends, and relatives (I turn to freedom in chapter 4). But in order to understand these claims about the sage, we need to first get clear about the function and structure of claims of the form 'Only the sage is X' in Stoic philosophy (sections 2 and 3). The results of this discussion can then be applied to Zeno's claim that only the sage is a citizen and a relative (section 4). The sage is a relative insofar as she fully belongs to what is perfectly reasonable in the cosmos; the conception of citizen-gods helps us to better understand what this means (section 5). Finally, I turn to friendship and to Zeno's claim that Eros provides safety in the city (sections 6 and 7).

1. Are Gods Sages?

The gods are, in all respects that relate to *virtue*, like the sage. Gods and sages are described with the same predicates—wise, virtuous, happy (*eudaimôn*), and perfectly reasonable. In this sense, the theses that only the sages are citizens and that the gods are citizens are largely equivalent. The core idea is that only a perfectly reasonable living being is a citizen. Chrysippus famously says that Zeus is not superior to a sage: "Zeus does not exceed Dion in virtue, and Zeus and Dion, given that they are wise, are benefited alike by each other whenever one encounters a movement of the other" (Plutarch, *On Common Conceptions* 1076A = LS 61J, translation LS).

Chrysippus's thesis is very strong: not only is Zeus not superior in virtue to Dion, but Zeus himself is called *wise*, and he can be *benefited* by a human being.[2] The Stoic theory about the likeness of sage and god stands within the context of an ongoing ancient discussion about an idea that is most famously discussed in *Theaetetus* 176b–c.[3] Here Plato has Socrates explain how one should try to become as much like god as possible. For lack of a simple English term, it has become customary to discuss the idea of becoming as much like god as possible without any real attempt at translation, by using the Greek expression *homoiôsis theô* (literally, 'assimilation to god'). We might say that Stoic claims about the likeness of sage and god constitute the early Stoic perspective on these matters. Sages and gods stand, as it were, next to each other as models of wisdom. Both of these models invite the ordinary progressor to become like them. The Stoic sage plays a role that, in Plato, only the divine model plays: he can be emulated by others. Within the Stoic theory,

---

[2]It is a difficult question how the idea that gods are virtuous or have virtue (*aretê*) is dealt with in Greek tradition and philosophy. God can be described as good, just, blessed, and so on, without being called virtuous. In many literary or mythological contexts, 'justice' is not understood as one of the virtues. Rather, it seems to refer to Zeus's way of distributing destinies and ordering human lives. On the other hand, there is the tradition of *aristeiai* of gods. Just as the heroic deeds of Achilles or Patroclos can be listed in an *aristeia*, Zeus's great deeds can be recounted in a text or depicted in art, and this can be referred to as an *aristeia*.

[3]Important passages in Plato on *homoiôsis theô* are: *Symp.* 207e–209e, *Th.* 176b–c, *Rp.* 611d–e, 500c–501b, 613a–b, *Lg.* 716c–d, *Ph.* 81a–84b, *Phdr.* 245c–249a, *Tim.* 41d–47c, 90a–d. On Plato's conception of becoming like god see Julia Annas, *Platonic Ethics, Old and New* (Ithaca, N.Y.: Cornell University Press, 1999), chap. 3; David Sedley, " 'Becoming Like God' in the Timaeus and Aristotle," in *Interpretion the Timaeus-Critias: Proceedings of the Fourth Symposium Platonicum*, ed. T. Calvo and L. Brisson (St. Augustin, Germany: Academia Verlag, 1997), 327–339. On earlier conceptions see D. Roloff, *Gottähnlichkeit, Vergöttlichung und Erhöhung zu seligem Leben: Untersuchungen zur Herkunft der platonischen Angleichung an Gott* (Berlin: de Gruyter, 1970).

there is no room for the virtuous human being to *further* emulate god. Later Stoic philosophy seems, to some extent, to fall in with the thought that even the most virtuous human being could still lead his life by modeling it after that of god. When Seneca asks 'What is a happy life?' he can sum up his description by saying: "To put it in a nutshell for you, the wise man's mind should be such as befits god."[4] However, this is not exactly the way the early Stoics would phrase their theory; on their account, it does not make sense to say that the wise man's mind *should* be in such and such a state. Rather, the progressor's mind should be in that state that is both the state of the sage and that of a god. The early Stoics use *both* the sage and the gods to explain the notion of perfect reason; they do *not* present the virtuous person as striving to become similar to a god.[5] In his book *On Nature,* Chrysippus writes that the virtuous are *in no way* surpassed by Zeus:

> Chrysippus, even though he has written much to the contrary, clearly sides with the view that neither anything bad surpasses anything bad, nor any wrong action another wrong action, nor virtue virtue, nor any perfect action another perfect action. He does say in the third book of *On Nature*: "As it befits Zeus to be proud of himself and his life and to be high spirited and, so to speak, carry his head up high and to give himself airs and to boast, since he is leading a life worthy of boasting, thus this also befits all the good, since they are surpassed in nothing by Zeus." (Plutarch, *On Stoic Self-Contradictions* 1038c = SVF 3.526)

Zeus's lack of superiority with respect to virtue is based on the Stoic thesis that all virtuous actions and all wrong actions are on the same level. If someone is virtuous, then she is virtuous *simpliciter*, not more or less virtuous. Therefore, if a human being is virtuous, and a god is virtuous, they are (in this respect) exactly alike. Given the Stoic conception of virtue, Zeus also is not superior

---

[4] Seneca, *Ep.* 92.3 = LS 63F, tr. LS.

[5] Another strand in early Stoic theorizing about the sage and gods starts off from the idea of 'having a god inside oneself.' Diogenes Laertius reports that the virtuous "are also said to be divine [*theious*]; for they have in them as it were a god [*hoionei theon*]" (DL 7.119). It is this idea that, as I argued in chapter 1, is relevant to the Stoic view on temples (that there "should be no temples").

in happiness. The virtuous or wise being is *eudaimôn*: if there are no degrees of virtue or wisdom, there can be no degrees of happiness. Only the virtuous and wise are happy; the inferior man or fool is miserable.[6] Thus any distinction between the blessedness of gods and some form of lesser happiness attainable by human beings cannot be integrated into Stoic philosophy. Whoever is virtuous is happy; and this does not allow for degrees.[7] Insofar as the Stoic conception of citizenship depends on perfect reason, and on the state of the virtuous person's soul, it can be explained equally well by reference to gods and by reference to sages.

However, the sage is no god; she is not the same kind of living being as a god. A well-known *scala naturae* of the Stoics focuses on how different entities *move*—whether they move (or: are moved) externally or internally, and if internally, through mere growth, through *impressions*, or through *assent to impressions*.[8] This scale ends with human beings. But Cicero presents a Stoic *scala naturae* that goes further and includes the gods as the highest kind of entity: "The fourth and highest scale is taken by those beings who are by nature good and come into being as wise, and who are already born with right and stable reason [*ratio recta constansque*]." These beings are the gods. They belong to god in the sense in that god is identified with the world, and the world is inhabited by perfect (*perfectam*) and full (*absolutam*) reason (*De natura deorum* 2.34). Thus there is a difference between the sage and god. God *is* wise, while a sage, even though she now is wise, had to first *become* so.[9]

Plutarch reports that, according to the Stoics, the gods are not only immortal and happy, but beyond this, friendly toward human

---

[6] Cf. DL 7.89 = SVF 3.39 = LS 61A; Alexander of Aphrodisias, *De fato* 199,14–22 = SVF 3.658 part = LS 61N.

[7] Cf. Stobaeus 2.98,17 = SVF 3.54. See also Proclus, *in Plat Tim.* P. 106F Schn. = SVF 3.252.

[8] Origen, *On principles* 3.1.2–3 = SVF 2.988, part = LS 53A.

[9] Cleanthes argues that there must be a higher being than human beings: if there are better and worse natures, there must be a best nature. A human being is afflicted in all kinds of ways, *and even if he attains virtue, then only late in life*. Therefore, there must be a better animal, namely god (SE M 9.88–91). In this argument, it seems that *if* a human being were virtuous from the very beginning, god would not be better.

beings, caring, and helpful.[10] On the one hand, this claim extends the comparison of sage and god: the gods' attitudes strongly resemble the rational feelings of the sage. But the caring and friendly nature of the gods is not only reminiscent of the rational feelings that replace the affections in those who are virtuous. It also refers to the gods' omniscience and hence providence: in order to *care* for human beings, the gods need to know beforehand what will happen. While the sage knows everything that pertains to the leading of one's life, the sage does not know *all causes*. Sages need to make use of *signs* when predicting what will happen; gods, on the other hand, can be caring and provident through their knowledge of causes.[11] Further, the gods have 'witnessed' previous worlds. Every world that is generated is identical with the previous world—the gods literally know what is going to happen. Each world-cycle is thought to be, in all respects, the same.[12] Divine reason is different even from the perfect reason of the sage. The fact that gods know causes *and* are eternal gives rise to a more robust kind of omniscience. Thus, while the *ethical* meaning of calling gods and sages citizens is very much the same—that only perfectly reasonable beings can live by the law that pervades the cosmos—in terms of physics, the citizen-gods are different beings from the sages, and this has implications for the way they possess knowledge. While we can, for the most part, explore the central conceptions of early Stoic political philosophy with respect to both the gods and the sages, we must keep these differences in mind. The gods are, physically speaking, different beings, and this may help us to understand some of the Stoic claims in political philosophy.

---

[10]*On Common Conceptions.* 1075E — SVF 2.1126 = LS 54K. This view is ascribed to Chrysippus in Cicero, *De divinatione* 1.81–82 and 2.101–102 The importance of this claim within Stoic theology is also emphasized in Cicero's presentation in *De Natura Deorum*, which elaborates this point in contrast with the Epicurean views to the contrary.

[11]Cf. Cicero, *De divinatione* 1.82, 1.118, 1.125–130.

[12]Nemesius, *De natura hominis* 309,5–311,2 = SVF 2.625 = LS 52C. As Ricardo Salles points out, this means that objects are the same in a very strong sense, including numerical identity; "Determinism and Recurrence in Early Stoic Thought," *Oxford Studies in Ancient Philosophy* 24 (2003): 253–272, 259. Given the Stoic theory of kataleptic impressions, for two things to be indiscernible, they must, strictly speaking, be the same. No two things *could* have the relevant kind of indiscernibility (*aparallaxia*; cf. SE M 7.409–410). Thus, the gods have seen the same things happening in the strictest sense.

But we may nonetheless be reluctant to engage with the citizen-gods. If it seems that the gods really are, in terms of ethics, like the sages, why should we not confine ourselves to the discussion of wisdom? After all, early Stoic political philosophy is a part of ethics, and perhaps we should not get too distracted with physics. Consider Chrysippus's claim about Zeus and Dion both being virtuous and wise. Should we take the reference to Zeus in any way literally? Why should we not focus on the ethical core of the claim, namely, that there are no degrees of virtue or vice, so that whoever is virtuous is virtuous, wise, and blessed in the fullest sense? It is tempting to think along these lines, and thus, in reconstructing the Stoic theory of the cosmic city, to lose sight of the gods as corporeal beings. However, even with respect to Chrysippus's statement—the comparison of Dion and Zeus—it is not quite clear whether we should adopt a purely ethical reading. The statement can be given a plausible physical interpretation: the universe itself is a living being; it has a soul, and, in a sense, the active principle, that is, Zeus, *is* this soul. Thus Dion would be compared to the rational soul of the universe. On this reading, Chrysippus's perplexing statement amounts to the comparison between two perfect souls, the soul of the sage and the soul of the universe. If we rephrase Chrysippus's thesis along these lines, the comparison between sage and Zeus (or: active principle) is, read as a physical thesis, still very striking, but it loses its implausibility. The perfect soul of a sage resembles the perfect soul of the cosmos. It relates perfectly to the soul (or: reason, law, etc.) that pervades the cosmos, and thus becomes a fully integrated part of the cosmos. And this is a key insight about how the sage relates *physically* to the cosmos; as we will see, this is the point that is at the core of the Stoic conception of being a relative.

2. The Sage Is 'Ignorant of Nothing'

Cicero reports the Stoic claims that only the sages are kings, rich, and beautiful; that everything, wherever it is found, belongs to the sages; that no one could be consul, praetor, emperor other than the sages; and finally that only the sages are citizens and free. He refers to these claims as paradoxes, adding that most of the Stoic paradoxes go back to Socrates.[13] The sage is also the only seer, poet, and priest.[14] It is clear how Cicero can find such Stoic claims paradoxical (in the sense in which several Stoic teachings appear paradoxical): how could anyone be at the same time a king, seer, priest, judge, businessman, poet, and so on? Would the sage be a king of the cosmic city, and at the same time hold all other key positions in this city? Or are we to think of the occasional sage living somewhere, who should be assigned all these tasks for which he uniquely qualifies?

Claims of the form 'Only the sage is X' have, as I will argue, a specific structure. They aim to add to our understanding of what wisdom is, and they aim to redefine X. The four claims of (S) follow this pattern. As I hope to show, even the claims of (S) are, in spite of the plural 'sages,' most centrally about wisdom as a condition of the soul. But we can only see this if we take the time to study the structure and function of claims of the form 'Only the sage is X.' In order to do so, we need first to turn to some relatively basic ideas in Stoic epistemology.

The Stoics famously hold that the sage is 'ignorant of nothing.' As Kerferd observes, it seems natural to rephrase this by saying that the Stoic sage 'knows everything.'[15] Other ancient theories take precautions against the wholly implausible idea of someone knowing every single thing that could possibly be known—by arguing that only certain kinds of things are the objects of knowledge, or by distinguishing between what is more or less universal, and so on. The Stoics offer no such qualifications, and thus it may appear that their sage is strictly omniscient in a quite implausible sense, that he knows everything in the past and present (and maybe even in the future) that can possibly be known. Such a conception of the sage's knowledge would be unable to recognize a difference between, for example, understanding the nature of fate and knowing what a random person at the other end of the world had been wearing last Friday.

<hr>

[13] *Academica* 2.136 = SVF 3.599.

[14] Stobaeus 2.67,13 and 20; cf. 2.114,16.

[15] G. B. Kerferd, "What Does the Wise Man Know?" in *The Stoics*, ed. J. M. Rist (Berkeley: Cambridge University Press, 1978), 125–136. Kerferd offers a brief introductory conspectus of views proposed earlier than 1978.

However, if we read the sources carefully, the Stoics do not describe the sage as omniscient in such an implausible sense.[16] What is more, the claim that the sage is 'ignorant of nothing' is not even adequately rephrased as the claim that he 'knows every-thing'—this is a statement that the Stoics do not make, and it is due to the different epistemological background assumptions of inter-preters that it can seem to them that not being ignorant of anything is the same as knowing everything. On Stoic premises, it is not. The Stoics hold that only the sage has knowledge, that he does not have opinions (SE M 7.151–157), and that knowledge is an overall condi-tion of the soul.[17] They propose four definitions of *epistêmê* (the term I translate, throughout, as knowledge), as follows. (1) Knowl-edge is cognition (*katalêpsis*) that is secure and unchangeable by reason; here, the term 'knowledge' refers to the *product* of an individual act of cognition of the sage (a new 'piece of knowledge'). (2) Knowledge is a system of such 'pieces of knowledge,' and (3) it is a system of such *expert* 'pieces of knowledge,' which has, like the virtues, intrinsic stability.[18] (4) Knowledge is a "tenor for the recep-tion of impressions which is unchangeable by reason, and consisting, they say, in tension and power."[19] The sage can only acquire individual 'pieces of knowledge' because of the stable system of knowledge that, as it were, structures his soul. Thus the notion of a system is integral to how the sage 'knows everything': everything he holds to be true is part of a system of assumptions, each of them having the status of knowledge.[20]

Like knowledge, ignorance is a condition or state of the soul, generated (and sustained, or reinforced) through assent to impressions.

---

[16]Cf. Michael Frede's remarks on how the sage is not omniscient in his introduc-tion to *Rationality in Greek Thought,* ed. M. Frede and Gisela Striker (Oxford: Oxford University Press, 1996), 1–28; see also Frede, "Stoic Epistemology," in *Cambridge History of Hellenistic Philosophy*, ed. Keimpe Algra et al. (Cambridge: Cambridge University Press, 1999), 295–322.

[17]For the claim that only the sage has knowledge, see Cicero, *Academica* 2.145 = SVF 1.66 = LS 41A; SE M 7.152 = LS 41C; on how knowledge is the overall condition of his soul, see Stobaeus 2.73,16–74,e = SVF 3.112, part = LS 41H.

[18]I cannot discuss here what the difference between (2) and (3) might be.

[19]Stobaeus 2.73,16–74,3 = SVF 3.112, part = LS 41H.

[20]On the notion of consistency see Michael Frede, "On the Stoic Conception of the Good," in *Topics in Stoic Philosophy*, ed. Katerina Ierodiakonou (Oxford: Oxford University Press, 2001), 71–94, esp. 83.

We can think of ignorance along the lines of the different definitions of knowledge. On the one hand, there are individual 'pieces of ignorance' (opinions); on the other hand, ignorance is the overall condition of the fool's soul (since this overall condition is not one where individual 'pieces of ignorance' would fit in with each other in any specific way, there is no analogue to [2] and [3]). Ignorance is a certain kind of assent: changeable and weak assent.[21] Every 'piece of ignorance,' (that is, every such changeable and weak assent) arises from (as well as reinforces) ignorance as a condition of the soul. The sage "never makes a false supposition," and he "does not assent at all to anything non-cognitive, owing to his not opining and his being ignorant of nothing."[22] The sage only assents to kataleptic (or: cognitive) impressions; if an impression is cognitive, he assents firmly.[23] Thus every assent that the sage gives is a new 'piece of knowledge' in his soul, just as every assent of the fool is a new 'piece of ignorance.'

According to this analysis, no one either has knowledge or is ignorant about content that has never presented itself to him. The fool, while being ignorant *tout court*, is not ignorant of things about which he has never had an impression to which he assented. Rather, he has no attitude at all with respect to such things. The sage has, in the same way, no attitude at all with respect to matters about which he has never had a kataleptic impression (he may have had a non-kataleptic impression, but since he will not have assented to the

[21]Stobeaus 2.111,18–21 = SVF 3.548 = LS 41G. Constance Meinwald explains rightly that, according to the Stoics, opinion is not restricted to assent to *incognitive* impressions; "Ignorance and Opinion in Stoic Epistemology," *Phronesis* 50 (2005): 215–231. The fool has 'cognition' (*katalêpsis*), i.e., assents to kataleptic (or: cognitive) impressions, but he always assents weakly. *All* assents of the fool are characterized by the overall disposition of his soul and thus must be 'weak'—the fool cannot assent in the firm and unchangeable way the sage assents. It is thus important to note that the Stoics do not envisage *two kinds* of opinion—assent to the incognitive and weak assent. Rather, all assent by fools is weak, which is why the fool is limited to opinions; and in some of these opinions, he assents to cognitive impressions, in some to incognitive impressions.

[22]Stobeaus 2.111,18–21 = SVF 3.548 = LS 41G.

[23]It is a difficult question whether the Sceptic challenges to this account or the Stoic replies are ultimately more convincing. For a recent discussion that relates different interpretations of the Stoic–Sceptic debate to contemporary theories in epistemology see B. Reed, "The Stoics' Account of Cognitive Impression," *Oxford Studies in Ancient Philosophy* 23 (2002): 147–180.

impression, he does not have any cognitive attitude with respect to it). To put this in another way, if the sage never had an impression regarding the color of the coat of some person unknown to him, there is, as it were, no *occasion* for him either to know what the color is or to have an opinion about it. If he had a blurred impression regarding the color of the coat, one to which he did not respond with assent, this impression, as it were, does not leave a trace in the overall condition of his soul. It would be incorrect (on Stoic assumptions) to say that the sage is ignorant about the color of the coat. 'Being ignorant of something' is a kind of assent and a state of the soul just as much as 'knowing something.' In the case of the color of some unknown person's coat, we would have to say that there is no aspect in the overall state of the sage's soul that relates to this content. Thus the sage neither has knowledge nor is ignorant about the color of the coat.

This has nothing to do with the idea that knowing the color of a coat would be too much on the level of particulars, while knowledge is in some sense about universals. It also has nothing to do with limiting knowledge to certain kinds of objects ('higher' objects of some kind). Neither of these conceptions plays any role in Stoic epistemology. Whatever impression the sage assents to, this will be an act of cognition, resulting in knowledge. As Plutarch remarks, if the Stoic sage has a memory of Dion sneezing or Theon playing ball, this is a case of knowledge (*On Common Conceptions* 1061C). The sage's knowledge is only limited by the fact that he is presented with a limited number of cognitive impressions. But is assent to the cognitive impression that Theon plays ball just as integral to the state of the sage's soul as an insight about the nature of fate? Even if assent, in both cases, results in knowledge, it might seem implausible to see no difference between how knowledge of some trivial, particular event and knowledge of a basic principle of reality affect the overall state of one's soul. However, we need not assume that we are left with such a picture.

The notion of a *system* of knowledge supplies us with a first clue as to how we might describe their different status. Knowledge of the color of someone's coat, or of Theon playing ball, is not going to be part of a systematic body of knowledge in a way that makes many other pieces of knowledge connect with it. The system of pieces of knowledge in the sage's soul will not be significantly altered by the addition, or the lack, of some such piece of knowledge. Compare this to how much the state of someone's soul would be altered if he came to understand the nature of fate. One could not be wise without doing so—such knowledge is deeply tied to the sage's overall way of seeing the world, and thus to the majority of his judgments. While it may seem evident to us that knowledge about fate or causes plays this kind of role, we have little explicit evidence on what is, in this way, integral to the overall state of the sage's soul. Plutarch seems to report a criterion: the sage does not mind whether he remembers that last year Dion was sneezing or Theon was playing ball; since he holds that among the many cognitions and memories arising from cognitions only a few have anything to do with him (*pros hauton hêgeitai*), he is unconcerned with the rest (*On Common Conceptions* 1061C). I cannot, at this point, enter into the question of how it is that the sage may forget something. What is important for present purposes is that the Stoics seem to have made a distinction between pieces of knowledge that contribute to the leading of one's life (as we may paraphrase the foregoing expression 'have anything to do with him'), and others that do not. Clearly, understanding the nature of fate is highly relevant for how one leads one's life. Knowing that someone is playing ball is, absent very special conditions, not at all relevant for how one leads one's life.

We can try to elucidate further which pieces of knowledge make up the core of the sage's system of knowledge by considering that the overall condition of knowledge is, at the same time, the overall condition of virtue. A Stoic definition of virtue brings out the way the Stoics subscribe to the Socratic tenet that virtue is knowledge:

> The Stoics said that wisdom is knowledge of the divine and the human, and that philosophy is the practice of expertise in utility. Virtue singly and at its highest is utility, and the virtues, at their most generic, are triple—the physical one, the ethical one, and the logical one. For this reason philosophy also has three parts—physics, ethics and logic. Physics is practiced whenever we investigate the world and its contents, ethics is our engagement with human life, and logic our engagement with discourse, which they also call dialectic. (Aetius 1, preface 2 = SVF 2.35 = LS 26A).[24]

---

[24]For a briefer report of this view see DL 7.92. The foregoing passage has up to now not received much scholarly attention (an important exception is Stephen Menn, "Physics as Virtue," *Proceedings of the Boston Area Colloquium in Ancient Philosophy* 11, ed. John J. Clearly and William C. Wians [1995]: 1–34). While Kerferd ("What

According to this account, the division into philosophical disciplines is at the same time the most generic division of virtues.[25] Thus virtue is most literally knowledge, but not *any* knowledge: virtue is knowledge in the three fields of philosophy. This conception of virtue is also attested in Cicero's *De finibus*. At the end of an exposition of key ethical theses of the Stoics, Cato says that in addition to *these* virtues (namely, the ethical ones) the Stoics called dialectic (i.e., logic) and physics virtues. Logic is a virtue because possessing it ensures that we never assent to anything wrong, are not deceived, and are able to hold on to the insights we gained with respect to the good and the bad. "If rashness [*temeritas*] and ignorance are, with respect to everything, vices, then it is right that the art which removes these is called virtue" (*De fin.* 3.72). Physics, on the other hand, is a virtue because life in agreement with nature is based on the world as a whole and its administration (3.73).[26]

That virtue is knowledge does not mean that knowledge is virtue; not every piece of knowledge is integral to virtue. The foregoing

---

Does the Wise Man Know") does refer to the Stoic account of virtue (and even to the Socratic tenet that virtue is knowledge), he only refers to the more conventional distinctions among justice, moderation, *phronêsis*, and courage. But the aforementioned distinction might be at least as important to the Stoic theory: it takes the claim that virtue is knowledge literally, and spells it out; it clarifies *what* knowledge it is that is identical with virtue. Cicero reports the identity of virtue and right reason as an essential tenet of Stoicism: virtue is a stable and integrated (*constans conveniensque*) state of the soul, making laudable those in whom it exists; "all fine [*honestae*] decisions, judgments and actions and all right reason [*recta ratio*] arise from it (even though virtue itself can, in the briefest possible way, be called right reason) [*recta ratio*]" (Cicero, *Tusc.* 4.34 = SVF 3.198).

[25]Chrysippus discusses Athena: the name "Athena" means "Athrena," and this in turn means "Tritonis" and "Tritogeneia." These names, according to his analysis, signify that wisdom (*phronêsis*) (i.e., what Athena stands for) is tripartite, consisting of logic, physics, and ethics (Philodemus, *De Pietate*, cols. 9.15–10.3; edition of A. Henrichs, "Die Kritik der stoischen Theologie in *PHerc.* 1428," *Cronache Ercolanesi* 4 (1974): 5–32 (hereafter abbreviated Henrichs 1974; see chapter 2, note 63). Even though Chrysippus's claim is about wisdom, not virtue, it confirms (given that it is the same disposition of the soul that is called wisdom and virtue) the earlier perspective on virtue.

[26]Cato, who presents the Stoic doctrine, runs off into an eulogy about the admirable order and harmony of Stoic philosophy, emphazising how each and every thought fits in with the rest. Not a single letter within this body of philosophy could be moved (*De fin.* 3.74).

account of virtue helps us to see how we can 'rank' the knowledge of the sage. Clearly, the knowledge that constitutes virtue is the knowledge that is integral to the conception of the sage. While it is important that the sage will not have opinions on anything, and will not assent hastily even when nothing more than the color of someone's coat is in question, his knowledge of such everyday particulars is not central to the fabric of the stable disposition of his soul.

According to this interpretation, 'knowing everything' means that the soul is in a state where everything that is held to be true is a piece of knowledge, and where all these pieces of knowledge form a system of knowledge. This system consists of knowledge that is integral to virtue, plus (a possibly very large number of) further pieces of knowledge, depending on the particular life of a given sage. This state is considered to be stable: any assent of the sage starts from this stable disposition. It will result in integrating a new piece of knowledge with what is already there. But the new 'pieces of knowledge' can only be relatively mundane things—the core pieces of knowledge must already be in place for someone's soul to be in the overall state of knowledge, and thus for him to assent accordingly. The idea that the sage is strictly omniscient is, once we see the basic structure of Stoic epistemology, quite absurd. It presupposes that the sage has kataleptic impressions of everything one could possibly have an impression of.

Assent does not only result in either knowledge or opinion, it is also identified with impulse to action, provided that what is assented to is the appropriate kind of impression. The sage's 'omniscience' goes hand in hand with his always acting correctly. Just as he does not fall prey to deceiving impressions outside of the sphere of action, the same applies when he assents to impressions that present possible courses of action: "Furthermore, the wise are unerring [with respect to action], not being liable to error" (DL 7.123).

Taken together, the ideas about knowledge and action—that the sage always assents so as to acquire knowledge, or, in the sphere of action, so as to act correctly—explain the way he is an expert in 'everything': "Furthermore, the wise man does all things well, just as we say that Ismenias plays all airs on the flute well" (DL 7.125).

The comparison with the musician who masters all airs on the flute helps to explain how it is that the sage is an expert in what, no doubt, will turn out to be a fairly wide range of things. Doing several

things well is like bringing the disposition of the perfectly rational
soul to bear on different tasks. It is *one* art that makes the musician
master the different airs. Similarly, it is the same state of knowledge
that makes the sage an expert in whatever he applies himself to. The
same claim is transmitted in Stobeaus, but in more detail:

> They [the Stoics] also say that the wise man does everything well—that
> is to say, everything that he does: for as we say that the flute-player or
> the lyre-player does everything well, with the implications 'everything
> to do with flute-playing,' and 'everything to do with lyre-playing,' so
> the wise man does everything well so far as concerns what he does, and
> *not of course also what he does not do* [my emphasis]. In their opinion
> the doctrine that the wise man does everything well is a consequence of
> his accomplishing everything in accordance with right reason [*kata
> logon orthon*] and with virtue [*kat' aretên*], which is expertise concerned
> with the whole of life. By analogy, the inferior man does everything
> that he does badly and in accordance with all the vices. (Stobaeus
> 2.66,14–67,4 = SVF 3.560 = LS 61G, tr. LS with changes)

The sage does not, strictly speaking, know everything. Rather,
every assent that he in fact gives is a piece of knowledge. It is exactly
this picture that we get with respect to action. The wise man does not
'do everything'; rather, whatever he does is right. He is not an expert
in *every* art—only in those arts he applies himself to. Just as it seems
nonsensical to assume that someone could *do everything* (perform
every possible action, engage in every possible art), it is, on the Stoic
theory, nonsensical that someone could know everything: that would
imply that he had given assent to every possible kataleptic impression.

3. *'Only the Sage Is X'*

It is with this general account in mind that we should approach Stoic
claims on how the sage is a king, military strategist, priest, judge,
seer, and so on. First, a brief list of passages that report these claims:

> Besides being free the wise are also kings, since kingship is rule which
> is answerable to no one; and this can occur only among the wise, as
> Chrysippus says in his work *On Zeno's Proper Use of Terminology*.
> For he says that a ruler must have knowledge of what is good and

bad, and that no inferior has this. Likewise only the wise are holders of public offices, judges and orators, whereas no inferior man is. (DL 7.122 = LS 67M, tr. LS)

Rather, he [the virtuous man] is in the highest degree happy, fortunate [*eutuchês*], blessed, well-off [*olbios*], pious, god-loved, worthy, kingly, military-leader-like, statesman-like, economist-like and good with finances. The inferiors are in all these things the opposite. (Stobaeus 2.100,2–2.100,6 = SVF 3.567)[27]

Only the sage is a good seer, poet, orator, dialectician and critic. . . . They say that also only the sage can be a priest, but not the inferior. (Stobaeus 2.67,13 and 20)

And the virtuous is also the only soothsayer. (Stobaeus 2.114,16)

[There are] also the theses that he [i.e., the wise man] legislates and that he educates people, and again that it is appropriate for the virtuous to compose writings which can benefit those who encounter the writings. (Stobeaus 2.94,11–14, tr. partly Schofield, 125)

As long as we think of all the different roles and tasks along the lines of how they are conventionally understood, the sage emerges as a varied person, seemingly doing all kinds of things. But once we assume that these claims really serve to spell out what it means to be fully reasonable—to have one's reason in the correct or perfect state (*orthos logos*)—they start to make sense. Like the musician's art, the state of the sage's soul is *one*, and it is part of its perfection that it can be applied in different spheres. The context of some of the quoted passages makes it clear that, in each case, it is due to his knowledge that the sage is uniquely so qualified. Each time, the knowledge is put to a different use. However, it is essentialy the *same condition of the soul* that is needed in, and for, all the various tasks.

Let us look, by way of example, at the claim about the sage being a priest. Only the sage can be a priest, because it is integral to being a priest that one has intimate knowledge of divine nature (Stobaeus 2.68, 2–3). This Stoic notion of what it means to be a priest is continuous with the conventional notion: a priest is an expert in divine matters. But at the same time, the Stoic notion is highly

---

[27]The predicates "kingly," "military leader–like," and so on, pose further questions, which, however, we need not engage with at this point.

revisionist. A priest in the conventional sense is not a philosopher who probes and develops theories in theology. His knowledge is perceived as—in one way or another—much more 'inspired' or 'intuitive' (he may be initiated into rites, trained to perform a public function, inspired through religious practices, etc.).

Those who have the roles of priest almost certainly do not have the knowledge that, according to the Stoics, priests have. But the Stoic claim is not that they should be fired and replaced by sages. The claim is rather that, if we come to understand what being a priest really involves, this radically changes our understanding of what a priest *is* and of *who is* a priest. We come to see that the persons who have the roles of priests *are no* priests. A priest, according to the suggested reading, really is a philosopher-sage, someone who has mastered physics and, given the interrelatedness of the disciplines, also ethics and logic. Things are similar with respect to divination: it is the sage's wisdom that enables him to read signs and thus predict the future. Both according to the conventional notion and according to the technical, Stoic conception, the soothsayer is an expert in predicting things. However, on the Stoic account, what enables him to do so is his knowledge—his knowledge of nature and his ability to draw conclusions from signs.[28]

The Stoics think that in *better* states, sages would take part in politics (Stobaeus 2.94,8-11). But they do not ask us to envisage a sage who, since he is so uniquely qualified, must be put into service at all kinds of civic and religious positions, *as they are conventionally understood.* Chrysippus discusses the claim that only the sages are kings in a work on Zeno's proper use of terminology (and rightly so: what is at issue is, in an important sense, the redefinition of a term). Chrysippus explains that only the wise are kings, since "kingship is rule which is answerable to no one," going on to say that "a ruler

---

[28]The Stoic sage cannot predict the future on account of his knowledge of causes; only god knows all causes. The sage needs to make use of signs (this is how Cicero presents the Stoic views on divination in *De divinatione*; see 1.82, 1.118, 1.125–130). As Michael Frede has pointed out, the Stoics seem to have emphasized how causes are hidden or obscure (*adêla*), which makes knowing causes of particular phenomena extremely difficult; some Stoics seem to have been charged with being extremely reluctant *ever* to venture into specific causal explanations; "The Original Notion of Causes," in Frede, *Essays in Ancient Philosophy* (Minneapolis: University of Minnesota Press, 1987), 125–150, 130–131.

must have knowledge of what is good and bad," which no inferior has.[29] The fact that only the sages can hold public offices and be judges and orators is introduced as an extension of this claim, and it is obviously supposed to rely on the same reasoning. Being a king, holding a public office, being a judge or an orator—all of these are redefined if we are to think of them as consisting of knowledge of what is good and bad. Knowledge of what is good and bad is at the core of ethical knowledge. We do not learn that the sage is in fact a king, orator, judge, and so on—we learn that being one of these in the true sense means having knowledge of good and bad. To say that the only judges and rulers are the sages is to explore the kind of knowledge that is needed for judging and ruling.

This discussion helps to bring out something important about Stoic theorizing. Claims of the form 'Only the sage is an X' do not add to our picture of the sage by telling us that he is, in addition to being all-knowing, virtuous, and wise, also an X. Rather, these claims become understandable and interesting elements of the Stoic theory only if we see that the explanatory direction is the other way around: *A thesis of the form 'only the sage is X' redefines X as involving wisdom (or knowledge, or virtue)*.[30] Thus we learn what X really is (a specific practice of wisdom), not that it is one of many tasks of the sage. And this means further that there is a sense in which all the tasks and roles that figure as X are in some sense the

---

[29]DL 7.122 = LS 67M.

[30]It would be very interesting to follow up on the Socratic heritage of this type of Stoic thesis. In her discussion of Plato's *Cratylus*, Rachel Barney coins, with respect to Plato, the notion of a 'project of the strict sense'. "This project is not an investigation into the dictionary meaning of a term, but a particular kind of 'real definition,' and one which typically has revisionist results. It is an attempt to work out what a correct naming convention for the term in question would be.... Part of the project of the strict sense, then, is to establish the relation to knowledge of the term under investigation, and to work out what sort of knowledge is involved." Barney mentions that Plato might have inherited this project from the historical Socrates and perhaps also the sophists, and, as she says, "a number of the paradoxes of Stoic ethics can be seen as expressions of this Socratic project run amok." *Names and Nature in Plato's "Cratylus"* (New York: Routledge, 2001), 14–15 and n. 23. I agree with Barney— the Stoic redefinition of terms seems to grow out of a Socratic, and possibly also sophistic, engagement with how we should properly understand terms—most important, those that are evaluative. The way wisdom and knowledge matter to the Stoic project seems to develop further the importance knowledge has in the Socratic project.

same—not insofar as they could not involve different fields of knowledge, but insofar as this knowledge will ultimately be part of the systematic knowledge of the sage. Further, the redefinition of X is on the one hand radically revisionist, but retains on the other hand some core element of the conventional understanding of X. A priest in the Stoic and in the conventional sense is an expert in divine matters, a soothsayer is an expert in predicting future events, and so on.

4. Citizenship and Being a Relative

If the foregoing argument is persuasive, Zeno's claim that only the sages are citizens, friends, relatives, and free spells out further aspects of what the knowledge and wisdom of the sage involve. Sages are the only citizens, the only friends, the only relatives, and the only ones who are free. This means that to become virtuous or wise *is* to become a citizen, a friend, a relative, and free. Accordingly, each of the notions in (S) explores an aspect of perfect reason (or wisdom). Note that the implication of this is that 'citizenship,' 'being a relative,' 'being a friend,' and 'being free' are to be understood as *kinds of expertise*, or ways in which wisdom plays out if we describe this or that aspect of the sage's life. This is already a significant revision of these notions: citizenship, being a relative, a friend, and free do not, according to this interpretation, primarily describe social positions or social relationships, but rather the perfect condition of the soul. To be a citizen, a relative, a friend, and free are *dispositions* of the soul, or aspects of one disposition or condition— that of perfect reason. Insofar as these dispositions (excluding, for the moment, freedom, which I discuss in chapter 4) are about the way we ideally *relate* to the world and other human beings, they are *relational* dispositions. But citizenship, friendship, and being a relative are *not* primarily *relationships* to other human beings; it is up to the individual agent to become virtuous, and thus a citizen, relative, and friend.

Just as the revised notions of a priest or a soothsayer are not totally discontinuous with the conventional notions, so, too, should we expect some continuity between the conventional notions in (S) and their technical counterparts. I have discussed citizenship extensively in chapter 2, and at this point, we only need to relate the results of chapter 2 to the analysis of claims of the form 'Only the sage is X.' With respect to citizenship, I propose that the common element in the Stoic and the everyday understanding of the term lies in the idea that to be a citizen is to be a *full* member of a political community, a member who in some sense is associated with the administration of this political community. There is a sense in which the cosmic city 'consists of' its citizens, which is similar to the way in which an ordinary polis is (in some sense) constituted by its citizens. These ideas, however, are reformulated in a deeply revisionary way, and especially the last aspect is, as I argue later, also relevant to the claim that only the wise are relatives.

Citizens in the full sense are those who have *perfect reason*, that is, the gods and those among humans who are wise. The cosmos is itself a living being, and it is made up of elements and of other living beings—of gods, human beings—and the things created for their sake. It is a system or complex organization of all of this. A full member of this lawful, perfectly organized system must be someone who is, as it were, 'up to' complying with the *law of this cosmic city*—a living being whose reason corresponds to the perfect reason of nature by being, itself, in a perfect state. And precisely this is a further claim that the Stoics make about the sage: only the sage is 'lawful' (*nomimos*); he does what the law prescribes and is its only exegete. And only he is *nomikos*, which we can translate as 'able to follow the law' (Stobaeus 2.102,4–9). One needs to be perfectly reasonable in order to live fully by the law— gods and sages live by the law "by the use of reason" (Cicero, *De Natura Deorum* 2.154). Sages and gods partake of reason and law (which are identical) to the fullest degree. As citizens and, accord ingly, those with the highest political status, they are able to 'rule.' As we will see in chapter 4, the core of this ability lies in the perfectly reasonable movement (or action) as a part of the cosmos, a part that is, through the perfect condition of its soul, perfectly integrated with the whole.

Note that nothing in the notion of a citizen, understood in this way, depends on there being several human sages, or even one. The claim that only the sages are citizens does not envisage a community of wise human beings. A single sage, if she existed, could be the only human citizen in the cosmos: the only human being who is, on account of her wisdom, able to live fully by the law of the cosmos.

With respect to the notion of being a relative, we might first note that the aspect of the ordinary understanding of the term that is reflected in the technical Stoic notion is that 'being a relative' refers to a relationship of *belonging*. Second, we should note that matters are somewhat complicated by the question whether Zeno develops a technical notion of *oikeion* that is the very notion that comes to be central in the theory of *oikeiôsis* (see chapter 2). As I have suggested, there is good reason to think that he did so.[31] If so, we have an excellent starting point for understanding his claim that only the sages are relatives. It would mean that only the sages have completed the process of *oikeiôsis*—have understood fully how they are parts of the cosmos, and by this have become fully integrated parts of the whole.

The relationship of belonging Zeno seeks to capture would thus be the relationship of belonging *to the cosmos*. With respect to citizenship, Zeno says that only the wise are citizens, not that they are each others' fellow-citizens. Similarly, with respect to being a relative, he does not say that the sages are *each others'* relatives (DL 7.32–33). Insofar as being a relative is a relationship, it must be a relationship with what is perfectly reasonable in the cosmos. Other sages are perfectly reasonable, and thus the sage is their relative. But more generally speaking, he is the relative of *everything* that is perfectly reasonable in the cosmos, and 'being a relative' refers to being a perfectly integrated part of the cosmos.

(The sage is not the relative of all human beings. It is one thing to maintain that the sage, by having completed the process of *oikeiôsis*, regards all others as relatives. This attitude is similar to regarding everyone as a fellow-citizen. But it does not make *others* into sages, and thus not into relatives [or citizens] in the technical sense. The sage can be everyone's relative insofar as she sees everyone as a relative; yet at the same time, the others are not going to be *her relatives*. In this weak sense, the sage is related to everyone. But in a stronger sense, a sense according to which all relatives are themselves relatives, only the gods and the cosmos can be relatives of the sage.)

Let me explore in some more detail what I mean by describing the sage and gods as a perfectly integrated part of the cosmos. The gods

---

[31] While we cannot be sure that the theory of *oikeiôsis* was already spelled out by Zeno, it nonetheless seems unlikely that his use of '*oikeiôn*' and '*allotrion*' should be *un*related to the role these terms come to assume within the theory of *oikeiôsis*.

(or their souls) are, as we shall see, portions or parts of the perfectly reasonable soul of the cosmos.[32] Both the sage and the gods are perfectly reasonable *parts* or *components* of the perfectly reasonable soul of the cosmos, and in this sense, they are relatives. The sage is also a relative of the perfect reason of the cosmos. In both cases, we are describing the same aspect of the Stoic notion of wisdom: there is a sense in which the perfectly reasonable soul belongs to whatever else is perfectly reasonable in the cosmos—perfect reason is ultimately not something that is achieved within an unreasonable world, but rather a perfection that, once achieved, integrates the human being with the perfectly reasonable soul of the world, and with what is divine about the world.

This, it seems to me, can be argued independently of what exactly we think about Zeno's contribution to the theory of *oikeiôsis*. It is clear that the conception of the cosmos as a living being with all living beings in it as its parts goes back to Zeno. This can, for example, be seen from direct quotations by Cicero in *De Natura Deorum*. Zeno argues for the claim that the world is sentient from the fact that it has sentient parts, and similarly for the claim that it is rational from the fact that the world 'gives birth' to those who are animate and rational (2.22). And it is also clear that already Zeno emphasizes the idea that the cosmos is one. This claim is at the center of Stoic physics: the cosmos is finite and, in this sense, one.[33] But it is also one insofar as it is pervaded and 'held together' by one force—albeit a force with many names: Zeus, creative fire, reason, law, and so on.[34] A human being who achieves wisdom becomes, as it were, part of this one force that 'holds the cosmos

[32]Progress in understanding what it is that connects one to others does not stop with human beings. If the relevant bond is that of reason, the largest circle must be that of humans and gods. While the theory of *oikeiôsis* is usually not presented in this light, Dirk Obbink mentions that it "links the individual . . . with the gods in the outer reaches of the concentric circles of the cosmos"; "The Stoic Sage in the Cosmic City," in Ierodiakonou, *Topics in Stoic Philosophy*, 191.

[33]The world suffers conflagration and then comes into existence again. But at a given point in time, the world is one (the Stoics envisage a unitary cosmos, with the void stretching out indefinitely around it; see SE M 9.332 = SVF 2.524 part = LS 44A).

[34]Michael White speaks of a "seamless, radical continuity"; "Stoic Natural Philosophy (Physics and Cosmology)," in *The Cambridge Companion to the Stoics*, ed. Brad Inwood (Cambridge: Cambridge University Press, 2003), 124–152, 146. See also Susanne Bobzien, *Determinism and Freedom in Stoic Philosophy* (New York: Oxford

together,' that pervades the cosmos and administrates it. Given this, it is not implausible to assume that Chrysippus argued in the third book of his *On Nature* that, in a sense, the cosmos *consists of the wise.*[35] All wise living beings are parts of perfect reason, which pervades the cosmos. Even though the world does not literally consist only of god or reason (matter being the other 'principle'), we might think that what Chrysippus says when he says that the cosmos is a single entity *ek tôn phronimôn* is that, *insofar as the cosmos is a single entity*, it is constituted by those who are wise. It is reason or god that sustains the cosmos as a *unified* entity.[36]

Each human being is a part of the living being 'cosmos,' and each human being's soul is a portion of the *pneuma* pervading the cosmos. Those whose soul can be in better or worse condition— that is, human beings—can relate to the cosmos's reason in a better or worse way. Reason (or soul) pervades every part of the cosmos, just as soul extends into every part of the human body (DL 7.138).[37] It is fundamental to the physics of how human souls relate to the world's soul that, according to the Stoics, the human soul is vapor (*pneuma*), just like the soul of the cosmos, and that *pneuma* comes in different degrees of density. These degrees of density are called 'tenors' (*hexeis*). If the human soul is in the condition of knowledge, wisdom, and virtue, it has the same tenor as the soul of the cosmos. That the human soul is *part* of the cosmic *pneuma* is by

---

University Press, 1998), 16–18. When Plutarch complains that Chrysippus begins his ethical inquiries by saying that Zeus is the source and origin of justice, he goes on say that, from here on, Chrysippus is very concise in his ethical writings. However, he then elaborates on the things Chrysippus puts at the beginning of all ethical writings: he does not only refer to Zeus but also to fate and providence, and he prefixes the thesis that the universe is *one and finite and held together by a single power* (*On Stoic Self-Contradiction* 1035B).

[35]According to a report by Philodemus, Chrysippus says in his third book of *On Nature* that the cosmos is a single entity of, or for, the wise (*PHerc.* 1428, col. 7,21–24. I am using Obbink's reconstruction of the text ("The Stoic Sage," 185) and Henrichs 1974.

[36]This line of reasoning is attested for Diogenes of Babylon. According to Diogenes, there is a sense in which the cosmos *is* Zeus. What this means, more precisely, is that the cosmos *encompasses* Zeus in the way [the body of] a human being encompasses the soul (Philodemus, *De Pietate*, col. 8.14–21; Henrichs 1974).

[37]Cf. DL 7.151 on how blendings occur 'through and through.'

no means a metaphorical claim. Rather, it is backed up by a very literal theory on the permanent generation and material reconstitution of the human soul. The human soul is in constant material flux. On inhalation, air causes the material of the soul to emerge from the blood, and on exhalation, parts of the soul are transported outside of the human body.[38] Thus the soul of *any* human being, whether wise or not, is in some sense continuous with the *pneuma* in the cosmos.[39] *Pneuma* can have different tenors, and what is generated in *every* human being is the degree of tension that makes a soul a *human* soul (or *pneuma* into human-soul-*pneuma*). This tenor is, as it were, a good enough starting point for further improvement, from which one might ideally reach the tenor of the cosmos's soul. While every human being belongs to the whole, one can do so in a deficient, or in a perfect, way. One only belongs to the whole in the fullest sense if the tenor of one's soul is in just as perfect a state as the tenor of the world's soul, or the tenor of a god's soul.

5. *The Citizen-Gods: Celestial Bodies and Portions of Pneuma*

This brings us to the gods. Why, first of all, should we take the claims about the gods as citizens literally? If we approach early Stoic political philosophy through the more recent studies in the field, we certainly do not expect the gods to play an important role. While no one disputes the testimony on how all human beings and the gods share life in the cosmos, the conception of citizen-gods receives very little attention. Schofield complains that the theory of

---

[38] For an excellent presentation of important sources on this process see Matthew Colvin, "Heraclitus and Material Flux in Stoic Psychology," in *Oxford Studies in Ancient Philosophy* 28 (2005): 257–272.

[39] Note that the Stoic-Socratic claim of the unity of the soul does not refer to these issues. When the Stoics or Socrates are said to hold that the soul is one, this is in contradistinction to Plato and Aristotle, or any ancient theory of the soul that distinguishes between rational and irrational parts or powers of the soul. For the Stoics, the soul is *not* one in a physical sense according to which it would consist of a persisting conglomerate.

the cosmic city is 'marred' by Stoic polytheism.[40] This may well capture a broadly shared modern response to the role of the gods. Even those who do not approach Stoicism in the hope of finding a protoversion of universalist cosmopolitanism seem to find the idea of citizen-gods too far removed from anything that could interest us.

But unlike the sages, the gods are physical entities in the cosmos that we can *observe* and *marvel at*. They thus provide a model of the blessed life that goes beyond (or: is partly different from) that of the sage. The study of perfectly rational parts of the cosmos may help us understand the physical side of the Stoic end, life in agreement with nature; a star's movements may exemplify what it means to enjoy an 'easy flow' of life. And the physical study of citizen-gods may also help with a second aspect of the theory. It might seem that, given the Stoic account of the soul as *pneuma* with a specific tension, once one's soul is perfect, it is no longer 'one's soul,' but *merely a portion* of the cosmos's soul. If the soul is understood as corporeal and as extending into all of the cosmos, how then can a part of this soul be confined to a particular entity, that is, a human being? Of course, a human being's soul extends through all of the human being's body, and the body offers, as it were, a limit to where a human soul begins and ends.[41] The souls of human beings who are not perfectly reasonable have a tenor that is different from (and deficient in comparison with) the perfect soul of the cosmos. But once one's soul is perfectly reasonable, how is it still one's *own* soul, rather than just a portion of the cosmos's soul? We might want a notion of a human soul's particularity that refers to its *actions*: The perfectly reasonable human being is conceived as making, by her rational powers, her own decisions, not as *dissolving* into the overall perfect movements of the cosmos. Thus we may wonder whether the

---

[40]While Malcolm Schofield does not engage with the question who the citizen-gods are, he does take the physical framework of the Stoic theory seriously, and discusses the Heraclitean heritage in Stoic philosophy; see *The Stoic Idea of the City* (Chicago: Cambridge University Press, 1999), chap. 3.

[41]Bodies are sustained by the tenor of the *pneuma* that pervades them (Plutarch, *On Stoic Self-Contradictions* 1053F–1054B = SVF 2.449 = LS 47M). On difficulties in Stoic physics relating to questions about cosmic cohesion and unity on the one hand and its constituents and entities in it on the other see White, "Stoic Natural Philosophy," 146–151.

conception of citizen-gods makes it easier to see how a perfect being can both be a part of the whole and be a particular entity in it.

The view that the gods *inhabit* the cosmos and have the highest status among the different animals living in it is ascribed to the early Stoics in thesis (HG).[42] The gods are perfectly reasonable, live in the cosmos as in a city, are the rulers of this 'city,' and exercise providence. Gods and human beings are tied together by reason and law.[43] It is this cluster of ideas that I refer to as the conception of citizen-gods.[44]

In order to approach this conception, we must first of all ask in what sense Stoic theology allows for a notion of a plurality of gods.[45] It has not gone unnoticed, either in antiquity or in modern scholarship, that Stoic theology is—at least on the surface—quite heterogeneous. The Epicurean spokesman in Cicero's *De Natura Deorum*, Velleius, criticizes Zeno, Cleanthes, and Chrysippus for identifying god with the mind of the world, aether, the stars, the cosmos, and a number of other things (1.36–41).[46] In his view, these identity-statements are a sign of inconsistency.[47] Philodemus complains that Stoic talk about several gods is misleading, since in fact the adherents of Zeno hold that there is one god (*De Pietate*, col. 10.14–18). The scholar of Stoic thought who does not share the uncharitable attitude of an Epicurean will assume that

[42]Arius Didymus, ap. Eusebius, *Praep. Evang.* 15.15.3–5 = SVF 2.528 part = LS 67L.

[43]Cf. Cicero, *De Natura Deorum* 2.154; *De leg.* 1.23 = SVF 3.339.

[44]The gods remain part of the Stoic picture in later Stoic thought. Seneca writes, very much in agreement with thesis (HG), that the truly 'common community' is that between gods and men (*De Ot.* 4.1).

[45]For a detailed discussion of the different sources on Stoic theology see Myrtô Dragona-Monachou, *The Stoic Argument for the Existence and the Providence of the Gods* (Athens: National and Capodistrian University of Athens, 1976). See also J. Mansfeld, "Theology," in Algra et al., *The Cambridge History of Hellenistic Philosophy*, 452–478. For a general account of Stoic theology as related to cosmology see A. J. Festugière, *La révélation d'Hermès Trismégiste*, vol. 2, *Le Dieu cosmique* (Paris: Gabada), 1949.

[46]Cf. Philodemus, *De Pietate*, col. 4.13–20, Henrichs 1974: according to Chrysippus, Zeus is reason, which is 'leading' everything, and is the soul of the whole cosmos.

[47]See the discussion of K. Algra, "Stoic Theology," in Inwood, *The Cambridge Companion to the Stoics*, 153–178, 169–170. Algra refers, for similar ancient objections, to Lactantius, *Div. Iust.* 7.3 (= SVF 2.1041), and Plutarch, *Comm. not.* 1085 B–C.

in theology, as in other fields of Stoic philosophy, these various identity-statements need much explanation, but can be spelled out as substantial and consistent tenets of one theory. To modern scholars, it will be more worrisome whether Stoic claims about god as the active principle allow for more than metaphorical talk about several gods.[48] It has often been observed that, for the ancients to speak both of god and the gods is less difficult than it would seem to us. But Stoic theology does not just go back and forth between a singular and a plural notion of god and the gods. The problematic aspect lies elsewhere: Stoic physics makes the singular notion of god so fundamental to all of Stoic philosophy that, comparatively speaking, talk about several gods appears to be merely metaphorical.

So, how do the Stoics arrive at a notion of a plurality of gods? To a large extent, Stoic theology truly *is* physics—god is understood as one of the two first principles of physics (*pneuma* or that which is active, as opposed to matter or that which is acted on) and conceived of as a corporeal entity (DL 7.134).[49] The principles are, unlike the elements of the world, ungenerated, indestructible, and everlasting (DL 7.134). God as the active principle pervades the matter of the universe (SE M 9.75–76). He is described as the manufacturer of the world (DL 7.137). Just as the soul of human beings is corporeal, god is corporeal. God is a designing fire, proceeding toward the creation of the world.[50] God is identified with reason, intelligence, and fate, so that 'god,' 'intelligence,' 'fate,' and 'Zeus' are different names for the same thing (DL 7.134–135). Finally, god is also identified with the cosmos

[48]For discussion of theories that recognize one main divinity but make room for several minor divinities see M. Frede, "Monotheism and Pagan Philosophy in Later Antiquity," in *Pagan Monotheism in Late Antiquity*, ed. Polymnia Athenassiadi and M. Frede (Oxford: Clarendon Press, 1999), 41–69; M. L. West, *Towards Monotheism*, in Athenassiadi and Frede, *Pagan Monotheism*, 21–41.

[49]A parallel text of the Suda gives 'incorporeal' instead of 'bodies.' However, according to Stoic physics, only corporeal entities can act, and—as active principle—god surely acts. Origen, *Against Celsus* 4.14 (= SVF 2.1052 part = LS 46H), affirms that the Stoics conceive of god as a body. See David Sedley, "The Origins of Stoic God," in Frede and Laks, *Traditions in Theology*, 41–83, and Michael Frede, "La Théologie Stoïcienne."

[50]Aetius 1.7.33 = SVF 2.1027 part = LS 46A.

(DL 7.137).[51] That the world *is* god follows from the fact that there is nothing better than the world. Cicero's spokesman for the Stoics in *De natura deorum* quotes Zenonian arguments:

> "That which has reason is better than that which does not have reason; but there is nothing better than the world; therefore the world has reason." It can be shown in a similar way that the world is wise, and that it is happy and eternal. Because everything which has these features is better than that which lacks them, and there is nothing better than the world. From this it will be inferable that the world is god.... He continues and argues even more concisely: "Nothing," he says, "which is without soul or reason, can generate out of itself anything animated and able to reason; but the world generates something animated and able to reason; therefore the world is animated [has a soul] and able to reason." (Cicero, *De nat. deor.* 2.21–22)[52]

If we consider how drastically Zeus is redefined—as one of the two principles of reality—we might well expect not to find a traditional picture of the other Greek gods either.[53] The spokesman for Stoic philosophy in Cicero's *De Natura Deorum*, Balbus, asserts that the Stoics dismiss any anthropomorphic picture of the gods (2.45). But the Stoic conception of the Olympians and other traditional Greek gods is still more revisionist than that. A passage in Diogenes Laertius gives *one* account of how the Stoics move from the conception of one god to that of several gods:

> [They say that] the god [*theon*] is an immortal living being, rational or thinking, perfect in happiness, not receptive of anything bad, provident with respect to the cosmos and the things in the cosmos. But he is not of human shape. He is the demiurge of the whole [*tôn holôn*] and, as it were, the father of all things, in general and in this part of him [*to meros autou*] which pervades everything, and which is called by many

---

[51]The second and third sense of *kosmos* are: (2) the world-order, and (3) what is composed of both god and the world-order.

[52]The universe, understood as a divine being, is also wise (2.37) and virtuous (2.39). Compare *De Natura Deorum* 2.32: if the universe were not reasonable, it would be inferior to human beings, which is impossible.

[53]Cf. DL 7.135–136 = SVF 1.102 part = LS 46B; Plutarch, *On Stoic Self-Contradictions* 1052C–D = SVF 2.604 part = LS 46E.

names according to its powers [*kata tas dunameis*]. They call him
[1] Dia because all things are 'by' [or: 'through' (*dia*)] him; they call
him [2] Zeus insofar as he is the cause of life [*zên*] or insofar as he 'runs
through' all of life; [3] Athena, because his commanding-faculty
extends to the aether [*aithera*]; [4] Hera because it extends into the
air [*aera*]; and [5] Hephaistus because it spreads into the creative [or:
masterful] fire [*technikon pur*]; and [6] Poseidon, since it stretches into
the sea; and [7] Demeter, since it reaches to the earth. (DL 7.147)[54]

What does it mean that a part of god, not god, pervades everything? Perhaps we can think about this along the lines of the human
soul. The soul pervades all of the body, but it is, strictly speaking,
not the commanding-faculty of the soul that extends into all regions
of the body, but the senses, and so on.[55] Similarly, it is not god in the
strictest sense who pervades all of the world. The part of god that
pervades everything is called by many names, according to its various powers (*dunameis*). But this part again has parts, or can be
divided up into regions of the world. 1 and 2 explicate what god is
by interpreting names that seem to refer to god in the narrow sense,
that is, the part of god we might think of as his commanding-faculty.
But 3–7 seem to refer to the part of god that pervades the cosmos.
The Olympians are presented as something like *portions* of god, who
extends into all regions of the cosmos—aether, air, sea, fire, and
land.[56]

Another context in which we learn about different gods is the
theory of successive worlds, destroyed by periodic conflagration.
During these periods, the destructible gods are mixed together into
one, or, to put it differently, the commanding-faculty of the world
assimilates all other gods into itself.[57] God continues to exist in his
commanding-faculty (*hegemonikon*) (Origen, *Against Celsus* 4.14).[58]

---

[54]Translation Hicks with changes; my numbers.

[55]The commanding faculty of the soul passes judgment on what the senses report;
see Calcidius 220 = SVF 2.879 part = LS 53G. On the parts of the soul see Aetius
4.21.1–4 = SVF 2.835 part = LS 53H.

[56]Hephaistus is a mixed case. It might seem that 'to be creative fire' or 'to be
designing/masterful fire' is a 'power' of god.

[57]Seneca, *Ep.* 9.16 = SVF 2.1065 = LS 46O.

[58]The *hegemonikon* is also described as that which has the dominant power in all of
nature, the best of everything, deserving like nothing else to have power and dominion
over all things (Cicero, *De Natura Deorum* 2.30).

The soul of the world 'feeds' on the world, growing until it has used up matter on itself.[59] This account seems to go along with an analogy between Zeus and the gods on the one hand and the commanding-faculty and the other parts of the soul on the other. But at least in some of the sources on periodic conflagration, the gods are not portions of *pneuma*, but are rather identified with the planets. While Zeus is everlasting, Chrysippus writes in the third book of *On the Gods* that "sun and moon and the rest of the gods" are subject to generation and destruction.[60]

Through Philodemus's treatise *On Piety*, we have some further insight into the Stoic conception of the gods.[61] Philodemus sums up the Stoic views by saying that the Stoics "deceive others into thinking that they leave us with many gods." But in his view, "if they have left us with any divinity at all," then they say that god is one (*De Pietate, col.* 10.8–15).[62] The general picture Philodemus paints explains exactly this: the Stoics describe the traditional gods in ways that suggest that ultimately their theology can only accommodate a single, unified divine force:

> But indeed Chrysippus, too, referring everything to Zeus, says in the first book of his *On Gods* that Zeus is the principle of reason that rules over everything and is the soul of the universe; and that by virtue of having a share in it,[63] all things—humans and beasts and even the stones—are alive, on account of which it[64] is also called Zena, and Dia, since it is the cause and the ruling element of all things. The world, he says, is a living thing and a god, and so is its ruling element and the soul of the whole; thus one gathers analogously that Zeus, and the universal nature of all things, and Fate, and Necessity are god, too. Eunomia and Dike and Homonoia and Eirene and Aphrodite and everything of this sort are all the same being. There are no male or

---

[59]Plutarch, *On Stoic Self-Contradictions* 1052C–D = SVF 2.604 part = LS 46E.

[60]Plutarch, *On Stoic Self-Contradictions* 1052A.

[61]I am using Henrichs's edition, but I follow mostly the reconstruction and translation of Philodemus's *De Pietate* by Dirk Obbink in his "All Gods Are True in Epicurus," in Frede and Laks, *Traditions in Theology*, 183–221.

[62]See Henrichs 1974, 20–1, see Obbink, "All Gods Are True," text 10a.

[63]As Obbink comments, "it" needs to be understood as referring to Zeus, and thus to reason, and the soul of the universe (Obbink, "All Gods Are True," 200).

[64]Again, as Obbink remarks, this refers to the principle of reason ("All Gods Are True," 200).

female gods, just as cities or virtues are really neither male nor female, but are only called masculine or feminine, though their substances are the same, just like Selene and Men. Ares, he says, is about war and Arrangement and Opposition.[65] Hephaestus is fire, Kronos the flowing of the flow. Rhea is earth, Zeus Aether, although some people say [sc, according to Chrysippus][66] he is Apollo, and Demeter is earth or the *pneuma* in it. It is simply childish to represent them, in speaking, in painting, or sculpture, in human form, the way we do cities, and rivers, and places, and ethical states. The air about the earth, he says, is Zeus, that in darkness is Hades, and that which goes through the earth and sea is Poseidon. He assimilates the other gods to lifeless things just as he does these, and he considers the sun, moon and other stars gods, and also the law; and he says that men change into gods.[67] (Philodemus, *De Pietate,* cols. 4.12–6.16, Obbink, "All Gods Are True," text 5, tr. Obbink)[68]

Philodemus charges Chrysippus with several closely related ways of reducing different gods to a single divine force. The presentation starts from what appears to be the basic, physical thesis: the world is alive and is a god, and its commanding-faculty and soul are a god. From this Philodemus concludes that the different traditional gods are just different names for this one divine entity. Second, Chrysippus seems to think of air as the pervasive divinity, which can be given different names depending on its location—thus, the traditional gods seem to be *portions* of one single, physical divinity. Thus far, Philodemus's report fits in relatively well with the account in Diogenes Laertius (apart from the fact that we do not hear anything about 'powers'). Some of the gods are (in a sense, quite traditionally) associated with the elements (again, this is similar in DL 7.147). According to Stoic physics, fire transforms—by way of air—into water, and from this into earth (air evaporating), and from this (air being 'subtilized') aether emerges (Plutarch, *On Stoic Self-Contradiction* 1053A). Thus air or *pneuma* is

---

[65]This seems to be in tension with the earlier statement that Zeus is war.

[66]Again, I follow the reading Obbink suggests ("All Gods Are True," 200).

[67]This last remark is difficult to reconcile with other texts on the sage's likeness with a god: in general, it seems that a human being is, if wise, in nothing inferior to Zeus, while still being a human being, not a god (and thus, still being different). The likeness thus refers to what is judged to be most important: the state of the sage's reason is the same as that of a god.

[68]The text is translated into Latin at Cicero, *De Natura Deorum* 1.39–40.

in some sense basic, and is the key to the transformation of one element into the other. Accordingly, it may seem that each sphere that corresponds to an element (earth, sea, etc.) represents a 'portion of divine *pneuma*'; and this is the reading that also seemed plausible for the account of the different Olympians in Diogenes Laertius's report. Finally, Philodemus mentions that Chrysippus considers the *stars* and the *law* to be gods.

While there are many difficult points in Philodemus's report, these are the key aspects for present purposes.[69] The traditional gods appear, according to this presentation of Chrysippus's views, in very untraditional ways. Not only is Zeus drastically redefined as a first principle of physics, pervading everything in the universe. Like Zeus, the other gods, too, lose their anthropomorphic shape and character. What is more, they seem to be reduced to portions of the divine principle, or to different names that can be given to this principle. Philodemus's presentation is part of a critique, and we may speculate that he does not present Chrysippus's theory in its most favorable light. However, the main ideas we can gather from Philodemus's presentation are fully consistent with the key thesis of Stoic theology that is attested in various places: that Zeus or god is an all-pervading, active, fiery principle.

On Philodemus's account, there is not much left of the *traditional* notion of the gods besides their names. If we do not fall in with Philodemus's charge that in fact there is only one god, and that the words that are taken to refer to *gods* are merely different names for him, then we are left with two conceptions of what the gods are: portions of *pneuma* and celestial bodies. How can we think of such gods as citizen-gods? Maybe this is easier to see with respect to the idea that the gods are celestial bodies.[70] Philodemus mentions that, according to Chrysippus, the stars are gods. Zeno describes the sun, the moon, and each of the other stars as intelligent and wise, and as having the fieriness of designing fire.[71] Balbus, who explains Stoic theology in *De Natura Deorum*, moves from a general account of

---

[69]It is not fully clear how the thesis that Ares is about war and arrangement and opposition can be fitted into the view of there being one physical divinity, which we can either refer to by different names or divide into physical portions.

[70]On the stars as gods, see Michael Frede, "La Théologie Stoïcienne," 230–232.

[71]Stobaeus 1.213,15–21 = SVF 1.120, part = LS 46D.

how the universe has soul and reason to a description of the stars as living beings with soul and reason.[72] His arguments for the existence of god already exploit the order and beauty of the universe as a *system* of celestial bodies; he professes that anyone who looks at the skies will understand that god exists. It is the very order in the movement of the stars that, if studied not as a whole, but with respect to the individual celestial bodies, serves as a proof for their individual, divine reasonableness. The *constantia* of the celestial bodies' movements makes them the object of reverence and wonder. Their *ordo* and *constantia* reveal that they *think* and *feel*:

> That the stars have senses [*sensum*] and intelligence reveals itself most clearly in their order and constancy [*ordo atque constantia*]—and there is after all nothing which could move in an ordered and regulated way without practical deliberation [*sine consilio*]—in which nothing is left unconsidered [*temerarium*], nothing is variable and nothing happens by chance. But the order of the stars and their constancy that lasts through all eternity neither points to nature[73]—since it is fully reasonable—nor to chance, which loves change and hates constancy. It thus follows that the stars are moved through themselves, out of their own sensibility and divinity. (Cicero, *De nat. deor.* 2.43)[74]

According to Cicero's report, the Stoics infer from the intelligence of the world as a whole that the celestial bodies, which account for movement within this world, are intelligent, ensouled, and divine.[75] Similarly, in the context of the comparisons between sages and gods in Cicero, some of which have been cited earlier, the gods are

[72]With respect to this aspect of their theology, the Stoics might be influenced by Plato, *Laws* 10; see Dorothea Frede, "Theodicy and Providential Care in Stoicism," in Frede and Laks, *Traditions in Theology*, 85–117. For discussion of how Stoic theology may seem to bear traces of Zeno's time as a student of Polemo, see Sedley, "Origins of Stoic God."

[73]This is a use of 'nature' that is not in agreement with Stoic philosophy, where nature itself is something ordered. Obbink argues convincingly that Cicero's account is not in all respects reliable ("All Gods Are True," fn. 36).

[74]See also *De Natura Deorum* 2.56 on how the sky has order, truth, calculation, constancy, and mind (*mens*).

[75]If we take the exposition of Stoic doctrine in Cicero's *De Natura Deorum* as, to some extent, indicative of the Stoics' *own* train of thought, it may seem as if Cicero's spokesman for the Stoics has been thinking of celestial bodies all along, while describing the gods as virtuous, happy, and so on.

identified as planets: the sages and the gods are both 'constant,' and this is explained, with respect to the gods, by referring to them as celestial bodies.[76] The train of thought in Cicero's presentation in *De Natura Deorum* suggests that the Stoic doctrine that compares sages and gods is most naturally understood as referring to celestial bodies. Celestial bodies move in the constant and regulated way that is comparable to the consistent choosing and acting on the part of the sage. In them, we find an obvious analogue to *action*. Like human beings, the celestial bodies are entities whose soul is confined by a particular body, and whose soul moves this very body.

Compared to portions of *pneuma*, referred to by the names of Olympians, the celestial bodies may seem to be more attractive candidates for a *physical* reading of what the citizen-gods are. In a sense, they live in the cosmos, they move through it, and they are separate entities within it. Like sages, they can be said to have right reason without being themselves identical to reason. And it is their perfect movement that makes us marvel at them, and that displays the ideal of life in agreement with nature. It is this idea of the citizen-gods as planets that, I propose, significantly adds to what we can learn about the Stoic ideal of citizenship and being a relative as compared to what we can gather from studying the conception of the sage alone. The sage is rarer than a phoenix and so is not available for our admiration. There is nothing besides the stars that can impress on us an image of perfect integration into the order of nature, of perfectly regulated movement, and of a full fit into the universe as a whole. When we look at the planets, we can better understand what life, or a life, in agreement with nature is.

The cosmos as a whole moves *through* the movements of its parts. Perfect reason pervades the world in such a way that the entities in the world may have perfect reason, imperfect reason, or only *pneuma* in such a tenor as to make this portion of *pneuma* fall below the threshold of what the Stoics call reason. Those entities that have

---

[76]Dorothea Frede starts her discussion of providence in Stoic theology from a summary account of *Laws* 10 ("Theodicy," 88–95). On her analysis, Plato's conception might have been an important point of reference for the Stoics. The claims about the celestial bodies as ensouled, rational, and so on indeed strongly recall Platonic ideas. Cf. also Francisco L. Lisi, ed., *Plato's "Laws" and Its Historical Significance. Selected Papers of the First International Congress on Ancient Thought* (Salamanca: Academia Verlag, 1998).

perfect reason move by themselves so as to fit so perfectly in the overall movement of the cosmos that they *constitute a part of its order*, and that everything that also moves perfectly is in complete agreement with them. Not only does each individual planet move regularly, but all the planets together move regularly. If we think of the cosmos as an entity in motion, then the movements of the planets are some of the most fundamental movements within the cosmos. As contrasted with, for instance, the running around of a rabbit, these celestial movements are, as it were, part of the backbone of the cosmos. It is within the framework of such regular movements that a rabbit can run this way or that. We can see from the contrast between planets and rabbits what the ideal of agreement with nature means. Ideally, we move in the cosmos so as not only to be its part, but to be, as it were, a part of it that helps to sustain its orderly, overall movement. The gods are individuals, but they ultimately belong to god. During conflagration, they are consumed by god. During the other periods, the planets are in a relevant sense particulars. They are not swept along by an overall cosmic movement. Rather, they move themselves and thus *constitute* part of this cosmic movement. This life of the planets is, I suggest, the best image for how perfectly reasonable human beings would on the one hand remain particulars who live their own life, producing their own actions, and on the other become fully integrated parts of the whole.

But once we acknowledge that one might think of planets as individual, thinking living beings, who act (or move) perfectly, it might seem that we can extend this line of thought to portions of *pneuma*. The portion of Zeus that may be called Poseidon is maybe just as identifiable a part of the cosmos as is a celestial body. As in the case of the human soul and the human body, such a portion of *pneuma* may be conceived of as a particular entity by reference to the physical realm it pervades—the sea, the earth, and so on. Perhaps we can understand the talk about the gods as individuals nearly as well when referring to portions of *pneuma* as when referring to the planets. Common to both pictures is that they depend on a corporeal conception of Zeus, who, qua spatial and corporeal being, has spatial and corporeal parts. The corporeal, all-pervading divinity can be divided into parts under different perspectives—either insofar as we look out for individual bodies, or insofar as we divide up this divinity into portions or regions of the cosmos.

The gods, understood in this way, offer a very concrete model of what it means to live and act in agreement with nature. Among the several versions of the *telos*-formula, Zeno's account of *eudaimonia* as a good flow of life (*euroia biou*) comes to mind.[77] The divine stars may offer a very concrete model of what it means to have one's life 'flow well,' to move in such a way as never to move, as it were, against the general flow of things, but harmoniously within it, fully integrated into the movements of the cosmos. There is no regularity of movement if not by deliberation, Balbus says; nothing within the movements of the stars is unconsidered or by chance—their movements reflect their perfect rationality. It is not as if being a part of nature would by itself make one's movements orderly. Living beings that are part of the large living being, the cosmos, are still individuals, and their movements will only be perfectly integrated into the overall movement if everything in them is well considered. Once it is, we can think of their life, too, as 'flowing well' within the cosmos.

According to Chrysippus, we are to live in agreement with human nature and nature as a whole by never doing anything the common law would forbid, the common law being identical to right reason and Zeus. Acting in accordance with law and right reason *is*, in some sense, *acting in accordance with Zeus*. And this means, according to Chrysippus, that "the virtue of the happy man and his good flow of life are just this: always doing everything on the basis of concordance (*kata tên sumphônian*] of each man's guardian with the will of the administrator of the whole" (DL 7.87, tr. LS with changes).[78]

Life flows well if one's own reason is such that it agrees with the will of Zeus, and since human reason can, *if it is perfectly ordered*, be described as part of divine pneuma, we can even use a term that associates the human soul with something divine—*daimôn*. The happy human being's soul is said to be (or to be associated with) a 'guardian' or divine spirit, a *daimôn*, that is in tune with Zeus's intentions.

---

[77]Stobaeus 2.77,21 = SVF 3.16 = LS 63A.

[78]On the different formulae see Gisela Striker, "The Role of *Oikeiôsis* in Stoic Ethics," in *Essays in Hellenistic Epistemology and Ethics* (Cambridge: Cambridge University Press, 1996), 281–297; and "Antipater, or the Art of Living," in *The Norms of Nature*, ed. Malcolm Schofield and Gisela Striker (Cambridge: Cambridge University Press, 1986), 185–204; as well as M. Frede, "On the Stoic Conception of the Good."

(Of course, this account leads to further questions: Most importantly, how can we, given Stoic *determinism*, think of movements that are integrated worse or better into the cosmos? Would it not seem, if there is a natural order of things, following on and succeeding one another, that every movement in the cosmos is fated, *as it is*? These matters deserve detailed discussion, and they lead beyond the scope of this book.[79] Very roughly speaking, the Stoics seem to envisage a crucial difference between acting in a genuinely well-considered way, and thus truly on one's own accord, as the stars do—their every movement reflects *perfect* deliberation—as opposed to being merely swept along in a course of action that one has not calmly and wisely decided on.)

6. *Friendship*

The Stoic conception of friendship has received considerable scholarly attention, much more than those of citizenship and being a relative.[80] This may be due in part to the fact that we have comparatively detailed evidence on friendship. But it is surely also due to the recent philosophical interest in theories of friendship, and the perplexing fact that friendship seems to be a *positive* notion in Stoic thought, while the emotions that are conventionally associated with

[79]For discussion of the many questions involved see Bobzien, *Determinism and Freedom*. While I cannot engage with the difficult questions concerning fate and determinism in Stoic theory, let me draw attention to one aspect that is perhaps particularly relevant to our discussion. As Cooper remarks, scholarly debate on Stoic determinism often does not seem to fully appreciate the idea that human souls are *portions* of Zeus's soul. As he suggests, we should not think of rational assent, which the Stoics say is 'in our power,' as somehow 'outside'—and possibly in conflict with—Zeus's administration of nature. "Given that we are portions—albeit disjoint ones—of Zeus's mind, Zeus's universal causality (i.e., Fate), and his responsibility for everything through having planned it, cannot threaten to remove the possibility of either our own causality or our own personal responsibility for our acts. Our causality, and our personal responsibility, are in fact *part* of Zeus's." John M. Cooper, "Stoic Autonomy," in *Knowledge, Nature, and the Good* (Princeton, N.J.: Princeton University Press, 2004), 204–244, 240.

[80]See Anne Banateanu, *La Théorie Stoïcienne de l'Amitié: Essai de Reconstruction* (Fribourg: Editions Universitaires Fribourg Suisse, 2001). Banateanu offers an extensive collection of texts, both in Greek and in French translations.

friendship are considered to be part of a foolish life. Friendship as the Stoics conceive of it—friendship that involves neither suffering on behalf of a friend nor grief at the loss of friendship or death of a friend, nor excitement at the prospect of getting together, nor pride in one's friends' success, and so on—just does not seem to be friendship to us. I will only engage with a narrowly circumscribed range of questions about friendship. To dicuss all the evidence would be a book-length project of its own. But it seems clear to me that we cannot (and should not try to) 'save' the Stoics from an interpretation of their theory that describes it as revisionist. Thesis (S) shows how *very* revisionist the Stoic notion of friendship is: like citizenship or being a relative, friendship is *an achievement of reason* or, as we might put it, a *dimension of wisdom*.

Like being a citizen and a relative, being a friend is, first and foremost, a disposition or state of the soul, not a relationship. Yet it is a *relational* disposition: the fact that the sage is a friend has certainly something to do with her being *friendly* toward everyone. Just as the sage considers everyone to be a fellow-inhabitant of the cosmos and to be related in the sense of *oikeiôsis*, she is also friendly toward everyone. But those she relates to and is friendly to are not citizens and relatives themselves, and they are not friends. Insofar as the sage is the friend of someone who is also *her* friend, she must be the friend of other friends, that is, other sages and gods. Note that one implication of this claim is that, in order to be someone's friend, one does not need to *befriend* this person. Sages are each others' friends in virtue of their wisdom, not in virtue of having come to know and like one another. The way one becomes a friend of all other friends is to become wise.

If a human being turns into a sage, she achieves a life that cannot be tainted by misfortune. But the Stoic *telos* does not envisage *autarkeia*—no matter whether one is wise or not, one is part of a larger living being, the cosmos, and in *this* sense, there is no self-sufficiency for anyone but Zeus.[81] Thus we may ask, if the sage's

---

[81] The comparison of god and sage and the conception of citizen-gods goes against the Aristotelian idea that gods do not *need* communities (see *Pol.* 1.2.1253a,26–29). According to this tradition, cities enable human beings to survive and to live well. For someone starting from such assumptions, the notion of a citizen-god is revolting— it seems to give up on the idea of divine *autarkeia*. But only god *understood as the cosmos* can count as self-sufficient within the Stoic theory. See Plutarch, *On Stoic*

happiness is unaffected by fortune and misfortune, is there anything that can *affect her life positively*? The answer of the Stoics is yes. The sage, who is able to live by the law, and who fully belongs to the cosmos, is benefited by whoever in the cosmos is perfectly reasonable. The achievement of wisdom is not the achievement of detachment from the world. It is, quite to the contrary, the achievement of being integrated into the world in the best possible way. And someone who achieves being thus integrated into the world, and into the perfect reason of the world, will be positively affected by everything that is good about the world.

Let us look in more detail at how those parts of the world that are perfectly reasonable benefit each other. Interestingly, the Stoics refer to the sage's friend in the context of their definition of the good *as benefit*:[82] good is defined as 'benefit or not other than benefit'; virtue and virtuous action *are benefit*; the virtuous man and his friend are '*not other than benefit.*' To be wise is to benefit. But whom does the sage benefit, and is he also benefited himself by anyone?

Virtue is good insofar as virtue benefits. This opens up the way to saying that whoever *has virtue* is useful or beneficial. This train of thought leads to the wise man, as the person whose soul is in this condition. But why does it lead to his friend? The wise man is beneficial. People in the sage's vicinity are quite generally benefited by his attitudes and actions. The affective disposition of the sage is

---

Self-Contradiction 1052D: "Of the cosmos alone can it be said that it is self-sufficient [*autarkês*], because it alone contains within itself all that it needs. It is fed and grows out of itself, whereas its parts are in mutual exchange with each other."

[82]"For virtue, which is a disposition of the commanding-faculty, and virtuous action, which is an activity in accordance with virtue, are benefit directly. But the virtuous man and his friend, while also themselves belonging to goods, could neither be said to be benefit nor other than benefit, for the following reason. Parts, the sons of the Stoics say, are neither the same as wholes nor are they different from wholes; for instance, the hand is not the same as a whole man, since the hand is not a whole man, but nor is it other than the whole since the whole man is conceived as man together with his hand. Since, then, virtue is a part of the virtuous man and of his friend, and parts are neither the same as wholes nor other than wholes, the good man and his friend have been called 'not other than benefit.' So every good is taken in by the definition, whether it is benefit or not other than benefit" (SE M 11.22–26 = SVF 3.75, part = LS 60G, tr. LS). For a collection of fragments on the Stoic theory of the *good* that relate to friendship see Banateanu, *La Théorie Stoïcienne*, chap. 3, 45–84.

such that he is kind, generous, warm, and affectionate.[83] But if we ask whether he *himself* can be benefited in any way, it seems he could, but only by interacting with an individual who is virtuous, as he himself is. Only virtue benefits, and if the wise man is ever to be benefited through anything, then it is only through the virtue of someone else. And if someone else is beneficial, he is, by virtue of benefiting others, a friend. As I am suggesting, the ability to benefit is at the core of what it means, according to the Stoics, to be a friend.

This conception of friendship is bound to be attacked as highly counterintuitive. Where does affection, acquaintance, and the shared life with others figure in this account? A considerable part of the testimony engages with a controversy on these questions.[84] The Stoics seem to have been put on the spot with respect to the question whether friends, according to their notion of friendship, even *know* each other. And they seem to have responded in good Stoic fashion, by insisting on the one hand on a basic continuity between their technical vocabulary and the ordinary use of a term and on the other hand on a highly revisionist theory. According to a report in Diogenes Laertius, "[the Stoics] describe friendship as a certain community [*koinônian*] of the things that belong to life [*tôn kata ton bion*]" (7.124). This claim responds directly to those who insist that friendship is a *koinônia*. Yes, the Stoics agree, it *is* a community. But the community the Stoics have in mind is not the community of a *shared life*. We can see these matters more clearly in a report in Stobaeus:

> All goods are common to the virtuous, and all that is bad to the inferior. Therefore a man who benefits someone also benefits himself, and one who does harm also harms himself. All virtuous men benefit

---

[83]DL 7.116 = SVF 3.431 = LS 65F.

[84]Some of the doxographical reports are shaped by preconceived questions, questions that do not necessarily derive from the Stoic theories themselves, but rather from the fact that certain issues have been prominent in the ancient discussions of friendship. Modern commentators tend to fall in with this mode of discussion, and sometimes present the Stoic account of friendship organized around questions that seem to derive more from an Aristotelian than a Stoic ethical framework. For a recent study that to some extent adopts this perspective see Glenn Lesses, "Austere Friends: The Stoics and Friendship," *Apeiron* 26.1 (1993): 57–75.

one another, even though they are not in every case friends with each other, or well disposed towards each other, or well meaning or accepting of each other, because they do not always get hold of [*katalambanesthai*] each other and may not live together at the same place. But generally they would be well disposed towards each other and friendly and well-meaning and accepting of each other. But the foolish are in the opposite situation. (Stobaeus 2.101,21–102,3 = SVF 3.626 = LS 60P, tr. partly LS)

The claim that all goods are common to the virtuous is deceptive: it recalls ideas about shared property. But if we fill in 'virtue' and 'virtuous action' for 'all goods,' we see that the thesis has nothing to do with property. Everything good is common to the virtuous insofar as each of them is equally virtuous. And everything good is common insofar as each of them is *affected by each instance of virtue*. Thus a first point we can learn from this passage is that, just as it seemed in Diogenes Laertius 7.124, the 'community of the things that belong to life' is a community of a very elusive kind. It has nothing to do with sharing one's life, or with sharing material possessions. Rather, it refers to the way all wise beings are commonly affected by the actions of any one of them, and how they hold the same views with respect to the things that pertain to the leading of one's life.

Second, we should note that the report makes use of a *conventional* notion of friendship. All sages benefit each other, *even though they may not be friends*. We can translate this into a claim that makes use of the technical and the conventional notion of 'friendship': all sages are *friends*, even though they may not be friends. Being friends in the conventional sense of spending time with each other is not integral to friendship in the technical sense. The same picture emerges from the famous passage in Plutarch according to which all sages in the inhabited world are benefited if a single sage somewhere extends his finger wisely. "This is their friendship's work [*tês philias ergon*]," Plutarch remarks, and we may feel that 'work' is here used with a good measure of irony. Stoic friends, Plutarch seems to tell us, are not really the friends we would wish to have when we are in trouble. They go to great lengths in helping each other—they extend their fingers wisely! Plutarch goes on to report that according to the Stoics, the sages receive an amazing benefit from "the virtuous motions of one another even if they are not together and happen not even to be acquainted."[85]

The technical notion of friendship is thus enormously revisionist. But, as with respect to the other notions that figure in claims of the form 'Only the sage is X,' there is an important element of continuity with the conventional notion. Friendship is *reciprocal*. Friends need not know each other, but even without acquaintance, there is a relationship of being benefited *by each other*. The sage is the other sage's friend because *the reciprocal relationship of 'being good for each other' exists only between sages*. Stoic friendship is reciprocal independently of whether a friend actually is acquainted with his or her friend. The Stoic conception of friendship thus proposes an answer to the question whether the wise agent, who is friendly, caring, and beneficial toward everyone, can *herself* be benefited—whether there is anything that can make the life of the virtuous human being even better. The answer is yes, other perfectly reasonable beings and their actions can make such human beings' lives even better.

But does this also hold for the life of Zeus? Can Zeus's life be made better by there being a human sage, acting wisely? Friendship is a relational disposition that, in effect, creates reciprocal benefiting between the wise, and the Stoics endorse all the implications of this thesis. One of the implications is that a sage is a friend even if there are no other sages. There are still the gods, and the cosmos, for the sage to be friends with. And these 'divine friends' are benefited by the sage's virtuous actions. Zeus is benefited by the actions of a sage. This is the upshot of Chrysippus's thesis that Zeus does not surpass Dion in virtue, is wise, and is *benefited* by Dion's movements.[86]

It is this idea of the reciprocal benefit between wise individuals in the cosmos that I take to be integral to the conception of the cosmic city. Full integration with perfect reason makes one the beneficiary of everything that is good about the world. And this idea helps us to see how the perfectly reasonable soul of a sage or god does not *dissolve* into the perfect reason of the cosmos. The Stoics seem to hold that every perfectly reasonable 'portion' of the world *contributes its own share* to the perfect reason of the world as a whole. It is not as if, once one were wise, one's actions would become

---

[85] *On Common Conceptions* 1068F–1069A, translation Cherniss with changes.
[86] Plutarch, *On Common Conceptions* 1076A = LS 61J.

incorporated into the perfect movements of god. Rather, the actions of each wise individual remain *her actions*, and they *add* to the rationality of the whole. Zeus benefits from the actions of a sage, and this is not a metaphor.

7. Eros—God of Friendship and Concord

The Stoics develop a technical notion of concord (*homonoia*): all virtuous men are in concord with each other by agreeing on the things that pertain to the leading of one's life (Stobaeus 2.94,1–4). Concord characterizes how sages are related to each other. But do the Stoics also subscribe to the conventional political ideal of concord, that is, the idea that institutions and policies are to be designed so as to promote concord, understood as the opposite of civil war? This is how two famous passages have often been interpreted. But, as I shall argue, this is misleading; for the Stoics, 'concord' is not what we expect as readers of ancient literature and political thought. I shall end this chapter by briefly discussing these passages, beginning with an extract from Plutarch.

> It was not this that was Lycurgus' main achievement, to leave the city exercising leadership over a great number of other cities. Rather, he thought that, as in the life of a single man, so happiness for a whole city comes into being from virtue and concord with itself.[87] So he ordered it and brought it into harmony with this in view, that having achieved a free and self-sufficient form of life they might continue in it for a very long time by practising self-restraint. This is what Plato too took as the principle of his constitution [or, of the *Republic*], and Diogenes and Zeno and all those who have tried to say something on these matters and win approval for doing so, even though they have left only writings and theories. (Plutarch, *Lyc.* 31 = SVF 1.263, 261; tr. Schofield)[88]

---

[87]According to H. C. Baldry, this clause is "the only general principle" mentioned in our evidence on Zeno's *Republic*; "Zeno's Ideal State," *Journal of Hellenic Studies* 79 (1959): 8.

[88]Andrew Erskine discusses how this point about Lycurgus may be a fabrication of Plutarch. As we have seen in the passage on Alexander, Plutarch has an interest in comparing the theories of philosophers with the practical achievements of statesmen; *The Hellenistic Stoa: Political Thought and Action* (Ithaca, N.Y.: Cornell University Press, 1990), 19–20.

The analogy of soul and city, which is presented as Lycurgus's idea, is obviously important to Plato.[89] According to Plato's Socrates in the *Republic*, soul and city are ideally *one* (or internally unified), a state that is also described as concord and harmony. Most scholars also think that a number of institutions, such as the community of women, are designed so as to enhance internal unity and concord. Plutarch refers to Plato first, and it seems to me that his reference to Diogenes and Zeno is more tentative. With respect to Diogenes, there is probably no analogy between discussing the 'constitution' of the soul and institutions Diogenes would design for a city.[90] Similarly, Plutarch's reference to Zeno must be somewhat more loose than his reference to Plato.

Insofar as the Stoics adopt a notion of concord (or related notions) with respect to the soul and life of an individual, they are discussing the ideal of a life that is in agreement with nature, and an ideal of consistency among all the pieces of knowledge that make up the sage's systematic knowledge.[91] This consistency is different from Plato's harmony—it is not a harmonious relationship between different 'parts' of the soul (the Stoics do not think that there are rational and irrational parts of the soul). Further, insofar as the Stoics conceive of concord as an ideal for relationships among several human beings, they define it as knowledge of the common goods.[92] All virtuous men are in concord with each other by agreeing

---

[89]Key passages on the method of investigating city and soul in unison are: *Rp.* 368c–d; 377c–d; 402a–b; 434c–d.

[90]Diogenes is associated with a line of thought on the notion of a *politeia* where on the one hand the cosmos is said to be the only true *politeia* (DL 6.72) and on the other the term *really* refers to the 'state of being a Cynic' (on how these two claims go together see Moles, *The Cynics*, 426–427). Thus there can be no analogy of *city* and soul—no city is being discussed. Instead, Diogenes invokes an analogy of the state of the cosmos and the state of one's soul.

[91]The latter point is, of course, very difficult to spell out in detail. For a very helpful discussion of the ideal of consistency, see M. Frede, "On the Stoic Conception of the Good."

[92]'Common goods' is a difficult notion—the conception of a 'common good,' or 'common goods,' does not figure in Stoic ethics. We might either think that they all have knowledge of the good, *and* all goods are *common to them* (insofar as they are all benefited by everything that is good). Or we could take the phrase to refer to the idea that they all have knowledge about how to life a good life, where the way one leads a good life is *one* way for all human beings, and in this sense *common*.

on the things that pertain to the leading of one's life (Stobaeus 2.94,1–4). *Homonoia* thus is quite literally like-mindedness among sages—the like-mindedness of having one's souls in essentially the same state, and thus having minds that are alike. Sages, gods, and god are in concord by having their souls in a perfect state. This conception of concord does not seem to envisage peaceful life in a well-governed city. Rather, concord seems to be a relationship among the wise, or a relationship between a sage and the world. Both the sage and the world are, by being virtuous, in concord—they are in concord with everything else in the world that is perfectly reasonable.

This, of course, does not mean that Zeno could not have talked about concord in an everyday sense. We have seen repeatedly that the early Stoics go back and forth between using their core terms both in their technical and in the everyday sense. In many cases in which a city's policy follows the advice of a sage, and in which a city improves its actual laws, its inhabitants may, as a result, be more in concord with each other, understood in an everyday sense. But this is a weak claim. The thesis I am arguing against is stronger. It says that, for instance, the claim on dress codes or the 'community of women' indicates that the Stoics suggest institutional reform for actual cities with a view to an ideal of concord in the traditional sense.[93]

The phrase 'community of women,' however, is not likely to refer to the same idea as in Plato's *Republic*—it does not seem that Zeno or Chrysippus suggests that we should abolish the family as a relevant community. Rather, it may reflect claims on how it does not make a difference whether one has sexual relations with this or that person, claims that are also suggested by a number of other Zenonian and Chrysippean theses. The claim about dress codes may rely on the fact that conventional views on how men and women are different and should live differently are not justified.

---

[93]Cf. Erskine, *Hellenistic Stoa*, 22–27. Schofield begins the second part of his study with a distinction between three general views of Zeno's *Republic*. Zeno's political proposal may appear as antinomianism, as revisionism, or as communism. Schofield sides with the third option: "What makes Zeno's community ideal is the degree of concord achieved in it through the political virtue of its citizens, which is in turn fostered by communist political institutions" (*The Stoic Idea*, 22).

These considerations, which the sage, if he were an advisor of a king, might raise, do not seem to *specifically* address concord. They reflect a range of philosophical insights. We have no sources that attest that Zeno or Chrysippus argue for the claim that it is better for a city to be in concord. (It might seem that this is a view that one need not argue for—is it not obvious that institutions and policies that prevent internal conflict in a city are to be desired? In the weak sense in which I suggested that the sage's advice is likely to improve the shared life in a city, this may be obvious. But if we think of some of the more extreme measures in Plato's *Republic*, it is by no means clear that *every* policy that enhances unity and concord is desirable. And it certainly seems that, should one hold the view that whatever law or practice enhances unity is to be instituted, one would have to offer very strong arguments in its favor.) Major differences between Platonic and Stoic philosophy—most important, perhaps, the Stoics' psychological monism—suggest that unity and concord could not be the kind of ideal for the Stoics that they seem to be for Plato in his *Republic*.[94]

Let me turn to a further piece of evidence on Zeno's views: "Pontianus said that Zeno of Citium regarded Eros as a god of friendship and freedom and the provider, in addition, of concord, but of nothing else. Eros is a god who contributes to the city's security."[95] Like Plutarch's comparison between Zeno and Plato, this passage is a major point of reference for those who think that Zeno discusses a city of sages, a city that is virtuous and in concord (on account of its wise inhabitants), a city whose laws and institutions enhance its concord.

For Schofield, this city is a 'city of love.'[96] The various Stoic claims on how it is 'no more and no less' appropriate to have intercourse with this or with that person and the elevated role of Eros seem to testify to this picture.

In order to assess this view, we must take a closer look at Zeno's account of Eros. Given the Stoic view of the Olympians, it may seem

---

[94]Note that it can certainly not be an ideal with respect to the cosmic city. The cosmos *is* one, and its soul is 'in concord' with all other perfectly reasonable beings.

[95]Athenaeus 561C = SVF 1.263 part = LS 67D. The context suggests that this is a quotation from the *Republic*; however, we cannot be fully sure.

[96]This is Schofield's expression (*The Stoic Idea*, 22).

that the invocation of Eros cannot be anything but a metaphor.[97] But what does this metaphor stand for? Zeno tells us explicitly: for friendship, freedom, concord, "and nothing else." The last bit of the quotation should not go unnoticed. What Zeno does, at this point, is radically to redefine who Eros is. Eros *does not stand for erotic passion*. Given Stoic thought on the affections (*pathê*), this seems to be the only way to integrate Eros into a virtuous, Stoic life. As a passion, *erôs* does not fit into the life of sages.

But is it true that the Stoics have such a critical view of *erôs*, a view that sees *erôs* as one of the affections (*pathê*) and thus as something that has no place in a good life?[98] According to early Stoic doctrine, the sage has no affections (*pathê*). The four most generic *pathê* are desire, fear, pleasure, and pain; *erôs* is a desire.[99] It is clear that the Stoics do not exclude sexual relations from the life

[97]However, it probably is a very forceful metaphor. As Paul W. Ludwig argues in *Eros and Polis: Desire and Community in Greek Political Theory* (Cambridge: Cambridge University Press, 2002), reference to *erôs* runs through much of Greek writing on politics.

[98]In her foreword to the second edition of Schofield's book, Martha Nussbaum remarks that both Zeno and Chrysippus wrote works "of ideal political theory entitled *Republic*, works that in some respects followed Plato, but that also sharply departed from Plato, especially in the treatment of desire, sexuality, and the body." In her presentation of Schofield's interpretation, she goes on to say that the Stoics "implicitly criticize the repression of eros and the body in Plato's ideal city. The ideal Stoic city is held together by strong erotic ties, and citizens are encouraged to form intense erotic relationships with other citizens, on the basis of virtue and the potential for virtue. All other passions are reproved in Stoicism. Stoic citizens will have neither anger nor fear, neither pride nor jealousy nor envy, neither grief nor pity. Eros alone is exempted from the critique." Nussbaum in Schofield, *The Stoic Idea*, xi and xiii. In his more recent account of the Stoic theory, Schofield writes: "Nowhere is the contrast between his [Zeno's] position and Plato's more striking than on questions of sexual relations, not least because Zeno apparently made his proposals on love and sex central to his whole theory"; Schofield, "Epicurean and Stoic Political Thought," in *Greek and Roman Political Thought*, ed. Christopher Rowe and Schofield (Cambridge: Cambridge University Press, 2000), 435–456, 444.

[99]In their list of desires, the Stoics list "*intense* erotic feelings, and cravings, and yearnings [*erôtes sphodroi kai pothoi kai himeroi*]" (my emphasis) (Stobaeus, 2.90,19–91,9 = SVF 3.394 part = LS 65E). However, this does not mean that they do not consider *erôs* in the conventional sense as intense, hence a desire. In any conventional sense, *erôs* goes along with craving and yearning, with the very affliction and suffering, inner turmoil and disturbance that make the *pathê* unfit to be part of the sage's life.

of the sage. However, every form of *erôs* that is a desire must count as a *pathos*. The Stoics are not likely to make an exception to their theory of the affections by assigning *erôs, understood in the conventional sense*, a significant role in the city.[100] Indeed, if *erôs* in a conventional sense had a place in the sage's life, the sage would not be *free* (and thus would be no sage). From the point of view of the Stoics, *erôs* in the conventional sense enslaves us to those with whom we are in love, it makes us act in worthless ways, unable to follow reason.[101] By defining Eros as the god of friendship, freedom, and concord, and *of nothing else*, Zeno transforms Eros. The kind of *erôs* that is part of the sage's life is friendship, freedom, and concord with his friend. This is the sense in which the sage loves: his love is friendship.[102]

But how is Zeno using the key notions of friendship, freedom, and concord in the foregoing quotation? Could he plausibly use them in the everyday sense? If so, then Zeno would say that Eros

[100]Schofield writes that Zeno cannot have thought of *erôs* as a *pathos*; he thus recognizes the difficulty (*The Stoic Idea*, 29).

[101]Seneca quotes a response by Panaetius to the question whether the sage would fall in love: "As to the wise man, we shall see. What concerns you and me, who are still a great distance from the wise man, is to ensure that we do not fall into a state of affairs which is disturbed, subservient to another and worthless to oneself" (*Ep.* 116.5 = LS 66C, tr. LS). This very description of what is to be avoided shows why *erôs* cannot be part of the sage's life. It also brings out that there is an element to *erôs*, in addition to the affliction and turmoil, that conflicts with freedom: *erôs* enslaves us to others (see Epictetus, *Discourses* 4.1.15–18, and William O. Stephens, "Epictetus on How the Stoic Sage Loves," *Oxford Studies in Ancient Philosophy* 14 [1996]: 193–210, 206; on the notion of freedom see chapter 4).

[102]Cf. DL 7.129 130 = SVF 3.716 and 718. A similar kind of redefinition is transmitted in a different context. The Stoics describe *erôs* as a 'chase' for someone young, who is undeveloped, but naturally apt for virtue—but a 'chase' that does not involve an affection (*pathos*). Plutarch complains that this definition is against the common conceptions—one ought to call love what all people call love (*On Common Conceptions* 1073C).

Stephens gives a detailed account of how the Stoic sage loves that is along the lines of what I am suggesting ("How the Stoic Sage Loves," 194–197). However, his analysis is limited to Epictetus, and he proposes that, while Epictetus agrees with Cicero and with Seneca and Musonius Rufus, he disagrees with the early, Greek Stoics. But neither Seneca nor Epictetus proclaims that, in this point, they disagree with the early doctrine. Stephens refers to Bonhöffer's interpretation of Epictetus, which takes Epictetus to agree with the early Stoics; A. Bonhöffer, *Die Ethik des Stoikers Epiktet* (Stuttgart: Frommann, 1894), 66.

stands for the kinds of friendships that ordinary people have, and the kind of freedom that citizens in the traditional sense have, and the kind of concord that is the opposite of civil war. He would say that all these things make cities safer. However, Zeno holds that people who are friends in the conventional sense are actually enemies, that 'free citizens' are slaves, and so on. It does not seem likely that, in an account of what a god stands for, he would use the notions in this everyday way. But if not, then Zeno's claim comes to mean something very abstract. It comes to mean that Eros represents dimensions of wisdom that are particularly relevant to how we *relate to others*, how we ideally *benefit* others, and how we ideally *relate to the world*. An actual city would honor Eros by making friendship, freedom, and concord its ideals as *what they really* are. This would be a city that adopts the virtue of its inhabitants as its goal.

4

Law and Reason

The three major early Stoics refer to the law as the *common* law. In Plutarch's words, it is Zeno's dream that all human beings live under a common law.[1] In his *Hymn to Zeus*, Cleanthes says that there is no greater prize than to praise with justice (*dikê*) the common law for ever.[2] According to Chrysippus, life in agreement with nature means not doing anything that is "forbidden by the common law, which is right reason pervading everything and identical to Zeus, who is the director of the administration of existing things" (DL 7.87–88).

The early Stoic conception of the *common* law (*koinos nomos*) is an ancestor of what has later come to be called the *natural* law. The law, as conceived by the Stoics, is common to all human beings, and exists independently from the actual laws and customs in actual cities. In this sense, we may call it a 'natural law.' But even though later conceptions of the natural law partly derive from Stoic thought, they also depart from it.[3] The law, as conceived by the Stoics, is a basic component of nature—it pervades the cosmos, and is identified with a corporeal god.[4] This *physical* dimension of the common law is foreign to later natural law theories.[5]

---

[1] Plutarch, *De virt. Alex.* 329A–B = SVF 1.262 part = LS 67A.

[2] This is the end of Cleanthes' *Hymn to Zeus* (Stobaeus 1.25,3–27,4 = SVF 1.537).

[3] For a summary account of what the term 'natural law' is usually taken to mean, see Gisela Striker, "Origins of the Concept of Natural Law," *Boston Area Colloquium in Ancient Philosophy* 2 (1987): 79–94, reprinted in Striker, *Papers in Hellenistic Ethics and Epistemology* (Cambridge: Cambridge University Press, 1996), 209–220, 209.

[4] Zeus *is* the law. See Philodemus, *De Pietate*, col. 7.7; edition of A. Henrichs, "Die Kritik der stoischen Theologie in *PHerc.* 1428," *Cronache Ercolanesi* 4 (1974): 5–32.

[5] See G. Watson for a different view; "The Natural Law and Stoicism," in *Problems in Stoicism*, ed. A. A. Long (London: Athlone Press, 1971), 216–238. According to

The Stoics identify law and reason.[6] It is a core claim of Stoic *physics* that law, or reason, pervades and regulates the cosmos, and is identical with Zeus.[7] It is a core *ethical* claim that law and reason are prescriptive. Since the term 'natural law' is usually taken to refer to a plurality of laws, and since the common law is an ancestor of the natural law, the most natural way to think of the law being prescriptive might be to envisage a body of rules.[8] It is this picture of the Stoic theory that I refer to as the rules-interpretation. The individual rules could be prescriptions, prohibitions, and permissions of types of action. Or they could instruct us on what to pursue and what to avoid. However, as I shall argue, the Stoics propose no such rules, neither of the former nor of the latter kind.

But how else can the law be prescriptive, if not through rules? Another view that also has considerable initial plausibility, given Stoic epistemology and theory of action, is that whenever the sage decides to perform an action, her reason issues a command to herself that has the status of law. This view, which I call the prescriptive reason-interpretation, can invoke the Stoic account of perfectly appropriate action. The fool can act appropriately, but the sage does so from the disposition of perfect reason. This makes her action perfectly appropriate, and *lawful*. As we saw, only the sage is 'lawful' (*nomimos*),

---

Watson, the Stoics invented the concept of natural law. Phillip Mitsis proposes that passages in which Chrysippus identifies the law with Zeus (DL 7.88) and calls law 'king' (Marcian, *Inst.* 1 = SVF 3.314 = LS 67R) make it "fairly clear that the notion of natural law was developed in the Stoa very early on"; "The Stoic Origin of Natural Rights," in *Topics in Stoic Philosophy,* ed. Katerina Ierodiakonou (Oxford: Oxford University Press, 2001), 153–177, 163–164.

[6]On the status of such identity statements see Susanne Bobzien, *Determinism and Freedom in Stoic Philosophy* (New York: Oxford University Press, 1998), 45–47

[7]It is clear that the identification of law and reason refers, strictly speaking, to *perfect* reason. Chrysippus equates law with *perfect* reason (DL 7.87). See Cicero, *De leg.* 1.23 = SVF 3.339. Further, the law is said to be good (*spoudaion*) (Stobaeus 2.102,11–12).

[8]The rules-interpretation has been made very plausible by Striker, "Origins of the Concept of Natural Law." The content of nature's laws could be deduced by the Stoics, as Striker suggests, "from the apparent purposes nature had followed in making man the kind of creature that he is." Nature has given human beings the first impulses of self-preservation and sociability. "Obviously," Striker says, "a lot of filling in will be needed to arrive from those two fundamental tendencies at a detailed set of rules of morality" (in *Papers*, 219 No. 9). In recent years, Phillip Mitsis has argued for the rules-interpretation in much more detail than Striker.

and only he is able to follow the law, as I have rendered *nomikos* (Stobaeus 2.102,4–9). Whatever the sage's reason prescribes has the status of law. But while this is correct, the prescriptive reason-interpretation misses an important point: the law of the Stoics is *substantive*. The prescriptive reason-interpretation cannot explain the fact that the Stoics have substantive views about a life in agreement with nature—that they have views about what is valuable and disvaluable that are essential to the theory of appropriate action.[9]

Neither the rules-interpretation nor the prescriptive reason-interpretation gets things right, or so I shall argue. If we want to understand what the Stoics describe as *lawful action*, we need to understand the way the theory of appropriate action incorporates substantive claims about value and the nature of human beings without formulating rules. The bulk of this chapter will be concerned with a discussion of the much-debated theory of appropriate action—a discussion that focuses on aspects of this theory that are particularly relevant to the interpretation of the Stoic conception of the law. My core thesis is that the theory of appropriate action makes claims about what considerations should count as relevant in action, and in this way provides a *substantive* guide to life. I shall argue for this thesis by relating the discussion of appropriate action to the Stoic conception of reason. It has long been acknowledged by scholars that the Stoics propose a substantive

---

[9]The prescriptive reason-interpretation is most forcefully presented by Paul Vander Waerdt. As he argues, appropriate action and the perfect action of the sage differ with respect to the *disposition* of the agent. According to Vander Waerdt, the natural law does not prescribe rules. Rather, the law prescribes *a disposition*, the disposition of virtue: the Stoics "advance a dispositional rather than a rule-following model of natural law." "[N]atural law prescribes the intensional rather than the extensional characteristics of virtuous actions"; "Zeno's Republic and the Origins of Natural Law," in *The Socratic Movement*, ed. Vander Waerdt (Ithaca, N.Y.: Cornell University Press, 1994), 275. Vander Waerdt writes: "This law has three features that are especially relevant here: (1) it is constituted by the sage's rational disposition, not by a code of rules or legislation; (2) it prescribes *katorthômata*, actions whose moral correctness is guaranteed by the disposition with which they are performed; and (3) its prescription is sufficient to ensure the agent's attainment of his natural end, namely, 'living consistently' or 'consistently with nature'" (287). Anna Maria Ioppolo proposes an interpretation that elaborates on the intensional side of right action; "Decreta e praecepta in Seneca," in *La Filisofia in Eta Imperiale*, ed. Aldo Brancacci (Naples: Bibliopolis, 2000), 15–36.

theory of reason.[10] To 'have reason' in the way human beings have reason, on the Stoic account, involves mastering a certain amount of *content*. The main components of reason, thus understood, are preconceptions, concepts that are naturally acquired in the early years of life and that are constitutive of human reasonableness. Nature guides us in acquiring preconceptions, and once this process is concluded, a human being is rational. As I shall argue, it is part of nature's guidance that nature shapes our rational soul so that we come to live a life that is adequate to the kind of being we are. In this way, nature makes us form preconceptions about what is harmful and useful, and about appropriate action, and this development is part of the acquisition of reason. If the sage's soul issues a command, her perfectly reasonable soul makes a decision that has the status of law. But the command does not merely have the status of law because the sage decides on the basis of her perfect rationality, assenting firmly only to such impressions as one should assent to. It also assumes the status of law—and here I differ importantly from the prescriptive reason-interpretation—because the sage has perfected these initial evaluative and normative notions, thus being able to fully take into account what is of value and of disvalue for human beings, given the kind of being they are.

I begin to set out this interpretation by discussing relatively general aspects of the Stoic theory of reason and action (sections 1–4). On this basis, I shall try to explain how the law, as conceived by the Stoics, is at once prescriptive and substantive in an evaluative and normative way (sections 5–9). Finally, I sum up my interpretation, offering an account of how all human beings are connected by the law—how the law is the *common* law (10).

1. *Human Beings Have Reason*

Human beings *have* reason (*logos*), or, they are rational. To be rational insofar as one *has* reason means that one is the kind of living being whose cognitive activities involve *rational* (*logikon*)

---

[10]See Michael Frede, "The Stoic Conception of Reason," in *Hellenistic Philosophy*, ed. K. J. Boudouris (Athens: International Center for Greek Philosophy and Culture, 1994), 2:50–61. My views about the Stoic conception of reason are strongly influenced by Frede's account. See also Frede's introduction to *Rationality in Greek Thought*, ed. Gisela Striker and Michael Frede (Oxford: Oxford University Press, 1996), 1–28.

impressions, impressions that have a linguistic counterpart.[11] These are called *lekta*, sayables. The Stoics can, by way of abbreviation, speak of an impression by citing the corresponding sayable, for example, the impression 'that it is day.' Strictly speaking, 'that it is day' is the *lekton* that corresponds to the impression that it is day. With rational impression comes thought (*dianoia*).[12]

While human beings are defined as rational in this sense, they are not thought to be born in such a condition. The capacity to have rational impressions depends on having *developed* reason.[13] Reason is acquired, according to Stoic doctrine, through a natural process within the first years of one's life. This process importantly involves the acquisition of preconceptions (*prolêpseis*).[14]

In "Stoic Autonomy," in *Knowledge, Nature, and the Good* (Princeton: Princeton University Press, 2004), 204–244, John Cooper argues that we can understand how the Stoic conception of law is substantive by studying how the Stoic conception of *reason* is substantive. While I disagree with Cooper in detail, this is very similar to the approach I propose. Cooper starts out from the question whether the Stoics, when they discuss 'self-action' (*autopragia*; tr. Cooper) think of *autonomy*. His main thesis is that, while the Stoics do not use the term 'autonomy,' they do hold that the wise live their lives "under each individual's own law, where that law is also, and indeed by its origin, Zeus's or nature's law" (212).

[11]SE M 8.70 = SVF 2.187 part = LS 33C.

[12]DL 7.49 = SVF 2.52, part = LS 33D; DL 7.55–6 = LS 33H.

[13]Alexander of Aphrodisias, *De anima* p. 150 28 Bruns = SVF 3.183. For a discussion of this passage see Jacques Brunschwig, "The Cradle Argument," in *The Norms of Nature*, ed. Malcolm Schofield and Gisela Striker (Cambridge: Cambridge University Press, 1986), 133.

[14]Chrysippus defines preconceptions as "natural notions"—i.e., notions we acquire in a natural process—of something "general" (*katholou*) (DL 7.54). When we, e.g., acquire the preconception of 'white,' we come to be able to refer to a variety of white things as 'white,' even though the shades of white may differ, and so on. For discussion of these matters see F. H. Sandbach, "Ennoia and Prolepsis in the Stoic Theory of Knowledge," in Long, *Problems in Stoicism*, 22–37, and Ralph Doty, "Ennoêmata, Prolêpseis, and Common Notions," *Southwestern Journal of Philosophy* 7.3 (1976): 143–148. For a recent, comprehensive discussion of concepts and preconception in the Stoa see Charles Brittain, "Common Sense: Concepts, Definition and Meaning in and Out of the Stoa," in *Language and Learning: Philosophy of Language in the Hellenistic Age: Proceedings of the Ninth Symposium Hellenisticum*, ed. Dorothea Frede and Brad Inwood (Cambridge: Cambridge University Press, 2005), 164–209. See also Brad Inwood, "Getting to Goodness," in *Reading Seneca: Stoic Philosophy at Rome* (Oxford: Oxford University Press, 2005), 271–301. Inwood begins his article, which ultimately engages with the Stoic conception of the good, with a very helpful collection of fragments on concepts and preconceptions.

When a man is born, the Stoics say, he has the commanding-part of his soul like a sheet of paper ready for writing upon. On this he inscribes each one of his conceptions. The first method of inscription is through the senses. For by perceiving something, e.g., white, they have a memory of it when it has departed. And when many memories of a similar kind have occurred, we then say we have experience. For the plurality of similar impressions is experience. Some conceptions arise naturally in the aforesaid ways and undesignedly, others through our own instruction and attention. The latter are called 'conceptions' [*ennoia*] only, the former are called 'preconceptions' [*prolêpseis*] as well. Reason [*logos*], for which we are called rational [*logikoi*], is said to be completed from our preconceptions during our first seven years. (Aëtius 4.11.1–4 = SVF 2.83 = LS 39E, tr. LS)

To be rational in the sense of having rational impressions involves the mastery of a certain amount of content, which enables us to refer in speech and thought to the things around us and to have some kind of basic picture of things in the world. Reason in this sense also enables us to develop reason further. For example, the preconceptions of trees and bushes provide the starting point for asking questions such as 'What distinguishes a tree from a bush?' It is difficult to see whether the acquisition of preconceptions is based primarily, or even exclusively, on sensory experience.[15] Even though the example in the foregoing report is 'white,' it is not clear to me that this is an accurate picture. The notion of sensory experience would have to be construed *very* broadly for this to be plausible. Anything a child *hears* would have to be classified as sensory perception. But what a child hears will importantly include the speaking of her parents, siblings, teachers, and so on, and the child will not only *hear* them but also gradually come to *understand* them. To some extent, the acquisition of preconceptions must involve the learning of language. No specific theory about the learning of language and its role in the acquisition of preconceptions is transmitted. In the context of early development, the Stoics may just think of language as a feature of the world one grows into. But acquiring reason must involve a progression from nonrational impressions (of the kind that

---

[15]Inwood thinks it does—however, with the proviso that sensory experience must be interpreted broadly ("Goodness," 271). On this interpretation, one would, e.g., observe an instance of virtue by meeting with a virtuous person and seeing her act.

animals also have) to rational impressions. And rational impressions have a linguistic counterpart. It seems that, for the child to not only 'store up' impressions but also gradually move to *rational* impressions, she must also gradually come to understand what her parents or educators say, referring, for example, to objects in the garden as trees and bushes.[16]

Further, it may be too narrow to think of sensory experience, even if interpreted broadly, rather than experience, or perception or 'sensing,' in an even broader sense. Through interaction with others, a child may learn to perceive her sister's way of eating all of the cake as unfair, her father's way of playing with her as caring, and so on. The example 'white' suggests that preconceptions supply us with *descriptive* content, but this cannot be the Stoics' position. One preconception that doxography refers to is that of god. The Stoics make the following argument against the Epicureans: a conception of god that denies providence (as Epicurean theology does) is against the *preconception* of god. This preconception, the Stoics say, includes the idea that god is caring, benevolent, and well-meaning.[17] It seems that, for there to be a preconception of god, there also need to be preconceptions of 'caring,' 'benevolent,' and 'well-meaning.' These are *evaluative* notions.[18] By living with her family, a young child will develop a preliminary notion of what it means to be caring, or benevolent, or just. It seems that such ideas are part of developing reason, just like acquiring the preconception of 'white.'

The Stoics disagree on how long it takes to develop rationality. But the two theses that are transmitted agree insofar as they place this transition to full human rationality at a relatively advanced age—seven and fourteen years.[19] Of course, this is advanced only

---

[16]On the intermediary stages of such development, and on the question whether animals and children (before they are rational) have some kind of 'quasi concepts,' see Charles Brittain, "Non-rational Perception in the Stoics and Augustine," *Oxford Studies in Ancient Philosophy* 22 (2002): 253–307, esp. 256–274.

[17]Plutarch, *On Common Conceptions* 1075E = SVF 2.1126 = LS 54K.

[18]Sandbach ("Ennoia") emphasizes that preconceptions are *not limited to* evaluative and normative concepts. However, if we start out with Inwood's assumption, that preconceptions are acquired though sensory experience (interpreted broadly), it might seem more difficult to account for evaluative and normative preconceptions than for descriptive preconceptions.

[19]Seven years according to Aetius 4.11.1–4 = SVF 2.83 = LS 39E, fourteen according to DL 7.55–6.

relative to the usual age of becoming able to speak or beginning to have just the most basic sense of what to want (food, rest, etc.) and what to avoid (cold, heat, hunger, etc.). With seven or fourteen years, human beings have usually mastered a relatively broad vocabulary, use and understand full sentences (e.g., 'this is a tree,' not just 'tree'), including the basic logical conjunctions. They are able to count, to add and subtract numbers, to decide between options in a way that may involve some notion of justice (e.g., giving equal shares of cake to themselves and their siblings) and moderation (e.g., refraining from the third helping of ice cream because one might get sick), and so on. Of course, there is no way of marking a clear transition to what counts as the result of instruction and attention, rather than a natural process of growing into the world. To some extent, it may be part of growing into the world to become able to differentiate between one tree and many trees, and to start to count, and to see, for example, that if there are two trees at each side of the garden, there are four trees in the garden. Even the most basic conversations with one's elders, who might, for instance, tell the child that there are four, not three, trees in the garden, carry an element of instruction. However, we need not worry about the details of the transition from the nature-guided process of 'growing into the world' to social processes of education. What matters for my purposes is that, to have reason in the sense of the Stoics is significantly more than a very rudimentary linguistic ability and orientation in the world that surrounds us. Nature guides us, as it were, a considerably long way.

2. Hormetic Impressions

Human beings have reason, first, insofar as their impressions are rational. But the fact that they have reason also determines how they are able to *respond* to impressions—how they, as compared to other things and beings, *move*. The lowest class of things is of such a sort that each of them needs to be moved from the outside. All things that are alive have the cause of movement in themselves. Plants move 'out of' themselves (e.g., by growing), while animals move 'by' themselves, responding to impressions. A rational animal has, apart from its 'impressionistic nature,' reason. By reason it judges impressions, rejecting some and accepting others, and is guided accordingly.[20] A rational animal is thus defined as an animal that is not simply guided by its impressions; human beings act by accepting or rejecting impressions.

The assent that is relevant to action must be assent to an impression of a specific kind. Assent to, for example, the impression that it is raining does not set off an action.[21] Only assent to impressions that present a course of action as to be done can do this. In agreement with recent scholarship, I shall refer to such impressions as 'hormetic.' Assent to a hormetic impression *is* impulse (*hormê*). Impulse is not yet itself the action or bodily movement; it is defined as a movement of thought toward something in the sphere of action.[22] According to Chrysippus, impulse "of man is reason prescribing action to him" (and this is, the *agent's* reason or rational soul).[23] By assenting to a hormetic impression we decide to perform an action.[24] If there is no external impediment, impulse sets off action.

As we have seen, all impressions that human beings have are rational and have linguistic counterparts. The Stoics distinguish between different kinds of sayables (*lekta*). Assertibles (like 'it is day') are self-complete or complete *lekta*.[25] But sayables can also be incomplete or deficient; for example, predicates are deficient

---

[20]Origen, *On principles* 3.1.2–3 = SVF 2.988, part = LS 53A. The term 'judges' may misleadingly suggest that we scrutinize and then judge impressions. The Stoic idea is that, by assenting to an impression, we accept that something is true—we do not, strictly speaking, accept the impression, but rather the truth of what it presents. On this point see Tad Brennan, "Stoic Moral Psychology," in *The Cambridge Companion to the Stoics*, ed. Brad Inwood (Cambridge: Cambridge University Press, 2003), 257–294, 262.

[21]For all of my discussion of Stoic theory of action, I am very much indebted to Inwood, *Ethics and Human Action in Early Stoicism* (Oxford: Clarendon Press, 1985).

[22]Stobaeus 2.86,17–87,6 = SVF 3.169 part = LS 53Q.

[23]Plutarch, *On Stoic Self-Contradictions* 1037F = SVF 3.175, part = LS 53R.

[24]Up to this point, this account is—in the wake of Inwood's influential study—more or less common ground in scholarship on the Stoics, and I have implicitly relied on this picture all along. See Inwood, *Ethics and Human Action*, 45–66, esp. 55–66; see also Inwood, "The Stoics on the Grammar of Action," *Southern Journal of Philosophy* 23, supp. (1985): 75–86.

[25]I am following Susanne Bobzien's translations of *axiôma* and *lekton*. Bobzien renders the Greek more faithfully than it is often done and distinguishes between self-complete and deficient sayables; many authors speak of complete and incomplete *lekta* ("Logic," in Inwood, *Cambridge Companion to the Stoics*, 85–123).

sayables (the idea is that, with a sayable like 'writes,' we can ask 'who?'—see DL 7.63; this is how it is elliptically deficient).

The Stoics define impulses as acts of assent.[26] Recall that on the Stoic picture of the soul, assent is a physical movement, and, in some sense, impulse is *this* movement.[27] When the initial assent to a hormetic impression and the impulse are thus considered separately, and as a sequence, they have different objects. When we assent, we assent to an impression that has a complete sayable as its linguistic counterpart; impulse, however, is directed at a predicate, not at the complete sayable.[28] I may assent to the impression that, since it looks like it may rain, I should take my umbrella. The impulse, insofar as it can

[26]Stobaeus 2.88,2–6 = SVF 3.171 = LS 33I.

[27]According to a report in Plutarch, impulse is *generated* by assent. Plutarch, *On Stoic Self-Contradictions* 1057A = SVF 3.177 part = LS 53S. See Inwood on the question whether impulse *is* assent or is *generated by* assent, *Ethics and Human Action*, 61. While I cannot argue for this point here, I think that impulse might, in this respect, be like opinion. Opinion *is* weak assent, but it is also true that weak assent, understood as the *initial* acceptance of an impression, *generates* opinion. Analogously, impulse *is* assent to a hormetic impression, but it can also be viewed as *generated* by the initial acceptance of the impression. (Suppose there is an external impediment to the action: in this case, impulse persists, and the continued assent to the impression that one should φ can be distinguished from the initial assent to it.) On assent and opinion see Constance Meinwald, "Ignorance and Opinion in Stoic Epistemology," *Phronesis* 50 (2005): 215–231.

Inwood further argues that assent is given to sayables, not to the rational impressions themselves. Michael Frede has contested this point: the sources suggest that assent is given to impressions, not to *lekta* (or rather, assent is given to *lekta* only in the indirect way *lekta* correspond to and depend on impressions) (SE M 8.70). Frede, "The Stoic Doctrine of the Affections of the Soul," in Schofield and Striker, *Norms of Nature*, 93–110, 103–107. Cf. Inwood, "Seneca and Psychological Dualism," in *Passions and Perceptions: Studies in Hellenistic Philosophy of Mind: Proceedings of the Fifth Symposium Hellenisticum,* ed. J. Brunschwig and M. Nussbaum (Cambridge: Cambridge University Press, 1993), 150–183, 168.

[28]"[A]cts of assent and impulses actually differ in their objects: assertibles are the objects of acts of assent, but impulses are directed toward predicates [*katêgorêmata*], which are contained in a sense in the statements" (Stobaeus 2.88,2–6). See Seneca, according to whom 'going for a walk' would be an example for what impulse is directed at (*Ep.* 133.18).

Rational impressions have complete *lekta* as their counterparts. While there are incomplete *lekta*, there are no 'rational incomplete impressions.' E.g., one does not have the impression 'red' or 'walking,' but the impression that X is red or that A is walking. My reasons for thinking that *rational* impressions have linguistic counterparts with a propositional structure are: (1) rational impressions are subject to assent;

be distinguished from the assent, is directed toward a *predicate*, namely, 'to take my umbrella.' This is the action I decide to take (to take my umbrella) when I assent to the impression that, since it looks like rain, I should take my umbrella. (Assent to this impression might be said to be two things: the opinion that, since it looks like rain, I should take my umbrella, and the impulse to take my umbrella.)

By assenting to a hormetic impression, we *make ourselves act*, or, as the Stoics put it, our reason issues a *command*. Assent to a hormetic impression has, as we might put it, normative force; it 'sets us off' (provided that there is no external impediment). Stoic philosophy is importantly characterized by a full endorsement of the thesis that the soul is a unity; what one holds to be true directly translates into motivation for action. If I hold it to be true that I should take my umbrella, I am motivated to take my umbrella. For the Stoics, to understand something that is relevant to action *is* to be motivated accordingly.[29]

The agent assents to an impression that presents something as *to be done*. This thought is expressed, by the Stoics, in the following terms: the cause (*to kinoun*) of the impulse is a hormetic impression of something appropriate (*kathêkontos*) (Stobaeus 2.86,17–18).[30]

---

(2) all examples of rational impressions that I have found in the sources have complete sayables corresponding to them; and (3) the claim that there are incomplete sayables like 'writes' does not imply that anyone ever has the impression 'writes.'

[29]Inwood suggests that predicates are, in Stoic theory, closely associated with commands. On his reading, impulse is directed at a predicate insofar as the agent assents to something like a command to herself (such as: 'walk!') (*Ethics and Human Action*, 62–65). This is how Inwood explains the motivational or normative force of assent. But as I argue, given Stoic psychology, there is no gap between judgment and motivation that would need to be explained in this way.

[30]Translations of the term *kathêkonta* are inevitably to some extent artificial and potentially misleading. Cicero and other Roman authors already faced this problem, and the terms they settled on have influenced the reception. It would seem that there cannot be many questions of *translation* that have shaped the history of ethics in more substantial and philosophically relevant ways than this: Cicero translates *kathêkonta* as *officia*. Thus *kathêkonta* stand at the outset of moral philosophizing about *duties*. It is highly likely that Kant primarily encounters Stoicism in these terms. When we find Stoic influences on Kant's thought, we have to be aware of the terminological shift that takes place through translation of Greek into Latin. It is partly for this reason that it could at the same time be true both that Kant is deeply influenced by the Stoics and that the early Stoics are deeply un-Kantian.

The hormetic impression thus does not only represent a course of action. Rather, the hormetic impression presents the course of action *as to be done*, and by assenting to it we prescribe this action to ourselves. Insofar as the command is issued by the *agent's* reason, it is the *agent's* reason that gives her an order, telling her what to do. To assent to a hormetic impression is, in this sense, to prescribe to oneself what one should be doing. In a minimal sense, every action is thus *prescribed by reason*. This sense corresponds to the sense in which all human beings and all human impressions are rational. Even assent to a hormetic impression that presents a lunatic course of action is, in this sense, rational. Reason is the faculty of decision-making, and decision-making is, roughly put, about telling oneself what to do. Stoic theory of action is thus fundamental to understanding the Stoic conception of the law: *perfect reason can be identified with law because reason is prescriptive*. This is true even for the reasoning of the fool. The perfect reason of the sage issues prescriptions that meet every standard for what counts, in the technical sense, as law—prescriptions that, in each and every instance, tell the agent what is in fact to be done.

We might think that this picture already answers all the questions we have about the Stoic law. If the sage assents from her perfect disposition, and assents only to impressions that one should assent to, then surely this is also the case with respect to hormetic impressions. Every assent to a hormetic impression of a sage has the status of law. It prescribes to the wise agent what she should be doing in a law-like fashion. This is the view I call the prescriptive reason-interpretation of the law. It is correct as long as we do not suppose that this is all there is to the Stoic conception of the law.

It is well known and noncontroversial in the interpretation of Stoic philosophy that the sage only assents to cognitive impressions, that is, impressions that make it clear through themselves that they present things exactly as they are. We might think that this is how the sage knows what to do: her hormetic impression makes it clear, through its very quality, that it presents the course of action that is in fact to be done as to be done. But do the Stoics argue that there are 'cognitive-hormetic' impressions? It would surely be a mistake to think that, according to the Stoics, cognitive impressions occur only in sense-perception. Cognitive impressions also occur in thought; a cognitive impression can be sensory or nonsensory. But what about hormetic impressions?[31] If we rely on the core thesis that the sage only assents to cognitive impressions, it would seem that there must be hormetic, cognitive impressions. However, I am not sure that we can settle this question. From the evidence we have, it is clear that the *factual* judgments that figure in the sage's actions (e.g., that an apple that is offered to him is in fact an apple) are assents to cognitive impressions. But it is not clear that the sage's assent to 'I should eat this' counts as an assent to a cognitive impression.

Independently of where we stand on this question, what is important for my purposes is that the prescriptive reason-interpretation implicitly relies on an implausible picture of the sage's assent: that the sage's assent to a hormetic impression is, as it were, a mere response to the quality of the impression. As I suggest, this is implausible. The sage's assent to a hormetic impression is not fully understood if we (supposing we could) settle the question whether the very quality of this impression makes it clear to the sage that the action that is presented as to be done is in fact to be done. If we want to understand why the sage assents when she assents, and thus get at the substantive side of the Stoic conception of the law, we need to study the deliberative route that takes the sage to her decision. We must ask what kinds of consideration count, from the point of view of the sage, as relevant to action.

3. Well-Reasoned Action

As we saw, hormetic impressions present a course of action as appropriate (*kathêkon*). Of course, we can be wrong about whether an action that seems appropriate actually is so. But even the fool

---

[31]Tad Brennan suggests that there are. He argues that the debates between Stoics and Sceptics make no sense if there are no hormetic, cognitive impressions, implying that the sage, when he, for example, assents to 'it is reasonable that this is an apple' assents to a hormetic impression (see DL 7.177; see also Cicero, *Academica* 2.99–100 for a similar example). But the debate between Sceptics and Stoics is about an impression that presents something as an apple that is actually an artificial apple—it is not about the sage's assent to the hormetic impression 'I should eat this.' Brennan, "Reasonable Impressions in Stoicism," *Phronesis* 35 (1996): 318–334, 324–325. Cf. Stephen Menn, "Physics as Virtue," *Proceedings of the Boston Area Colloquium in Ancient Philosophy 11*, ed. John J. Clearly and William C. Wians (1995): 13.

very often acts appropriately, and in these cases, her actions can *in retrospect* be given a well-reasoned justification. Action that is adapted to the way nature works, and is therefore appropriate, is defined as "consequentiality in life, something which, once it has been done, has a well-reasoned (*eulogon*) justification [*apologia*]."[32]

The Stoic theory of appropriate action raises a number of difficult and controversial questions.[33] I begin discussion of the theory with the following questions: (1) How should we interpret *eulogon*, the term I have rendered as 'well-reasoned' but is traditionally translated as 'reasonable' or 'plausible'? (2) Which considerations are relevant to deliberation and justification?

In response to question 1, here is an explanation for what would count as justification that is *eulogon*: one might justify an action by explaining that it is *in accordance with life*, which also pervades plants and animals (DL 7.107). We can easily see that this is not the kind of explanation a fool would ever give for an action. The notion of something being 'in accordance with life' and, what is more, the reference to how 'life' also pervades plants and animals are highly theoretical, and involve knowledge of physics and ethics. Only the sage can give this kind of explanation. As Brennan has convincingly argued, the standard of reasonableness is not what we consider ordinarily as well-argued (a standard on which several different courses of action might count as reasonable in a given situation, while, on Stoic assumptions, only *one* course of action is). In Brennan's words, "the standard of reasonableness in the *kathêkon* is the rationality of the Sage."[34] *Eulogon* is thus best translated as 'well-reasoned,' and 'well' here has the full force of 'good.' An instance of good reasoning can only be offered by the sage. That the fool can nevertheless act appropriately means that the Stoic theory takes, to an important extent, an *extensional* and *agent-independent* perspective. It assesses *actions*, not the deliberative

---

[32]Stobaeus 2.85,13 = SVF 3.494 = LS 59B, tr. LS.

[33]Insofar as the conception of appropriate action is fundamental to all of Stoic ethics, I will by no means be able to discuss everything that pertains to it. The *telos*-formulae (e.g., 'life in agreement with nature') can be read as accounts of what it means to live a life in which one consistently acts appropriately.

[34]"Reasonable Impressions," 328. Brennan convincingly challenges an interpretation that has been enormously influential (see Long and Sedley's commentary on the fragments; LS, 1:365).

route that leads up to the decision for action. No matter how the agent *arrived* at the decision to perform the appropriate action, insofar as the action is appropriate, it can be given a well-reasoned justification.

Chrysippus describes the life of the virtuous person as a life of *appropriate* actions: "The man who progresses to the furthest point performs all appropriate actions without exception and omits none."[35] The difference between a sage who performs an appropriate action and a fool who does so lies in the overall state of their souls. If the action is done from the disposition of expertise or knowledge, it is not only appropriate but, over and above this, right or correct.[36] Like appropriate actions (and *as* appropriate actions), correct actions (*katorthôma*) can be given a well-reasoned justification.[37] But the sage's reasoning, which leads her to decide for a particular course of action, makes use of the same considerations as the well-reasoned justification that can, in retrospect, be given for her action.

Appropriate actions are defined as those that reason dictates.[38] Deciding to perform an action is assenting to the impression that one should φ. The clause 'I should φ' is, as we can see from a number of texts, just another way of putting 'it is appropriate for me to φ.' Insofar as the fool decides to φ, *her* reason dictates to her to φ. But the clause 'reason dictates' does not refer to actions that *appear* to the fool to be appropriate, while in fact they may be inappropriate. Like the notion of well-reasoned justification, the clause must be taken to refer to *perfect* reason (the cosmos's reason or the sage's reason).

Given that the Stoics describe the fool as completely doomed, unhappy, and living a bad life, it might seem that none of her actions

---

[35]Stobaeus 5.906,18–907,5 = SVF 3.510 = LS 59I, tr. LS.

[36]The Stoic theory is further complicated by the notion of 'intermediates.' For my present purposes, it is not necessary to engage with this notion. See Stobaeus 2.85,13 = SVF 3.494; Cicero *De fin.* 3.58 = SVF 3.498; Stobaeus 2.86,12 = SVF 3.499.

[37]See M 11.200–201 = SVF 3.516 part = LS 59G part. Appropriate actions *include* right actions—*perfect* appropriate actions *are* right actions. See Anna Maria Ioppolo, *Aristone di Chio e lo Stoicismo antico* (Naples: Bibliopolis, 1980), 96–101, and *Opinione e Scienza: Il dibattito tra Stoizi e Accademici nel III e nel II a.C.* (Naples: Bibliopolis, 1986), 126–134; for a different view see Brad Inwood with P. L. Donini, "Stoic Ethics," in *Cambridge History of Hellenistic Philosophy,* ed. Keimpe Algra et al. (Cambridge: Cambridge University Press, 1999), 729.

[38]DL 7.108–9 = SVF 3.495 and 496 = LS 59E.

could count as 'to be done.' This, however, is not at all the case—at least not insofar as her actions are described extensionally, without reference to the state of her soul. The fool may even do many appropriate things. This view is, it would seem, quite plausible: however bad one might be, one still does many things that are, in the Stoic sense, appropriate. One might be a criminal and still put on a coat when it rains, eat and drink fairly healthy things, and so on. The bulk of one's daily activities could be appropriate, and there would still be room for being far from virtuous. And we can see why it is important to insist on an agent-independent assessment of these actions: the fool does none of these things on the basis of the reasoning that is ultimately needed in order to see why they are appropriate. In the end, one must understand nature and one's own nature in order to fully see why and how eating and keeping warm, and so on, are (under the relevant circumstances) appropriate. *Kathêkonta* are activities that are adapted to the way nature works (DL 7.108). What is appropriate follows from the nature of a living being; it is adapted and adequate for the living being and sustains it.[39] Of course, one can also understand these things partially, and in many cases a partial understanding is enough in order to arrive at appropriate action. But in order to explain *why* this action is appropriate, much more is needed.

In response to question 2: let us consider what it is that is *relevant* to deliberation and justification. The Stoics regard things like health, illness, life, death, wealth, and poverty as indifferent (*adiaphoron*).[40] Things that are indifferent do not contribute to our happiness or misery; but, other than, for example, the number of hairs on one's head, they are *not irrelevant to action* (DL 7.104). Indifferents provide considerations for action. It is part of the very definition of what indifferents are that they relate to action, and that the field of decision-making is concerned with indifferents (DL 7.105).

---

[39]Not only humans but also animals can act in this way: they, too, show behavior that 'follows from their nature' (Stobeaus 2.85,13 = SVF 3.494 = LS 59B). For similar claims on plants see DL 7.107 = SVF 3.493 part = LS 59C.

[40]The plural is *adiaphora*. Since it is a little awkward to talk of the 'indifferent things,' it has become customary to either speak of 'indifferents' or use the Greek *adiaphora*.

The theory of indifferents can be approached from the Stoic account of the *telos*. The end is life in agreement, or life in agreement with nature, or life in agreement with the experience of what happens by nature.[41] Some indifferents are in accordance with nature, others are contrary to nature, and still others are neither of these. Things like health and strength are in accordance with nature; illness and weakness are contrary to nature; neither in accordance with nor contrary to nature are states of the soul and the body such that the soul is open to receive wrong impressions and the body is liable to harm.[42] Things that are in accordance with nature are to be taken (*lêpta*); those that are contrary to nature are not to be taken (*alêpta*).[43] The former have value (*axia*), the latter disvalue (*apaxia*).[44] What is valuable can have more or less value, and what is disvaluable can have more or less disvalue. Things that have much value are preferred (*proêgmena*), those that have much disvalue are dispreferred (*apoproêgmena*). What is preferred is selected on the basis of *preferential reason* (*kata proêgoumenon logon*), that is, on the basis of reason leading us toward the things it prefers.[45]

If we add up these definitions, we see that preferred indifferents are what is valuable and at the same time what is in accordance with nature.[46] Preferred indifferents bear on action; the fact that they are in agreement with nature accounts for the fact that reason

[41]See chapter 3. It has been debated whether Chrysippus intends his version to be an elucidation of Zeno's, or disagrees in a substantial way. See Gisela Striker, "Following Nature: A Study in Stoic Ethics," *Oxford Studies in Ancient Philosophy* 9 (1991): 4–5.

[42]Stobaeus 2.79,18–80,13 = LS 58C part.

[43]Stobaeus 2.82,20–1 = LS 58C part.

[44]Stobaeus 2.83,10–84,2 = SVF 3.124 = LS 58D. I am adopting the translation of *apaxia* from LS. 'Disvalue' is clearly an artificial term. It aims at capturing the way *apaxia* relates to *axia*.

[45]Stobaeus 2.83,10–85,11 = SVF 3.124 and 128 = LS 58D and E. I am grateful to David Sedley for discussion of this phrase, which is, in LS, translated as 'on the basis of a preferential reason.' Sedley himself argued in conversation that the Stoics do not have room for a use of *logos* in the sense of 'a reason' (and no notion of 'reasons').

[46]Rachel Barney, "A Puzzle in Stoic Ethics," *Oxford Studies in Ancient Philosophy* 24 (2003): 333, calls into question whether we should equate these notions in this way. On the distinction between things of value and things of much value see later.

prefers them.[47] There are facts of nature that tell us what to prefer and what to disprefer. Right reason understands these facts of nature, and accordingly prefers preferred indifferents, and disprefers dispreferred indifferents. Deliberation is thus a kind of weighing or balancing with a view to everything that pertains to a given situation, and that is preferred and dispreferred (or natural and contrary to nature).

Note that what is 'to be taken' or 'not to be taken' are not courses of action, but rather indifferents—states like health or strength, or events such as catching a cold or the prospect of inheriting money. It is striking that, in the reports on the Stoic doctrine that bear on the Stoic conception of deliberation, there is such emphasis on selecting and deselecting indifferents, rather than on considering courses of action and eventually deciding to perform a specific course of action. Deciding which action is appropriate, it seems, *is* selecting and deselecting indifferents.

4. *Appropriate Action, Law, and Nature*

To live perfectly appropriately, and thus in agreement with nature, is to live by the common law.[48] The Stoic conception of the law is substantive, insofar as it integrates Stoic thought about value— thought on what it is that should count as relevant considerations for action. The law is 'by nature,' insofar as whether something is of value or disvalue is a *fact of nature*. When the sage considers valuable and disvaluable things, she considers the things that are natural and contrary to nature—natural or contrary to nature for a human being. But the law is also by nature, insofar as the law is identified with reason. As we have seen, there is a sense in which human reason is 'by nature.' Human beings acquire preconceptions, which constitute their rationality or reasonableness, in a natural process.

---

[47]The Stoics hold that the theory of the indifferents *starts out* from the 'first things in accordance with nature and contrary to nature' (Stobaeus 2.80,6–8). That means: while the terms 'the valuable,' 'the preferred,' 'that which is in accordance with nature' refer to the same things, the valuable is valuable and the preferred is preferred *because* they are in accordance with nature.

[48]See DL 7.87–88 on the identification of life in agreement with nature and life in agreement with the law.

The law can thus be seen as the perfection of a naturally acquired reasonableness. To be able to live lawfully is to have perfected one's reason, which is naturally acquired. It is this side of the Stoic conception of the law that I turn to now: the sage's perfect reason, insofar as it is practical, and identical with the law, has developed out of tendencies for action that nature instills in human beings *as part of making them rational beings.*

It has long been acknowledged that, according to the Stoics, 'nature guides' human beings, and that the theories of *oikeiôsis* and first impulse explain important aspects of this guidance. But the acquisition of reason on the one hand and the theory of *oikeiôsis* on the other are rarely seen as intimately connected. There is little discussion of the ways in which, *by acquiring reason*, human beings acquire evaluative and normative notions. However, if nature instills certain tendencies of action in human beings, this must be part of the way nature guides the development of the human soul. The human soul, according to the Stoics, does not have several parts or powers, one of them associated with reasoning and the other with motivation for action. The leading-part of the soul is rational, and if nature instills tendencies of action, it must be possible to describe this as part of the *cognitive* development of human beings. As long as a human being is not yet rational, his first and early impulses cannot be explained in terms of concepts, or in any other way that already involves human rationality. But insofar as nature guides human beings with respect to tendencies in action, this guidance must ultimately lead us to master evaluative and normative preconceptions. The result of nature's guidance must be explicable in terms of the rational soul, that is, the soul that is rational, insofar as grown-up human beings have acquired preconceptions and are able to have rational impressions, to think, and to assent.

As others have noted, this field of Stoic theory is perhaps even less accessible to us than others.[49] The limited goal I would like to achieve here is to suggest that according to the Stoics, human beings naturally acquire evaluative and normative preconceptions—most important, the preconceptions of benefit and harm, of appropriateness ('something should be done'), and of 'belonging.' We might

---

[49] A very helpful contribution to the reconstruction of relevant texts is Charles Brittain, "Non-rational Perception," esp. sec. 1.

think that this range of notions is not necessary in order to explain the actions of a human being who is just barely rational, that is, rational in the minimal sense of having acquired reason. It is well known that, according to the Stoics, fools think of health, wealth, and so on as good, and of illness, poverty, and so on as bad. Would it not seem that nature thus leads us to develop preconceptions of good and bad? On this picture, a minimally rational young person perceives some things as good and some as bad. We might add that to see something as good is to be motivated to move toward it, and to see it as bad is to be motivated to avoid it.[50] There are, however, a number of difficult questions relating to this picture. Most important, it is a complicated question whether, according to the early Stoics, human beings are generally motivated by perceiving something as good.[51] We have seen that impulse is generated by assent to an impression that presents a course of action as *appropriate*, rather than presenting a course of action (or an object of desire) as *good* (Stobaeus 2.86,17–18).[52] Motivation, it seems, is—at least in an important sense—discussed in terms of what seems appropriate, not in terms of what seems good.[53]

[50]This is roughly what John Cooper suggests ("Stoic Autonomy," 216–218). Cooper's analysis is importantly based on an excerpt from Epictetus (*Discourses* 3.2.2). According to Epictetus, it is in the nature of human beings to 'nod to' the true, and it is equally in the nature of human beings to be moved with desire for the good. Epictetus discusses how human beings have preconceptions of the good, and disagree in how to apply them (*Discourses* 2.17.1–13; see esp. 7). I am very grateful to John Cooper for discussion of these matters. In "On the Stoic Conception of the Good," in Ierodiakonou, *Topics in Stoic Philosophy*, 71–94, Michael Frede argues that, according to the Stoics, to be motivated is to see something as good.

[51]For a brief discussion of different positions on this question see Tad Brennan, "Stoic Moral Psychology," esp. 283–290.

[52]This point is also made by Charles Brittain in response to Frede, "On the Stoic Conception of the Good," in "Rationality, Rules, and Rights," *Apeiron* 34.3 (2001): 247–267, 247–253.

[53]This, of course, does not mean that the way things appear good and bad to the agent does not figure in the Stoic theory of action and movitation. I suspect that it does, but for my present purposes, we need not pursue the question. It is difficult to say whether, according to the *early* Stoics, we acquire a preconception of the good. As I hope to argue in an article entitled "The Good Is Benefit," I think they must. Chrysippus claims that the Stoic conception of the good 'connects best with our preconceptions'; he is not referring to a preconception of the good, but rather to other preconceptions that, as he claims, the Stoic concept of the good agrees with

Let us briefly recall some aspects of *oikeiôsis*: a human being develops the disposition of counting her own body and constitution, her family members, and gradually all others and the world as 'belonging to' her (DL 7.85); whatever 'belongs' to the human being is affiliated or endeared to her. Self-preservation is tied to love of one's constitution (*suum statum*) and the things that preserve this constitution, and is also tied to alienation from one's death and those things that seem to lead to death (Cicero, *De fin.* 3.16). According to the account in Cicero, the 'functioning of the soul' is as relevant as that of the body: cognition (*katalêpsis*) is naturally pursued, just as is the preservation of one's body. As soon as the first impulse of self-preservation is generated in human beings, nature also endears human beings to those closest to them. Plutarch complains that Chrysippus wearies us to death by writing in every book on physics and ethics that we have the disposition, as soon as we are born, to regard ourselves, our parts, and *our offspring* as belonging to us (*On Stoic Self-Contradictions* 1038B).

(Plutarch, *On Stoic Self-Contradictions* 1041E = SVF 3.69 = LS 60B; on Chrysippus's view of preconceptions as criteria see DL 7.54). We cannot conclude from this that there is *no* preconception of the good, and it would seem that, for fools to be able to refer to health and wealth, etc., as good, they must have some kind of notion of the good that is not the concept of the genuinely good. But the early Stoics seem to avoid reference to a preconception of the good when they discuss early development. Rather, they lead us gradually from notions like benefit and harm, and appropriate action, to the notion of the good. The reason for this is, I suspect, that the story we would have to tell about the way the preconception of the good relates to the scientific concept of the good is highly complicated—not that it could not be told. However, it involves considerable difficulty: in the case of the good, a complete change in perspective is needed in order to understand that none of the things that previously appeared to be good actually is good. Compare this to the preconception of trees. With respect to trees, the expert biologist and the barely rational child differ greatly with respect to the conception of trees they have, but, at least for the most part, they call the same kinds of objects 'trees.' Not so in the case of the good. Once we see that the good is something like consistency, or perfect rationality, we understand that the things we used to regard as good (health, etc.) really are not good at all. The Stoics give elaborate accounts of how we arrive at the notion of the good, and it seems to me that they are aware of the specific difficulties relating to a preconception of the good (see Cicero, *De fin.* 3.20, 3.33–34). Seneca (*Ep.* 120.3–5, 8–11 = LS 60E) says that nature could not have supplied us with a notion of the good; it takes much thought to arrive at it.

Where, in this process, do we find something like conceptual content and the formation of concepts? First and early impulse is not yet *rational* impulse. The human being is set into motion without *assent* to impressions, and whatever is represented to it is not represented in *rational* impressions. The young human being does not yet have preconceptions. But clearly, the Stoics envisage a gradual development; they assume that infants and children are aware of something like 'quasi-cognitive content,' and that they gradually develop preconceptions, which, prior to the completion of the process, must be something like quasi concepts.[54]

Cicero has the spokesman for the Stoic theory argue that, if given the choice, all of us would prefer the parts of our bodies to be sound rather than defective. This kind of judgment is presented as proof for the fact that there is something like a primary impulse, an impulse created by nature in living beings (*De fin.* 3.20). In the infant, this 'judgment' cannot be a judgment in the sense of assent to a rational impression. But the theory seems to say that there is a prerational, naturally acquired counterpart to this judgment, something like a prerational *preference* for the parts of one's body to be intact. The formation of such preferences (and the corresponding aversions) is explained in terms of endearment and affiliation: nature guides the infant to become affiliated with his constitution and those closest to him. This affective disposition is, again, part of the formation of the rational soul, and it must include something like quasi concepts of 'belonging' or 'being alien' to oneself. It is on the basis of this affiliation that the prerational being rejects what is harmful and takes what 'belongs to it' (*ta oikeia*) (DL 7.85). Note that *ta oikeia* here is the opposite of what is harmful. This seems fully adequate: the useful, which is the more standard counterterm to the harmful, really *is* that which belongs to the animal or prerational human being— that which sustains it in a state that is, given what kind of being it is, natural for it. When a human being first becomes endeared to her constitution, faculties, and capacities, as well as those who are very

---

[54]See Brittain, "Non-rational Perception." Brittain discusses the in-between state of development where impressions are not yet rational, but already have some kind of internal structure. He addresses the difficult questions of how we should think of these transitional stages, and argues that, according to the Stoics, there is something like sensory 'quasi concepts.'

close to her, she thus begins the process of acquiring notions of what it means that something is useful and harmful to her. Early notions of something being to my benefit or harm relate to the very things that seem to have these effects. Health, illness, strength, weakness, and so on appear to be things that benefit and harm us; they appear as 'dear' or 'alien,' and thus as valuable and disvaluable.[55] Closely related to this, these objects appear as objects to be pursued and to be avoided. Courses of action that secure them or avoid them appear in some initial sense as appropriate, or as sustaining what belongs to us.

We can perhaps understand the cognitive element of this process better by considering the role of *perception* and *awareness*. First impulse involves *perceiving* one's own constitution and *becoming aware* of what sustains and what harms one. The primary impulses of self-preservation arise out of a cognitive process based on perception. Hierocles points out that an animal, as soon as it is born, perceives itself.[56] It perceives not only its own parts but also their functions. For instance, a human being will strain his eyes when he wants to see something, because he perceives not only that he has eyes but also what he can do with his eyes (i.e., see).[57] Hierocles compares human beings with animals who are aware of their own weapons, that is, of those parts of their bodies (horns, etc.) that will serve them as weapons. He seems to spell out an idea that, in the early theory, is referred to as 'consciousness' of one's constitution. On a first reading of the sources, 'consciousness' is a somewhat surprising and mysterious notion; the texts on the early theory do not offer much explanation. But it seems highly plausible that something like Hierocles' account must be at work. The human being's *awareness* of her constitution would, on this picture, be a component of endearment. Being 'endeared' to oneself by nature would involve perceiving one's own body and the functions of arms, legs, ears, and so on. On the basis of perceiving oneself and what different organs

---

[55]According to Seneca, 'being familiar with bodily health' is a starting point in our cognitive development that may eventually lead to an understanding of the good. *Ep.* 120, 3–5, 8–11 = LS 60E.

[56]Hierocles 1.34–39, 51–57, 2.1–9 (= JLS 57C). On the way the argument in Hierocles seems less concise than in earlier Stoics see Brunschwig, "The Cradle Argument," 139.

[57]This kind of perception can be called 'proprioception'; see Brittain, "Non-rational Perception," 267–269, and Brunschwig, "The Cradle Argument."

and body parts are for, one would be enabled to protect oneself from harm and pursue that which preserves one's constitution. What is more, the distinction between cognitive development (becoming aware, etc.) and affective development (becoming endeared, etc.) that *we* are prone to draw does not fit into the Stoic picture. The affective dispositions of the soul *are* cognitive dispositions; they are deeply related to and reliant on judgments, or, in the early stages of life, the prerational precursors of judgments, and it seems that awareness of one's constitution is among these.

In the absence of any detailed evidence on the early Stoics, we can perhaps add to this picture by drawing on Seneca's *Letter* 121.[58] As a whole, the letter engages with the question whether living beings have a perception of their own constitution (*constitutionis suae sensus*). Seneca defines 'constitution' as 'the commanding-faculty of the soul related in a certain way to the body' (*principale animi quodam modo se habens erga corpus*) (*Letter* 121.10). To be aware of one's constitution involves being aware of how the commanding part of the soul and one's body are related. To be aware of, for example, the function of the eyes is to be aware of how one's eyes are connected to the main part of the soul, to have some awareness of, loosely speaking, 'where sight comes from' (i.e., that it is through the eyes that one sees). Seneca makes points similar to those of Hierocles. No one, he says, has difficulties activating himself (e.g., setting his limbs into motion); animals enter "life with this knowledge." Being conscious of one's constitution is compared to the 'knowledge' that the tortoise has when it lies on its back and wants to get back onto its feet. Such 'knowledge' is of course not knowledge in the technical sense. However, it does supply some kind of content, some kind of direction as to what to strive for.[59] Seneca connects this discussion with the notions of benefit and harm. An animal senses that it is made of flesh, and it senses that flesh can be burnt, cut, and so on; thus the animal is forced into 'understanding' (*intellegere*) what harms it. It has impressions of things harmful to it *as hostile*. Through this kind of development, the animal comes to avoid what harms it and to pursue what is useful to it (*Ep.* 121.21).

---

[58] Brunschwig discusses this letter in detail in "The Cradle Argument," 137–143.

[59] Brunschwig calls it a "tendency, a guiding principle of our conduct"; "The Cradle Argument," 137.

It thus seems that, according to the Stoics, the most relevant evaluative and normative notions that nature makes us acquire grow out of concepts of the useful and harmful, that which belongs to us and is alien to us, and that which we should be doing. Taken together, these quasi concepts add up to a sense of appropriateness, a sense of what is appropriate for us to do (avoid the harmful, etc.).[60] Appropriate action must, at least to some extent, be *continuous* with the evaluative-normative content that we acquire in a nature-guided process, just as knowledge is in agreement with preconceptions. As I suggest, the evaluative-normative preconceptions that relate to appropriate action (and thus the law) are early notions of benefit and harm, notions of what belongs to us and which parts of us have which functions, and a notion of what it means that a course of action is appropriate. These notions are part of minimal human rationality. If they are developed further, and perfected, they become essential to the sage's knowledge and her perfect, lawful action.

5. Prescriptive Reason and Freedom

Before we turn to the question whether the Stoic law consists of laws, let us look more closely at the law-like quality the Stoics ascribe to the sage's decision, and the idea that the appropriate is that which reason dictates (*logos hairei*). This clause brings out the *prescriptive* nature of reason: the appropriate is that which reason (and that is: right reason) chooses, dictates, and presents to us as something to be done. Given the identification of law and reason, what *right* reason dictates is what the law prescribes. Let me cite the famous beginning of Chrysippus's *On Law* (*Peri nomou*):

> Law is king of all things human and divine.[61] Law must preside
> over [*prostatēn te einai*] what is honorable and base, as ruler
> and as guide, and thus be the standard of right and wrong

---

[60]Brittain suggests that "the only secure cases of *conscious* complex non-rational perception Seneca and Hierocles inform us of are animals' sense of their nature and external objects as harmful and beneficial" ("Non-rational Perception," 271).

[61]The claim that law is king is, in Greek thought, almost proverbial. It goes back to Pindar, and was reinterpreted by several authors, including, for example, Herodotus. Chrysippus is taking up a phrase from poetry, offering yet another interpretation of it.

[*dikaiôn kai adikôn*], prescribing [*prostaktikon*] to animals whose nature is political what they should do [*hôn poiêteon*], and prohibiting [*apagoreutikon*] them from what they should not do [*hôn ou poiêteon*]. (Marcian 1 = SVF 3.314 = LS 67R, tr. LS)

The main point of this text is, as I suggest, that law is prescriptive. Note that the text does not suggest that there are *several* laws. (1) Chrysippus's treatise is called *Peri nomou* (On law), and not *Peri nomôn* (On laws) or *Nomoi* (Laws). (2) Throughout the text, law is discussed in the singular. We do not hear of some laws that prescribe and of others that forbid. Rather, law in the singular is said to prescribe and forbid. (3) The word *kanôn*, which Long and Sedley translate as 'standard,' should by no means be interpreted to mean *canon* as in a canon of books or of laws. The word is, in early Hellenistic philosophy, used very much like 'criterion' (*kritêrion*).[62]

The perfect reason of the sage prescribes to her what is to be done. But how does it prohibit actions? First, caution (one of the rational feelings of the sage) is defined as 'prohibitive reason' (Plutarch, *On Stoic Self-Contradictions* 1038A). Second, the sage is envisaged as an *advisor* (see later); he issues prohibitions for the inferior. The Stoics seem to have said that each such prohibition is also a prescription (e.g., 'do not φ' is the prescription not to φ and the prohibition against φ) (1037D). A prohibition of this kind is the mere flip side of a prescription. (Note that in both cases, no general prohibitive *rules* are at issue. When the sage is cautious, she is, in a given situation, 'held back by her own reason' from engaging in a certain activity. If she instructs a fool, this is on a particular occasion, and with respect to a particular action.)

Zeno declares that only the virtuous are citizens, friends, relatives, and free men (*eleutheroi*). In chapter 3, I discussed citizenship, being a relative, and being a friend, but postponed the discussion of freedom. Freedom seems, at first sight, to take us into the context of actual cities—the free men in a city would be those who have a specific political status. But like citizenship, being a relative, and

---

[62]Epicurus uses *kanon* in the sense of criterion of truth. As the Hellenistic debate on the criterion of truth develops, *kritêrion* becomes the more standardly used term. In Hellenistic philosophy, the term is not only used in the context of epistemology: something might be a criterion of *action* (rather than truth).

being a friend, freedom is concerned with and located in the soul.[63] On the basis of Stoic theory of action and appropriate action, we can now see what freedom amounts to. Diogenes Laertius reports the main thesis:[64] "Only he [the wise man] is free, but the inferiors are slaves. For freedom is the power of self-action [*autopragia*],[65] but slavery is the lack of self-action" (DL 7.121 = LS 67M).[66]

The sage's freedom has something to do with how he acts—he 'acts out of himself' or 'through himself.' To be a slave (as are all nonsages) is to be unable to act in this way. The notion of *autopragia* is difficult to translate and interpret. But if we think back to the Stoic *scala naturae*, we can remind ourselves that the higher a living being is, the more it moves or acts 'by' itself. Plants move, when they grow, in some sense 'out of' themselves. Animals set themselves in motion by following impressions, and human beings by assent to impressions. 'Self-agency,' as we may translate *autopragia*, seems to perfect and complete this scale. To be able to act by oneself in the best possible sense is the mark of perfect rationality.

We can add to these considerations by integrating some of the testimony on the Stoic theory of affection. The sage's freedom can be described as her deliberative disposition, which is unperturbed by affections.[67] Galen quotes Chrysippus: a rational animal follows

---

[63] As with other such revisions of how to understand an important concept, there are predecessors in earlier philosophy. In this case, we are reminded of such discussions as Socrates' ideas about the tyrant's soul in Plato's *Republic*, where freedom and slavery are presented as states of one's soul, ways of mastering oneself or being controlled by one's desires. We may also think of Socrates' remark in the *Meno* to the effect that Meno tries to rule Socrates, while not even being able to rule himself.

[64] This report can be supplemented by a number of brief texts that emphasize how the sage is free, no matter what the external circumstances of his life are: Plutarch, *On Listening to Poetry* 33D (SVF 1.219, LS 67O), and Philo, *Quod omnis probus liber sit* 97 (SVF 1.218, LS 67N).

[65] I am following the translation of this term by Cooper, "Stoic Autonomy."

[66] The report continues by explaining how only the sage is king, judge, etc.

[67] I will not be able to discuss these matters in the detail they deserve—the Stoic account of the affections has been subject to subtle and detailed scholarly discussion. For my own views on some of the controversial questions, see my "Die stoische Theorie der Emotionen," in *Zur Ethik der älteren Stoa*, ed. Barbara Guckes (Göttingen: Vandenhoeck und Ruprecht, 2004), 69–93, and "Anger, Present Injustice and Future Revenge in Seneca's *De Ira*," in *New Developments in Seneca Studies*, ed. Gareth Williams and Katharina Volk, Columbia Studies in the Classical Tradition (Leiden: Brill, 2006), 57–74.

reason naturally; it acts in accordance with reason as if reason were its guide. But human beings can also disobey reason, and affections, defined as excessive impulses, make them do so. There is no affection without assent to an impression (e.g., 'he has offended me'). Assent to such impressions sets off an excessive impulse—it generates both an affection (e.g., anger) and an action (e.g., seeking revenge). The impulse is so strong that it has something like momentum—even at a point where the agent might already be able to see things differently, she is pushed forward by this momentum, rushing on with her passionate action.[68] In this context, we can see how the sage 'acts by herself.' For the sage to have no affections is to be *free* in her agency—she sets herself into motion so as to be able to stop or change track immediately. She is a master over her own actions. For the fool, the Stoics use the image of a runner: someone who runs fast cannot stop instantly; she will have to make some more steps before coming to a halt. Figuratively speaking, these few further steps are a symptom of the fool's slavery. She is not in full control of her impulses and actions.

The claim that only the sage is a ruler accompanies the idea that only he is the full master of his own actions, and thus is closely tied to the claim that only he is free.[69] Only the virtuous man 'rules' (*archei*), even if not in fact, but in his disposition and in general (*kata diathesin de kai pantôs*). But it is also only the sage who complies with rule (*peitharchikos*) and follows the ruler (*akolouthê-tikos ôn archonti*) (Stobaeus 2.102,13–16). If the only ruler is the only one who is ruled, we must be dealing with the idea of ruling oneself.[70] The core of the Stoic notion of freedom is a conception

---

[68]Galen, *Plac.* 4.2.10–18 = SVF 3.462 part = LS 65 J.

[69]Cleanthes describes *enkrateia*—literally 'the state of mastery (of oneself)'—as a 'power' (*kratos*) of the soul, at the same time using this notion of power to describe the *tension* (*tonos*) of the perfect soul (Plutarch, *On Stoic Self-Contradictions* 1034D). See Francesca Alesse, *La Stoa e la Tradizione Socratica* (Naples: Bibliopolis, 2000), 309–312

[70]Cf. Plato's *Republic*: the best person has a divine ruler within himself (590c8–d1). We can see that the wise man is not conceived as a ruler over others from a further passage in Stobaeus: "He [the virtuous man] is neither forced by anyone nor does he force [*anankazei*] anyone; he is neither being hindered, nor does he hinder anyone; neither is any violence done to him by anyone nor does he do violence to anyone; he neither rules [*despozei*] nor is he being ruled.... The inferiors are in all these things the opposite" (Stobaeus 2.99,19–100,6 = SVF 3.567)

of ruling oneself that refers to how one is able to make decisions—unperturbed, undistracted, fully in accord with knowledge. The sage's action is 'unhindered' by any ailments of the soul, and in this sense, the sage is free.[71]

6. Appropriate Action and Rules

Stoic theory of action and of the soul explains how a perfectly appropriate action is law-like, and how the sage's impulses are lawful prescriptions to herself. This is the *prescriptive* side of the Stoic conception of the law. But we need to turn in more detail to the *substantive* side of this conception and examine more closely the thesis I have put forward—that the law does not consist of laws. In order to do so, we need to study the Stoic examples for appropriate action. *Kathêkonta* are honoring one's parents, brothers, and native country, or spending time with friends. Actions that are contrary to appropriate actions are those that reason tells us not to do, like neglecting one's parents. Actions that are neither appropriate nor contrary to appropriate action are such as to be neither dictated nor prohibited by reason, like picking up a twig. Taking care of one's health, taking care of one's sense organs, and so on are a subclass of *kathêkonta*: *kathêkonta* that do not depend on the circumstances. *Kathêkonta* that depend on the circumstances are, for example, mutilating oneself and throwing away one's property.[72] Further, to preserve oneself in one's natural constitution is considered the first *kathêkon*; the second is to pursue things that accord with nature and to avoid the things that are contrary to it.[73]

These examples raise the question whether the Stoics describe *types of action* as appropriate. It certainly looks as if they do. And if they do, then it would seem that the theory of appropriate action is concerned with rules—that for every type of action that the Stoics

---

[71]Of course, there are a number of questions about these matters that we could follow up more closely, both with respect to the Stoic account of 'self-action' itself and with respect to the later development of ideas about self-legislation and autonomy. For a detailed discussion of these questions see Cooper, "Stoic Autonomy."

[72]DL 7.108–9 = SVF 3.495 and 496 = LS 59E.

[73]Cicero, *De fin.* 3.20 = LS 59D.

would regard as appropriate, there is a rule that spells this out.[74] There would, for example, be a rule that one should take care of one's health. Interpreted in this way, the examples of appropriate action speak in favor of the rules-interpretation. But as we saw, Stoic theory of action strongly suggests that the Stoics think of particular actions. For every occasion and agent, one action is appropriate. If this is correct, then it seems that there *can* be no rules: what is appropriate is determined, in each given occasion, by the perfect judgment of the sage. On this picture, the Stoic examples for appropriate action merely *look* as if they referred to types of action; actually, they refer to tokens (e.g., on a given occasion, it is appropriate for A to honor her parents).[75] This view amounts, with respect to the Stoic conception of the law, to the prescriptive reason-interpretation: whatever the sage decides to do is appropriate and lawful in a given situation.

The Stoic conception of what is appropriate offers a situation-specific account of what we should do; so much seems right about the prescriptive reason-interpretation. But the texts describe a close link between the Stoic theories of *value* and of appropriate action. Even if claims of what is *kathêkon* do not translate into rules, they reflect what is of value and what is of disvalue, and they thus go beyond addressing particular situations. What we need to understand is exactly this—in what way the Stoic conception of appropriate action proposes a *substantive guide* to how we should live.

Let us look in more detail at the examples. First, we should note that the examples do not actually talk of *types of action*. Taking care of one's health is not a type of action. Rather, for any given agent, this will amount to doing something specific, an action that might

[74]This is what David Sedley proposes: "There is an exact one-to-one correlation between *kathêkonta* and *praecepta*. That is, to every proper action there corresponds a verbalizable rule recommending that action; and vice versa. So, for instance, to the unconditional obligation to respect your parents there will correspond the precept 'Always respect your parents'; to the 'circumstantial' obligation to give away your possessions there will correspond one or more rules beginning 'Give away your possessions if . . .' "; "The Stoic-Platonist Debate on *Kathêkonta*," in Ierodiakonou, *Topics in Stoic Philosophy*, 128–152.

[75]This is the view Brennan suggests ("Reasonable Impressions," 331). On his reading, the 'type-descriptions' are "merely illustrative." Brennan does not, in this context, discuss the Stoic conception of the law. However, his interpretation challenges the more traditional view on which the examples for appropriate actions are examples for Stoic rules (e.g., 'one should honor one's parents').

not be advisable for anyone else. Similarly, honoring one's parents
can amount to very different courses of action; in an extreme case,
it might be done by cutting off one's ties to one's parents. Further,
verbs like 'neglecting' are, in themselves, loaded with ideas about
virtue. Whatever a sage does, it will never amount to an instance of
neglecting something or someone (even if she were never to see her
parents again, she would not be neglecting them).[76] In all of these
cases, the Stoic examples do not seem to prescribe or forbid types of
action—they do not actually mention types of action. (This also
means that they do not *seem* to refer to types of action, while
actually talking of tokens, as the prescriptive reason-interpretation
supposes.) Rather, they are best understood as saying that, for
example, health and our sense organs have *value*, and should be
taken into consideration accordingly when we decide what to do.

However, this might seem to reintroduce the rules-interpretation
in a new variant. The Stoic examples for appropriate action do not
translate into rules that prescribe types of action. But perhaps they
prescribe the *pursuit and avoidance of things that have value and
disvalue*? Why should we not rephrase 'it is appropriate to take
care of one's health' as 'one should pursue health'? With respect to
what Cicero calls the 'second *kathêkon*,' the Stoics do seem to speak
of pursuits and avoidances or something of this kind (trying to get
hold of something, etc.). But we should note that Cicero's account of
the earliest *kathêkonta* is part of a developmental picture. Once a
human being makes progress, the language of pursuit and avoidance
is replaced. Progressors *select* and *deselect* with respect to natural
things and their opposites, that is, things of value and disvalue. We
should thus hesitate to say that, according to the Stoics, it is appropriate to pursue health and avoid illness. Rather, it is appropriate to
act in a way that perfectly selects and deselects things of value and
disvalue. The difference is subtle, but crucial. 'Pursuit' and 'avoidance' are, in the end, terms that are too strong, given that health,
sickness, and so on are not good and bad, and we should not,
ultimately, spend our lives pursuing and avoiding things that are
merely of value and disvalue. The way the other examples are

---

[76]The examples that come closest to mentioning types of action are those relating
to what is appropriate depending on the circumstances: mutilating oneself and discarding one's property. I will discuss these examples in detail later.

phrased recognizes this difference. It is appropriate to take care of our health, our sense organs, and so on. The Stoics seem to say that our actions should adequately recognize the value of our health, intact sense organs, and so on, not that we should *pursue* these things.

If this is how the Stoics give examples for appropriate action, then they formulate neither rules that prescribe types of action nor rules that prescribe the pursuit or avoidance of indifferents. Of course, we might think that these are not all the types of rules we should consider when asking whether the Stoics envisage rules. They might formulate *formal* rules of practical reasoning. Perhaps we should say that 'do not assent hastily' might be such a rule. But whether we should describe such norms of reasoning as rules or not, it is clear that this does not go to the heart of the interpretation of the Stoic conception of the law—the question whether the law consists of laws. For the Stoic law to consist of laws, we would have to find rules that are, in a strong sense, action-guiding—rules that tell us in a contentful way what we should be doing. Within Stoic philosophy, it seems to me that the two most plausible candidates for such rules would be rules that prescribe (or permit, or prohibit) types of action and rules that prescribe pursuits and avoidances. But neither of these comparatively plausible candidates seems to be part of the Stoic picture. Let us look briefly at three possible objections to this reading.

First, Diogenes Laertius reports a distinction between *kathêkonta* that are always to be done and others that are not always to be done (7.109). Is this in conflict with our assessment of appropriate action? The one thing that is said to be *always* appropriate is living virtuously. This, of course, is not a *type of action*. Viewed extensionally, all kinds of action can be part of living virtuously. We get a seemingly more specific list in a report on perfect action: being prudent (*phronein*), being moderate (*sôphronein*), acting justly (*dikaiopagein*), being cheerful (*chairein*), doing good deeds (*euergetein*), being in a good mood (*euphrainesthai*), going for walks prudently (*phronimôs peripatein*), "and everything which is done according to right reason [*kata ton orthon logon*]" (Stobaeus 2.96,18–22 = LS 59 part). This list, however, only translates talk of virtue in the singular into talk about several virtues (being prudent, moderate, just) and those moods or affective conditions that belong to the sage's rational feelings (being cheerful, etc.). To say that it is always appropriate to live virtuously is the same thing as saying that engaging in the different virtues is correct. And any given type of action, if performed wisely, can be part of the virtuous life. Thus, the notion of *kathêkonta* that are always to be done is not in conflict with the claim that the Stoics do not envisage rules.

A second concern might be that there might be types of action that are under *no* circumstances appropriate.[77] In the report in Diogenes Laertius, some *kathêkonta* are listed as 'against the appropriate' (*para to kathêkon*): treating one's parents with disrespect, neglecting one's friends, and so on (7.108). Could there ever be an occasion where the sage does these things? Again, it is important to note that 'treating one's parents with disrespect' is not a *type of action*. Rather, it captures an attitude of not valuing one's parents' concerns, and thus not recognizing a value—the value of the concerns of those who belong to us (see section 7). We should, in *all* particular situations, take this value into account. However, this does not amount to rules that prescribe types of action. Rather, we are dealing with claims about what is of value, and what, accordingly, provides us with relevant considerations for action.

Third, recent scholarship has regarded the interpretation of two notions that are central to Seneca's *Letters* 94 and 95—*decreta* and *praecepta*—as a key starting point for assessing the role of rules in Stoic ethics. (Since Seneca discusses what he presents as an earlier debate, the letters may to some extent reflect earlier Stoic views.)[78]

---

[77]Long and Sedley (LS, 1:365) suggest, on the basis of a passage in Cicero (*De fin.* 3.32), that an action like 'showing violence to one's parents' is contrary to appropriate action, "but such an action will also betoken a morally and emotionally bad disposition, irrespective of what is done." However, it is not clear that Cicero is fully in tune with orthodox early Stoic doctrine. Cicero's examples for what is wrong are—by the choice of verbs—heavily moralized: to *steal* from temples, do *violence* to one's parents, and so on. These types of action do not fit well into early Stoic discussion. The Stoics might ask whether there could be an occasion where one should take some property from a temple, and might say that there could be such an occasion; or they might ask whether there could be an occasion where one should cut off one's mother's arm, and again say that this could be the case.

[78]Recent debates on whether Stoic ethics envisages rules have importantly been initiated by Ian Kidd, "Moral Actions and Rules in Stoicism," in *The Stoics*, ed. J. Rist (Berkeley: University of California Press, 1978), 247–258. Kidd points out that it is

If we want to know about rules in Stoic ethics, it seems, we need to understand how Seneca characterizes *decreta* and *praecepta*. Since Kidd's influential study, the terms *decreta* and *praecepta* have often been translated as 'moral principles' and 'precepts,' respectively.[79] Both moral principles and precepts may seem to be rules. Understood in this way, *decreta* and *praecepta* have been central to the rules-interpretation. Phillip Mitsis has repeatedly made a case for finding rules in Stoic ethics.[80] Mitsis proposes that, for the Stoics, "moral judgment and development are structured at every level by rules." The Stoics "are convinced that moral development depends solely on a deepening cognitive grasp of both universal and more determinate moral principles."[81] According to Mitsis, both *decreta* and *praecepta* represent rules, the former being universal, the latter more specific.[82]

Next to their abstract discussions of reason, nature, and so on, it is very likely that the early Stoics went into considerable detail on what is appropriate in what specific situation, or for agents with this

---

not easy to pin down how exactly Seneca is using these notions. But in the course of his discussion, Kidd suggests that both can be understood as some kind of rules. *Praecepta* relate to preferred things, and are, on his reading, "summary descriptive rules of the human condition"; they are precepts, and do not take all cases into account. *Decreta*, on the other hand, are "like principles or general truths," and are "more like rules of practice" (252–253).

[79]Kidd, "Moral Actions and Rules in Stoicism."

[80]The most recent article by Mitsis is "The Stoic Origin of Natural Rights," in Ierodiakonou, *Topics in Stoic Philosophy*, 153–177. See also Phillip Mitsis, "Moral Rules and the Aims of Stoic Ethics," *Journal of Philosophy* 83 (1986): 556–558, and then "Seneca on Reason, Rules and Moral Development," in Brunschwig and Nussbaum, *Passions and Perceptions*, 285–312, and with J. DeFilippo, "Socrates and Stoic Natural Law," in Vander Waerdt, *The Socratic Movement*, 252–271. For a critical discussion of Mitsis, "The Stoic Origin," see Brittain, "Rationality, Rules and Rights."

[81]Mitsis, "Seneca on Reason," 290.

[82]Mitsis also argues that the Stoics conceive of individual rights ("The Stoic Origin"). Much depends on how we understand the notion of a right. We might want to say that the conception of all human beings as 'fellow-parts' of the universe makes them something like equal agents, which might be taken to lead up to ideas that, in a loose sense, could be described in the language of rights. But, as will emerge from my discussion, I do not think we can find rights in a more determinate sense in early Stoic political philosophy.

or that role and station in life.[83] Apparently even the earliest Stoics devoted some of their writing to what we might call practical ethical teaching.[84] Accordingly, the debate on the role of rules in Stoic ethics must deal with what seem to be different theoretical endeavors: ethics properly speaking, and discussions containing advice and 'case-studies,' as well as reflection on the usefulness of such lower level ethical reasoning.[85] The Stoics seem to think that fools can benefit from philosophizing that is not only abstract and general but also invites them to think their way through a number of specific situations.

With this distinction in mind, let us turn to Seneca's *Letters* 94 and 95.[86] Seneca's topic is *not* the theory of action, or the analysis of decision-making in the sage and the progressor. *Letters* 94 and 95 ask us to envisage ordinary progressors leading a tumultuous life, distracted by the superficiality of the lifestyles they see around them. They need philosophy to help them find a better life for themselves. Seneca's question is thus whether, for such agents, *decreta* will be enough, or *praecepta* have a limited, but useful, role to play. Seneca associates the former position with Aristo, a dissenting pupil of Zeno, and the latter with Cleanthes.[87]

---

[83]See Sedley, "The Stoic-Platonist Debate." While we know titles of treatises of the early Stoics that indicate that there were whole books devoted to *kathêkonta*, we do not know much about the contents of these books. Cicero's *De officiis* might be a treatise of this kind (*officium* is Cicero's translation of *kathêkon*). If it is, then such treatises have a broad scope, discussing very general questions alongside more particular ones. Cicero's discussion is presumably indebted to an important degree to Panaetius's treatise on *kathêkonta*. Thus, we have *some* idea of Panaetius's treatment of these questions. However, it is difficult to assess how close Panaetius is to the earliest Stoics.

[84]See Sedley on Zeno, "The Stoic-Platonist Debate," 130.

[85]As Sedley points out, there can be substantial philosophical disagreement on the use of precepts as compared to the use of teaching by example, and it is likely that such disagreement ultimately depends on fundamental assumptions in philosophical psychology ("The Stoic-Platonist Debate," esp. 152).

[86]In agreement with widespread current consensus, I regard Seneca as largely orthodox. On Seneca's views about how insight into more abstract questions of philosophy (e.g., logical puzzles) matter to developing virtue, see Cooper, "Moral Theory and Moral Improvement," in Cooper, *Knowledge, Nature and the Good*, 309–334. On Seneca's discussion see also Ioppolo, *La Stoa* and *Aristone di Chio*, as well as N. White, "Nature and Regularity in Stoic Ethics," *Oxford Studies in Ancient Philosophy* 3 (1985): 289–305.

[87]We do not know to what extent Seneca constructs these positions; it may seem that Cleanthes is just a placeholder for orthodox Stoicism as Seneca sees it. For similar

But what are *decreta* and *praecepta*? In the beginning of *Letter* 95, Seneca says that *decreta* (or *scita* or *placita*) are what the Greeks call *dogmata* (95.10), philosophical doctrines (in 94.4 Seneca speaks of the *decreta ipsa philosophiae et capita*). From an overall reading of both letters, it becomes clear that *decreta* is not well translated as 'principles.' While there is a sense in which we might say that the main tenets of a theory are its principles, these are not *practical* principles. As Inwood remarks, *decreta* seem to be general physical and ethical theses of the Stoics.[88] There clearly is a strong focus on evaluative questions: everything relating to what is good and bad seems to belong to the core of *decreta* (see 95.58). But any theoretical claim can count as a *decretum*. Seneca remarks that someone who proposes that precepts are sufficient and that *decreta* are not needed is contradicting himself by uttering a *decretum* (95.60).[89] *Decreta*, it turns out, are not rule-like. When they are said to be 'general' (94.31), this does not refer to the idea of general rules. Rather, *decreta* are general because they do not take the low-level perspective of analyzing a particular situation, but the general perspective of trying to understand how things really are.

But *praecepta* might have been the more plausible candidate for Stoic rules to begin with. Let me suggest a threefold distinction with respect to Seneca's examples for *praecepta*. As we shall see, none of these kinds of precept constitutes rules of the relevant kind.

1. *Advice for particular actions.* Someone tells us how to walk, how to eat, how to behave as a husband, and so on. The advisor might tell us very specific things, for example, that this afternoon, given our provisions, the weather, our health, etc., we should eat some watermelon. Such advice surely does not qualify as the kind of rule we would need to find in Stoic ethics in order to rightly say that, for the Stoics, deliberation involves the application of rules. Rather, it tells us that the Stoics envisage persons ('advisors') who

---

remarks see Inwood, "Rules and Reasoning in Stoic Ethics," in *Topics in Stoic Philosophy*, ed. Katerina Ierodiakonou (Oxford: Oxford University Press, 2001), 113.

[88]Inwood, "Rules and Reasoning," 118.

[89]Just as any theoretical thesis can be called a *decretum*, any advice can be called a *praeceptum*. Someone who says 'do not take precepts seriously' utters a precept (95.60).

are able to come up with the appropriate course of action for a particular occasion.[90]

2. *Precepts that relate to preferred and dispreferred indifferents, that is, things of value and disvalue* (see the end of *Letter* 94 and the earlier sections of 95). If anywhere, it is here that we should find examples for Stoic rules—rules that engage with health, wealth, and so on. But Seneca's examples for precepts do not instruct us on how to remain healthy or wealthy. Rather, in line with what I have argued about the inappropriateness of *pursuing* preferred indifferents, they remind us that we should *not pursue* health, wealth, and so on. Given the world we live in, we need someone who 'whispers in our ear,' reminding us that, for example, money is not really good and will not bring happiness. The advisor thus *discourages* us in our pursuit of wealth and avoidance of poverty (or other indifferents). We are in danger of pursuing and avoiding these things as if they were good and bad. A proverb like "Wealth does not bring happiness," as Seneca suggests, appeals to our better knowledge and thus helps us, no matter how simple it is.

3. *Precepts that are formulated by a teacher, rather than an advisor.* In some passages, we get the sense that a student is confronted with *praecepta* about situations that one might be in, independently of whether one is right now in any of these situations. The idea seems to be that, if one has thought about, say, all kinds of things that are advisable for husbands and wives with different biographies, one will, as a result, be better prepared for marriage. In this case, what one would learn might be rule-like. But rules in this sense do not tell us anything about the Stoic conception of decision-making, or at least they do not tell us that decision-making would involve such rules. What these passages contribute to our understanding of Stoic thought about deliberation is showing that part of the point of such training would be *coming to see how differences matter* (e.g., coming to see that husbands should behave differently toward a wife who has

---

[90] And it seems that even with such immediate instruction, the Stoics insisted that the teacher's advice is elliptical. If, e.g., a medical doctor tells his student to cut, he implicitly means to say "in due time and with measure." If the student does not perform well in following the instruction, he can be criticized—the instruction to do this-and-that really is the instruction to do this-and-that "correctly" (Plutarch, *On Stoic Self-Contradictions* 1037E).

been married before and one who has not). At least to some extent, we are dealing with a general exercise in thinking about the relevance of differences. The rules that might be discussed would, if the students make progress, be superseded by the capacity to judge situations as they arise.[91]

7. *Appropriate Action and the Concerns of Others*

Let me turn to another question that the examples for appropriate action raise. Reason dictates that one honor one's parents, brothers, and native country, or spend time with friends. The examples may seem surprising. In section 3, we looked at the sources on what provides relevant considerations for action—things of value and disvalue, things that are natural or contrary to nature. This account makes it easy to understand why taking care of one's health is appropriate. But how do other people enter the picture? Why care for our parents or brothers or compatriots? What do they have to do with any of the things that are of value or disvalue?

In discussing appropriate action, it is tempting to think primarily of situations in which the agent weighs, for example, considerations of her health versus considerations of her wealth. And it is also tempting to think that, once the concerns of others enter the picture, then *virtue* makes demands on the agent—virtue now must be weighed against one's health and wealth, and virtue, the only good, trumps these values. This, however, is an anachronistic picture that misconstrues the early Stoic conceptions of the good and the valuable.[92] Before we return to the question how the concerns of others figure in deliberation, we must first address this point.

[91]At one point it does seem as if Seneca said: the agent who has mastered the core tenets of philosophy is able to 'form a precept' in any given situation. This, in turn, may seem to mean that this person formulates for herself a rule about what this kind of situation requires. However, this is not what Seneca says. Seneca uses the verb *praecipere* (94.3). To paraphrase Seneca in a more literal way, the knowledgeable agent is 'able to prescribe for herself' what is to be done.

[92]The anachronistic picture is related to modern ideas about the relationship between moral and nonmoral reasons, and the thesis that moral reasons trump nonmoral ones.

The sage chooses among indifferents in *each and all* of her choices. The *task* of wisdom is to choose among the things that have something to do with how one leads one's life (*quae ad vitam degendam pertinerent*); if there were no relevant differences between these things, it would not be clear what choosing means.[93] Only insofar as these things differ is there a specific task of wisdom, namely, the selection and deselection of things with value and disvalue. Perfect deliberation with respect to indifferents makes for the kind of consistency that characterizes the sage. This consistency is, in the end, the only thing that is in itself to be desired (*solum per se expetendum*) and good (*solum bonum*) (*De fin.* 5.20).

It is of key importance that the sage is not weighing indifferents versus the good.[94] She chooses consistently well with respect to indifferents, and *only* with respect to these.[95] This is brought out even more clearly by the *telos*-formulae of the second-century Stoics Antipater and Diogenes. Both define the *telos* as 'reasoning well [*eulogistein*] in the selection and deselection of the natural things.'[96] Antipater also puts forward the formula 'doing everything in one's power, constantly and unwaveringly, to obtain the preferred natural things.' While these formulae seem to be in agreement with the earlier ones, they put more emphasis on the idea that the good life is a life in which one chooses consistently well *with respect to indifferents*.[97] Wisdom and virtue do not go beyond acting in the sphere of indifferents. It is not as if the sage, once she has turned wise,

---

[93]Cicero, *De fin.* 3.50 = SVF 1.365 = LS 58I.

[94]For discussion of this reading of Stoic ethics see Barney, "A Puzzle," 330–332.

[95]The task of wisdom is not only to not care about preferred and dispreferred things as if they were good, it is also to *not* select things that do not merit the status of being preferred and dispreferred, e.g., pleasure. See Barney, "A Puzzle," 314.

[96]Note that, according to this definition, we sometimes select and sometimes deselect natural things (not: always select natural things, always deselect things contrary to nature). This seems to capture the fact that, in deliberation, we may select wealth over health, or the other way around. The formula still seems consistent with Diogenes' formula. In the end, such selection and deselection aims at obtaining preferred natural things, or those of the natural things that are more relevant to one's well-functioning as a human being. For a summary of the different versions of the Stoic *telos*-formula see Stobaeus 2.75,11 = SVF 1.179, 1.552, 3.12 = LS 63B part. See Gisela Striker, "Antipater, or the Art of Living," in Schofield and Striker, *The Norms of Nature*, 187.

[97]On the different formulae, and their basic agreement, see Striker, "Antipater."

would 'choose the good' in the sense of 'choosing the good by weighing it against the indifferent.' Rather, she *chooses* the good by selecting perfectly with respect to indifferents.[98]

The sage is ultimately oriented toward consistency, and thus toward virtue or the good. She understands how consistency or agreement (*homologia*) is the only thing that is to be desired; this insight shapes all of her decision-making (Cicero, *De fin.* 3.21–22). The valuable is the object of *selection* (*eklogê*); only the good is the object of *choice* (*hairesis*).[99] The term 'choice' thus describes the way the sage relates to the good. But as the object of choice in this technical sense, the good is not on the same level as the indifferents. The sage does not choose the good by deciding *against* some indifferents. Rather, she chooses the good by selecting perfectly among indifferents.

But if the concerns of others do not enter deliberation through the demands of virtue, how then are they relevant? How do indifferents insofar as they pertain to *others* (e.g., the lives, health, wealth, and so on of others) enter the picture? In chapter 3 I argued that the political philosophy of the early Stoics does not rely on an account of just interaction with others, or a theory of what we owe to others. Rather, I argued, it relies on an argument about how all human beings *belong together* in the strong sense of being parts of a large living being, the cosmos. We can now add to this picture by considering how the Stoic theory of values and disvalues is connected to *oikeiôsis*: the things that have value are an extension of those things that nature initially instructs us to seek out.

Nature guides us to lead a natural life, in which we ourselves must learn how to follow nature's instruction and how to further develop the first impulses nature supplies, so as to ideally lead a life in agreement with nature. Our own health, wealth, and so on relate

---

[98]I develop these points in greater detail in Vogt, "Die frühe stoische Theorie des Werts," in *Abwägende Vernunft*, ed. Ch. Schröer and F.-J. Bormann (Berlin: de Gruyter, 2004). For a detailed discussion of the different ways scholars have interpreted the relationship of value and the good see Tad Brennan, *The Stoic Life: Emotions, Duties, and Fate* (Oxford: Oxford University Press, 2005).

[99]Stobaeus 2.75,1–6, 2.78,7–12, 2.79,15–17. The same distinction is reported by Cicero in terms of what is to be selected (*seligendum*), and what one is to strive for (*expetendum*) (*De fin.* 3.22). Similarly, Epictetus explains that the soul has a natural desire (*orexis*) for the good (*Discourses* 3.3.2–4).

back to the first impulse of self-preservation, which helps us to avert harm and secure what we need to survive. The Stoics directly connect the first impulse of self-preservation with another, equally fundamental impulse: endearment to our offspring.[100] Obviously, the point of this thesis cannot be that, when we are born, the first impulse we have is to be endeared to our offspring. No one has offspring when just born. If affection for one's offspring has the same 'natural' status as the first impulses of self-preservation, it seems that what nature equips us with is something that stays with us, as a piece of the soul's primary equipment.[101] And it seems highly likely that, in a newborn child, the corresponding impulses must be directed toward those who care for it and on whom it depends for its preservation (even if they are in relevant ways different from the endearment that parents have for their offspring). Part of the point must be that regarding one's closest relatives as belonging to oneself is as basic a human impulse as self-preservation, and one that is acquired through nature. Nature equips us with *two* first tendencies in action, and we cannot make sense of the sources if we do not assume that *extensions* of these two tendencies provide relevant considerations for deliberation.

And we can see how this would play out. Those one is closest to are regarded, through the direction of nature, as 'belonging to one.' Since they belong to us, their concerns are relevant considerations for us. This is exactly parallel to why our health provides a relevant consideration. The impulse of self-preservation is also about endearment— about becoming endeared to one's body with all its functions and capacities, so that, as a result of this endearment, one does not want there to be any impediment to them. Health, life, wealth, strength, and so on have value because they help us keep up these functions and capacities. Most generally put: whenever we regard something (our body, our brothers, etc.) as 'belonging to us,' we take whatever it is that sustains it or is an impediment to it as relevant considerations for our deliberation. If this is so, we can see why, for example, 'honoring our parents' is dictated by reason, just as much as 'taking care of one's health.'

---

[100]Plutarch, *On Stoic Self-Contradictions* 1038B, Cicero, *De fin.* 3.62. My views on these issues are much indebted to Gisela Striker, "Following Nature," in *Papers*, 221–280, esp. 248–261, and Brunschwig, "The Cradle Argument."

[101]Cf. Brunschwig, "The Cradle Argument," 113–144.

According to this picture, health and wealth and life, etc., provide relevant considerations for action, but not only our own health, wealth, life. When we say that values and disvalues provide considerations for action, this must be a shorthand for saying that the health and wealth and life, etc., of *those who belong to us* are relevant to our actions. But why is it appropriate to take care of brothers, parents, compatriots? Should it not rather be appropriate to concern ourselves with *all other human beings*? In later Stoic thought, first and foremost in Epictetus, we find the suggestion that we can think about this question along the following lines.[102] Caring for one's parents is *appropriate* because we are, in addition to being a part of the world, located at a specific place in it, a place that imparts something like 'special obligations,' relative to our roles as parents, siblings, and so on. Strictly speaking, we are to consider the concerns of all those who belong to us as our concerns, and all human beings belong to us. But the way this is best done may involve much interaction that responds to the roles we happen to have in our particular lives. We are, like all other human beings, a part of the world, but we are a *particular* part in it, with a particular location. It is not the case that we should take care of our parents, *rather than* considering the lives, health, and so on of all human beings. The way we are to concern ourselves with all human beings involves taking care of those we are connected to by the various roles we have in our lives. These remarks must remain tentative. We have too little testimony on early Stoic thought about these issues. It seems clear enough, however, that the early Stoics endorse both ideas—that all others belong to us, and that we should take care of those who are, in the conventional sense, related to us.

8. *A Hierarchy of Values?*

The *substantive* side of Stoic law is thus captured in the Stoic theory of value, but not through a canon of laws. In this and the next section I shall consider two further objections against this interpretation:

---

[102]Epictetus discusses how someone is first and foremost a human being, second a citizen of the world, and then third a son, fourth a brother, fifth, perhaps, a town administrator; one is old or young, a father or not a father, and so on (*Discourses* 2.10.1–12 = LS 59Q). Cicero discusses similar questions in *De officiis* (see 1.16–18; 1.30).

first, the idea that there might be a fixed hierarchy of values, and second, the idea that the Stoic notion of *circumstances* may imply that the Stoics conceive of a canon of rules or laws. I begin with the question whether the Stoics envisage a fixed hierarchy of values. Such a hierarchy might not account for rules that prescribe types of action or pursuits.[103] But it might suggest that there are rules of a different kind—rules of preference such as 'prefer life over health.'

The Stoics talk of things having *more* or *less* value or disvalue, and this may seem to indicate that they rank values. But the fact that value is a comparative notion does not amount to a fixed ranking of values. A well-known report that indicates that there are degrees of value discusses something like a *threshold* that needs to be met for something to count as valuable or disvaluable: there are some things that are of value, but not enough value to fall into the category of being preferred, and again some that are of disvalue, but not enough disvalue to fall into the category of being dispreferred. Only what has *much* value is preferred; only what has *much* disvalue is dispreferred.[104] All things in accordance with nature have value, are 'to-be-taken,' and are preferred; all things contrary to nature have disvalue, are 'not-to-be-taken,' and are dispreferred.[105] Value and disvalue thus are comparative notions, insofar as some things of value (or disvalue) do not reach the threshold of being relevant to one's life in agreement with nature.[106] But this does not introduce a hierarchy among values and disvalues themselves.

---

[103]If we do not allow for the arguments I have presented against these two types of rules, a hierarchy of values might be taken to speak in favor of a version of the rules-interpretation that Striker briefly considers. In an oral reply to a presentation of her article "Origins of the Concept of the Natural Law," Inwood raised the point that, if we conceive of the Stoic law as consisting of laws, then these laws must be such as to allow for exceptions. In a concluding note to the published article (219–220), Striker responds that cases that look like exceptions to rules might be explained as conflicts of rules, in which the higher order rule prevails. This kind of hierarchy of rules, it seems, might be explicable in terms of a hierarchy of values.

[104]Stobaeus 2.82,20–1; 2.83,10–85,11.

[105]See also the less detailed reports in Diogenes Laertius (7.105, 106). These reports say that everything of value and disvalue is to be preferred and to be dispreferred.

[106]For a different reading of these passages see Gretchen Reydams-Schils, "Human Bonding and *oikeiôsis* in Roman Stoicism," *Oxford Studies in Ancient Philosophy* 22 (2002): 221–251, 229–230.

And this seems only plausible. We can see this by asking at what level of generality or particularity indifferents play a role in deliberation. Does the agent weigh, for example, health against wealth? This only appears to be the case when we describe cases in abbreviated ways. If we spell them out, then the agent does not consider health, but rather, for example, the danger of catching a cold; she does not weigh wealth, but, for example, the danger of losing her home. If this is how health, wealth, and so on enter deliberation, it is easy to see that a fixed hierarchy of values does not make sense. On some occasion, it might be appropriate to risk catching a cold, if, by doing so, for example, one can save the roof of one's house from collapsing under an unusual amount of snow. And if one indeed catches a cold while shoveling the snow from one's roof, it might be appropriate to invest in cold medication. Deliberation does not engage with health and wealth in general, but with specific matters of health, wealth, and so on.

However, some kind of ranking may seem to be implicit in these examples. Catching a cold is, to most people, a relatively minor matter, and having the roof of one's house collapse under the weight of snow is, to most people, a major incident. How do we make these judgments about what counts as minor and major concerns? Do not these evaluations, ultimately, rely on a hierarchy of values, a hierarchy that ranks, for example, mental illnesses, chronic illnesses, illnesses of a brief nature from which one fully recovers, and so on?[107] However, even with respect to such a fine-grained ranking, the same kind of considerations applies. Suppose we think that our cognitive faculties have more value than our bodily health. Again, it seems that, in particular situations, an agent does not weigh her cognitive faculties in general against her bodily health in general. Faced with the question whether she wants to lose her memory or have a cold, she should most probably choose the latter. If, on the

---

[107]A report in Stobaeus may seem to suggest a fine-grained ranking of this kind, but insofar as it does, I think it is misleading. According to this report, there are mental preferred things, bodily preferred things, and external preferred things. Mental preferred indifferents have more value than bodily ones and external ones (Stobaeus 2.80,22–82,4 = SVF 3.136). However, the threefold distinction is suspicious—it accords too well with traditional distinctions between goods of the soul (internal goods), goods of the body, and external goods. This distinction is not fundamental to Stoic philosophy.

other hand, she can have heart surgery only if she agrees to a kind of anesthesia that robs her of her cognitive faculties for a few hours, taking the anesthesia will probably be the appropriate course of action.

Rather than rely on a fixed ranking of values, such considerations seem to rely on (1) assumptions about facts, and (2) a *standard* against which to measure the importance of indifferents on each given occasion. The assumptions about facts concern the constitution of human beings, what affects them in what way, what kinds of remedies are available, and so on. The standard is, I submit, a 'natural life,' or the *ability to function well as a human being* (in the sense of living a characteristically *human* life, a life in which the physical and cognitive capacities human beings typically have are employed for a variety of activities), considered under the specific circumstances in which a particular human being lives. When a sage is weighing the danger of catching a cold versus the danger of losing her house, she is weighing the indifferents that are involved against the standard of her well-functioning as a human being, on the basis of her understanding of how human beings function, or, in the spirit of Chrysippus's *telos*-formula, on her understanding of human nature and nature as a whole. (And perhaps we should add: on the basis of her own place in the community; e.g., for someone with profession A, it is appropriate to ascribe more importance to her right arm than her right leg, while for someone with profession B, the reverse is true.)

Consider the example of suicide. One of the reasons the sage might commit suicide in a well-reasoned way (*eulogôs*) is incurable illness (DL 7.130).[108] When weighing illness and life, the sage does not consider in the abstract whether the value of life is greater than the disvalue of illness. Rather, he thinks about two indifferents with a view to *his* 'well-functioning' (see Cicero, *De fin.* 3.60–61). If the sage's health is in such a terrible state that it keeps him from functioning well as a human being, he will end his life. This kind of

---

[108]Cooper proposes an analysis of the Stoic claim that the sage may commit suicide that is very much in agreement with my reconstruction of the Stoic theory; "Greek Philosophers on Euthanasia and Suicide," in his *Reason and Emotion: Essays on Ancient Moral Psychology and Ethical Theory* (Princeton, N.J.: Princeton University Press, 1999), 515–541.

decision would not be explicable if life were in general to be ranked higher than health. The appropriate action is the action that sustains or recovers the natural things needed for functioning in the highest degree; if there is no appropriate action that can sustain his functioning well, and if there is a preponderance of things contrary to nature in the sage's life (3.60–61), it is appropriate for him to commit suicide. Neither health nor life has more value; the sage considers how both relate in a specific situation *to his well-functioning*.

9. *Appropriate Action and Circumstances*

Finally, let me turn to a last intuition that, to many scholars, seems to speak, in one way or another, in favor of the rules-interpretation: the fact that, apparently, the Stoics discuss *exceptions*. If there are exceptions, it seems, these exceptions must be exceptions to rules.

The interpretation I have presented up to this point is, in many ways, close to Inwood's views.[109] However, I have been assuming that there is a constraint of the following kind on our reading of the Stoic theory: not every kind of rule can count as a rule that is part of the common law; the only such rules are those the sage adheres to (or applies in deliberation). Since Inwood does not start out from this constraint, a different kind of rule can, on his view, count as relevant. Inwood argues that the Stoics conceive of defeasible, general rules, and these are "constraining rules" or "generally stable guidelines for ordinary decision-makers"; sages can set aside rules.[110] The presence of rules is, on this view, supposed to be fully compatible with the need for considering all features of a particular situation when deciding how to act.[111]

---

[109]Inwood, "Rules and Reasoning."

[110]Inwood, "Rules and Reasoning," 108. Inwood also refers to non-universal generalizations as defeasible rules of thumb (107).

[111]My views on these issues are much indebted to Inwood's work. See also several of Inwood's articles in *Reading Seneca: Stoic Philosophy at Rome* (Oxford: Oxford University Press, 2005), esp. "Natural Law in Seneca" (224–248), "God and Human Knowledge in Seneca's *Natural Questions*" (157–200), and "Moral Judgement in Seneca" (201–223). In the latter two articles, Inwood discusses questions relating to epistemic modesty (to how one should be aware of the fallibility of one's judgments, etc.). My brief discussion of this idea (not with respect to Seneca, however) is influenced by Inwood's views.

More particularly, Inwood invokes two kinds of *exceptions*. First, we might think that the sage is an exception; rules apply to everyone *but the sage*. Second, rules might be defeasible insofar as they do not apply to *exceptional circumstances*; even for ordinary decision-makers, rules are merely 'generally stable guidelines.' If the Stoics conceive of such exceptions, then it might seem that we should reconsider the question whether they formulate rules that prescribe types of actions. Quite generally, if we found any evidence for *exceptions*, this would indicate that there must be a rule with respect to which these exceptions are formulated. We should further note that both ideas about exceptions matter to the interpretation of the disturbing theses. It may seem that some scandalous acts like incest are permissible for the sage, and for no one else. Or, it may seem that these acts are to be done under the stress of *exceptional* circumstances. The disturbing theses, on this account, present exceptions to rules.

First, let us turn to the idea that the sage is an exception. As Inwood remarks, the idea that Stoic ethics falls into two parts, one part discussing the sage, the other the lives of fools, has been shown to be deeply flawed.[112] The point I am adopting from Inwood's discussions is more subtle. We might think that only someone who knows herself to be perfectly reasonable should *trust* her own judgment to the extent that she decides, for example, to commit suicide. As long as one is not a sage, one should be aware that one's selection of indifferents is likely to be flawed, and one should thus abstain from such grave measures as taking one's own life. Similarly, one should rather hold on to a general prohibition of anthropophagy, and not trust one's judgment that this is the time to eat one's arm.[113] The sage, who is able to weigh all indifferents perfectly, does not need rules. The ordinary progressor, however, is safer is she sticks to them.

Inwood's point about epistemological modesty seems important. The task of deliberation extends to being aware that, if one is not a sage, one might, for example, be unduly given to grief and the violence of one's emotions might cloud one's judgment. Being aware of this kind of distortion might lead one to reassess one's evaluations, or to hesitate in trusting one's own judgment on what is

[112]"Rules and Reasoning," 95 and 99.
[113]"Rules and Reasoning," 100.

to be done. One might draw the conclusion that, given that one is in such miserable shape, it is best to trust someone else's judgment and to adopt the advice of a person one generally trusts. Similarly, one might stick to a precept, suspecting that, at this point, it is better to rely on a general precept than on one's own judgment. However, insofar as the progressor aims to become virtuous, she must model her deliberation on that of the sage. From this point of view, the most important task is to calm down. More generally speaking, she should try to acquire a disposition that enables her to perfectly assess all relevant features of a given situation so as to perfectly select and deselect indifferents. Rules, as far as they figure in the progressor's life, do not figure in it insofar as the progressor strives to be like the sage. But for the interpretation of the Stoic conception of the law, this is what matters. Only rules that are relevant to perfect deliberation could be rules of which the law consists.

Even though the early Stoics specifically discuss the sage's suicide, they do not seem to prohibit suicide for progressors.[114] They could plausibly warn progressors not to trust their hasty judgment. But the task of acquiring virtue is to try and decide as one ideally should, even if this means that one might fail. Similarly, the Stoic claim about eating amputated limbs, if we interpret it as I suggested in chapter 1, instructs *ordinary progressors* to not be held back in their assessment of all relevant features of a situation by conventional or even superstitious beliefs.

But what about the assumption that the Stoics distinguish between standard and exceptional circumstances? This assumption (and here I am not referring to Inwood's discussion) brings us back to the examples for appropriate action:

Of activities in accordance with impulse [i.e., all actions in the full sense, set off by impulse], some are appropriate, others are

---

[114]Charles Brittain makes this point in his discussion of Inwood's article in "Rationality, Rules and Rights," 255–256. As Brittain argues, the texts on suicide focus on the sage because they engage with the striking idea that suicide may be appropriate for the sage even though he is, as a sage, happy (fools being miserable) (Cicero, *De fin.* 3.60–1; Plutarch, *On Stoic Self-Contradictions* 1042C–D, and *On Common Notions* 1063C–1064C).

inappropriate [*para to kathêkon*], and others belong to neither type. Appropriate [*kathêkonta*] are ones which reason dictates [*logos hairei*] doing, such as honoring parents, brothers and country, spending time with friends; inappropriate are ones which reason does not dictate doing, such as neglecting parents, not caring about brothers, not treating friends sympathetically, not acting patriotically and so on. Neither appropriate nor inappropriate is what reason neither dictates doing nor forbids, such as picking up a twig, holding a pen or a scraper, and such like. Some appropriate [activities] do not depend on circumstances [*kathêkonta aneu peristaseôs*], and others depend on circumstances [*ta de peristatika*]. The following do not depend on circumstances [*aneu peristaseôs*], looking after one's health, and one's sense organs, and such like. Appropriate [activities] which do depend on circumstances [*kata peristasin*] are mutilating oneself and disposing of one's property. And so analogously with what is inappropriate. (DL 7.108–109 = SVF 3.495, 496 = LS 59E)[115]

The distinction between *peristatika* and actions that are appropriate *aneu peristaseôs* has often been interpreted as if it proposed a distinction between *exceptional* and *standard* circumstances. Some actions are *generally* to be done, but *exceptional* circumstances occasion exceptions to these rules. Things that are usually of value and disvalue are not so under exceptional circumstances, and therefore other courses of action are appropriate. We can pursue this line of thought in two ways, but both of them seem to me unpersuasive.[116] (1) If the good is at stake, indifferents 'switch' from being valuable or disvaluable to being strictly indifferent. The good trumps the valuable by annihilating the fact that the valuable is preferred. (2) In *exceptional* circumstances, what is usually

[115]Translation LS with changes. In translating *kathêkonta*, we need to supply 'activities' or 'actions.' I am supplying 'activities,' the term used in the beginning of the report.

[116]To some extent, I am constructing these views. The distinction between standard and exceptional circumstances has been an influential assumption in the interpretation of the disturbing theses; see Dirk Obbink, "The Stoic Sage in the Cosmic City," in *Topics in Stoic Philosophy*, ed. Katerina Ierodiakonou (Oxford: Oxford University Press, 2001), 178–195. Inwood ("Rules and Reasoning"), too, uses the notion of 'special circumstances.' View (1) is implicit in much of the older literature on Stoics ethics, and is discussed in detail by Tad Brennan (*The Stoic Life*, 182); see also Barney, "A Puzzle," 330; (2) is a further theoretical option we might explore.

valuable switches to being disvaluable.[117] On this reading, what is in accordance with nature, and therefore has value, is determined by the circumstances.[118] For example, having one's limbs intact is only valuable if, in a given situation, it actually promotes the proper functioning of a human being.

According to both (1) and (2), circumstances affect the value or disvalue of the things that are at stake in a given occasion. In order to see that (1) is implausible, we need to remind ourselves that wisdom consists in choosing among indifferents, *not* in weighing the good against the indifferent. The Stoics do not discuss cases where, for example, health would switch from being preferred to being strictly indifferent (in the sense of irrelevant to action) because, in a given situation, virtue is at stake. Virtue *is* choosing consistently correctly among indifferents, not a separate consideration that could be weighed against indifferents. Thus the presumed switch from (dis)preferred indifferent to strictly indifferent does not take place. In order to see that (2) is implausible, we need to go back to the testimony on what is in accordance with nature or naturally choice-worthy, and what is contrary to nature. At no point do we hear that natural things can, at times, be against nature. Similarly, it is at no point implied or suggested that what has value might turn into something of disvalue. We thus need an interpretation of the distinction between *peristatika* and what is appropriate *aneu*

---

[117]As I hope to argue in more detail in "The Good Is Benefit," the idea that the Stoics conceive of such a switch partly derives from a confusing section in Diogenes Laertius (7.103). After reporting the distinction between good, bad, and indifferents, the text goes on to explain that indifferents (1) no more benefit than harm, and (2) can be used in a good and a bad way. These additions recall passages in Plato's dialogues, and have been interpreted as part of the Stoic engagement with Socrates. However, neither (1) nor (2) is, as it stands, consistent with the Stoic theory (at least not if 'no more' is not interpreted as 'neither'). Strictly speaking, indifferents bring neither benefit nor harm, and the Stoics do not employ a notion of correct or good *use*. As long as we take these remarks in Diogenes Laertius as central to the doctrine, it seems that indifferents can have different value (can 'switch' from having value to having disvalue).

[118]Sedley ("The Stoic-Platonist Debate," 132) proposes that one should, e.g., care for one's health as a general policy, "not as a response to this or that particular circumstance. On the other hand, mutilating yourself, giving away your possessions, and so on, are 'circumstantial'... even they have natural value, but only as a response to very special circumstances."

peristaseôs that takes into account the fact that the valuable and disvaluable *remain* valuable and disvaluable, independently of the circumstances, and independently of what is to be done. (And this seems only plausible: why should we, for example, not continue to value health even if we decide on a course of action that involves the risk of catching a cold?)

Both readings (1) and (2) stipulate that what is appropriate *depending on* the circumstances is appropriate *depending on exceptional* circumstances. They also stipulate that what is 'independent of the circumstances' depends on *standard* circumstances. But this is not what the text says. The Stoics do not distinguish between what is appropriate in *standard* circumstances as compared to what is appropriate under *exceptional* circumstances. Rather, they distinguish between appropriate actions that depend on the circumstances and those that *do not*. It is not surprising that scholars have had difficulty taking this literally; it does not seem to fit at all with the Stoic theory of action. There it seems that *all* deliberation must take the circumstances into account—this is quite obvious from the Stoic account of the sage's assent to impressions. Correct action involves assent to impressions that fully present the situation as it is. It thus seems that there just *cannot* be a category of what is appropriate *independently of the circumstances*. It is thus tempting to think of the distinction as one between *standard* and *exceptional* circumstances. But this is not what the text says.

We can arrive at a clearer picture by considering that the term *kathêkonta* is used in a twofold way. At some points, it is used to refer to particular actions. In a given situation, a particular action seems appropriate to us. But as we saw, the term also occurs in Stoic claims that are best interpreted as saying what we should consider to be of value (e.g., 'it is appropriate to take care of one's health'). As I suggest, the difficult distinction between what is appropriate depending on and independently of the circumstances implicitly relies on this twofold use of *kathêkonta*. The examples for noncircumstantial *kathêkonta* are activities like taking care of one's health. The examples for circumstantial *kathêkonta* are on a much more particular level (e.g., to mutilate oneself). And it is clear that they must ultimately be on the most particular level, i.e., that of an individual action: it is only appropriate to mutilate oneself in such-and-such a case, not generally.

Thus I would suggest that certain *kathêkonta* are *independent* of the circumstances, insofar as one should, in each deliberation, assign value to things of value and disvalue to things of disvalue. That some things are valuable and others disvaluable to human beings is a fact of nature. Insofar as we can consider values and disvalues under a perspective that does not engage with any particular situations, we can speak of *kathêkonta* that are independent of the circumstances. As long as we think about preserving our health or life independently of specific circumstances, it is clear that these things are appropriate. The distinction between *peristatika* and things that are *aneu peristaseôs* takes care of a question that might be posed to the Stoics at this point of their theory. What about, one might ask, the actions that, if we consider them in the abstract, seem to be *inappropriate* (because they, for example, endanger our health), but that are, according to you, the Stoics, nevertheless sometimes appropriate? And now the Stoic can reply: these are 'appropriates depending on the circumstances,' *peristatika*. *Peristatika* are actions we can only describe as appropriate when we think of specific circumstances. Absent such a context, we would say that there is a relevant consideration *against doing them*. It is in this limited sense that only some, not all, particular actions are appropriate depending on the circumstances.

Let us consider an example. Suppose a mountain climber has an accident in which her arm gets stuck between two rocks. She waits for a few days, hoping that help will arrive. However, no help arrives, and she faces a choice between dying and cutting her arm off with her knife. She decides to do the latter (i.e., to mutilate herself), climbs back down, recovers, and a year later is back climbing in the mountains, with only one arm.[119] According to the Stoic analysis, it is not the case that 'having all one's limbs intact' stops being of value in such a situation. The climber does not think that her arm has no value or even disvalue. However, she thinks that, with only one arm, she will still be able to lead a human life in which she functions in the most relevant respects. Taking care of one's health (or of 'having all one's limbs intact') is appropriate independently of

---

[119]A similar case has been reported in the media. Of course, I am not claiming to know anything about the reasoning of the actual climber who acted in this way, and who is supposedly indeed back climbing in the mountains.

the circumstances: at no time during her deliberation and during her climbing back down, seeking medical help once she is back, and so on does the climber stop to consider her health as being of value. Cutting off her arm is appropriate depending on the circumstances. Only because of the circumstances in which she finds herself is it appropriate to cut off her arm.

Now it might seem that, in the end, my reconstruction of the Stoic theory is not so different from the interpretation I argue against. Is not the climber's accident a quite *exceptional* situation? What is the difference between claiming that cutting off her arm is appropriate depending on the circumstances (as I do) and claiming that it is only appropriate in *exceptional* circumstances? The difference becomes most relevant once we connect this discussion to the question whether the law consists of laws (or rules). The point of the Stoic distinction between things that are appropriate depending on and independent of the circumstances is *not* a distinction between standard and exceptional circumstances. The distinction thus does not lend itself to the reasoning that, if there are exceptions, there must be rules. The point of the distinction is that the things that appropriate action deals with (health, wealth, etc.) have *value* or *disvalue* independently of the circumstances, and that we can only explain why it is sometimes appropriate to put one's health or property at risk if we consider a specific case, with specific circumstances.

10. The Common Law

While the Stoic law is 'by nature,' the epithet the early Stoics choose for the law is not 'natural,' but rather 'common' (*koinos*).[120] Let me sum up my discussion by commenting on the way the law

---

[120]We find the term 'common law' as early as in Zeno's *Republic*—human beings should live one kind of life and in accord with one order, like a herd nourished by the *common law*. Plutarch, *On the Fortune of Alexander* 329A–B = SVF 1.262 part = LS 67A. For detailed discussion of this passage, see chapter 2. In his *Hymn to Zeus*, Cleanthes takes up the notion of a common law. He speaks of *god's* common law and about the righteousness (*dikē*) of praising the common law. Cleanthes characterizes both law *and reason* as *koinos*, shared. Stobaeus, 1.25,3–27,4 = SVF 1.537 = LS 54I.

is common—this characterization relates to and further illuminates the Stoic conception of the cosmic city, the way the world has reason, and the way the law lays out a substantive guide for human life without consisting of rules.

The law, which is identified with reason, 'divides itself up' insofar as it is a physical entity with parts: it spreads out among the souls of all perfectly reasonable beings—the cosmos, the gods, the sages. But it is not only common to those whose perfect souls are, as it were, portions of it. The common law is also common to all human beings. The rudimentary correlate to law that every rational being possesses is part of what makes up one's rationality. It constitutes a community among all, and lays out one way of life for all. As *rational* beings, all human beings are connected by what is, for them, natural and contrary to nature, and thus by what provides them with relevant considerations for action. This means that essentially *one way of life*, the life according to nature, is a bond between human beings. For all human beings, there is a community that consists in sharing one way in which the good life can be accomplished—by selecting correctly among things of value and disvalue.

Law is a substantive guide on how to select indifferents. Indifferents are *relevant to action* and provide us with *considerations for deliberation*. They have value *for the agent*, but not in a narrow sense. Everything that 'belongs to the agent' counts as what concerns the agent. And ultimately, all other human beings belong to the agent. The concerns of other human beings thus provide considerations that are relevant to whether the actions of an agent are appropriate. In many instances of deliberation (witness the climber, or suicide), all or most relevant considerations will relate to how the agent *herself* can lead a life that agrees with nature. But in other instances, the fact that other human beings belong to us makes it the case that the ways *they* are affected by things of value and disvalue are relevant considerations. To regard all human beings as fellow-inhabitants of the cosmos is a way of regarding them as 'belonging to us.' Regarding them in this way involves, as far as I can see, two things: (1) understanding that their concerns matter to us, and (2) understanding that they are faced with the same task as we are, leading a life in agreement with nature. The way nature sets us and them on the right track for pursuing this task makes it the case that all human beings share 'one way of life.'

Let me connect these ideas about the substantive nature of law and reason to the way both law and reason are prescriptive. If an ordinary progressor decides to do something, her reason issues a command for her. Each agent's reason has a law-like quality for her, insofar as the agent (understood as her rational soul) issues commands that set off her actions.[121] In this sense, *her* reason is *her* law, insofar as it tells her what to do. But this is not the technical, Stoic sense of 'law.' While every agent's reason is prescriptive for her through the very structure of how human beings set themselves into motion, one's reason can, in issuing commands, go wrong, while the law does not.

If the action an agent prescribes to herself is appropriate, it is prescribed by reason in the following sense: the activity that the agent decides on could be justified by right reason. The action is prescribed by the very way things are. That reason can defend something means that the indifferents involved in a given situation pertain to the agent's life in such a way as to justify her action. In this sense, the actions of inferiors, if they are appropriate, are dictated not only by their own reason but by perfect reason as well. In these appropriate actions, the agent's particular decision (but not the overall state of her soul) is in tune with what perfect reason—to be thought of either as the reason of a sage, or a god, or the cosmos—dictates.

The most straightforward identity of law and reason is to be found in beings that have perfect reason—sages, gods, the cosmos. Every decision of the sage issues a command of what is *in fact* to be done. Since the sage's reason is fully in agreement with the perfect reason of the cosmos, her reason can issue a command that truly *is law*. The rational soul of the sage is not inferior to that of god with respect to virtue or wisdom; what it issues is in full agreement with reason as it regulates the cosmos. Similarly, we can think of the celestial bodies as moving rationally in the sense that, since their movement is directed by their fully rational souls, it is exactly as it ought to be, completely integrated with the movements of the cosmos as a whole. This is what *homonoia* is: the full like-mindedness of those who are wise. Insofar as the soul of the cosmos is the source of the movements of the cosmos, it determines everything in the

---

[121]See Cooper, "Stoic Autonomy," on how the Stoic notion of *autopragia* is related to the idea of self-legislation.

cosmos. And while this determination is, in a way, simply the fact that the cosmos as a living being moves itself, we can think of it as 'regulation,' and thus, as law. It is, on another level of Stoic description, Zeus and his thoughts that move everything in the cosmos, and since Zeus is equated with reason, we may also think of the law as Zeus's law.

But while the law is Zeus's law, the commands it issues must be issued by each individual's reason. The way one 'obeys' Zeus's law is not by coming to see what something external to oneself tells one to do. Zeus's law is not a law-code, given with divine authority. The way one enables oneself to be guided by Zeus's law is to become perfectly reasonable. Becoming perfectly reasonable can be described in terms of the extent of the knowledge that perfect reason involves, and the corresponding overall condition of a soul that is fully consistent. Perfect reason is not being able to perfectly apply some formal principles of reasoning. Of course, there are characteristics of perfect reasoning that have nothing to do with any specific content—to not assent hastily, to only assent to cognitive impressions, and so on. But to be able to live by the law is to understand nature fully, to acquire a substantive body of knowledge that will constitute the perfect disposition of one's soul. And this is different from obeying a law that is external to oneself, or adhering to formal principles of reasoning. The knowledge of understanding nature will both make up the state of one's own soul and be the disposition from which one assents and acts. The task of wisdom is to become perfectly reasonable in a substantive sense—to fully understand nature.

Bibliography

Editions of Primary Texts

Note: Abbreviations (shown in brackets in the entries) are used throughout to cite the following editions: Diogenes Laertius, *Lives of the Eminent Philosophers*: DL; H. Diehls and W. Kranz, *Die Fragmente der Vorsokrater*: DK; Sextus Empiricus, *Outlines of Scepticism*: SE PH, *Against the Mathematicians*: SE M; A. A. Long and D. N. Sedley, *The Hellenistic Philosophers*: LS; Johannes von Arnim, *Stoicorum Veterum Fragmenta*: SVF.

Aristotle. *The Complete Works of Aristotle*. Edited by Jonathan Barnes. 2 vols. Princeton, N.J.: Princeton University Press, 1984.

——. *The Works of Aristotle*. Edited by Sir David Ross. The Oxford Aristotle. 12 vols. Oxford: Oxford University Press, 1908–52.

Cicero. *Rhetorica, De fato, Paradoxa Stoicorum, De partitione oratoria*. Text with English translation by H. Rackham. Loeb Classical Library. Cambridge, Mass.: Harvard University Press, 1942.

——. *De finibus bonorum et malorum*. Text with English translation by H. Rackham. Loeb Classical Library. Cambridge, Mass.: Harvard University Press, 1931.

——. *De legibus*. Text with English translation by C. W. Keyes. Loeb Classical Library. Cambridge, Mass.: Harvard University Press, 1928.

——. *De natura deorum and Academica*. Text with English translation by H. Rackham. Loeb Classical Library. Cambridge, Mass.: Harvard University Press, 1933.

——. *De officiis*. Text with English translation by W. Miller. Loeb Classical Library. Cambridge, Mass.: Harvard University Press, 1913.

Diogenes Laertius. *Lives of the Eminent Philosophers*. Translated by R. D. Hicks. Vols. 1 and 2. Loeb Classical Library. Cambridge, Mass.: Harvard University Press, 1991 [DL].

Diogene Laerzio. *Vite dei Filosofi*. Translated and edited by Marcello Gigante. Bari: Laterza, 1987.

Philodemus. *On Methods of Inference*. Edited with translation and commentary by P. and E. De Lacy. Naples: Bibliopolis, 1978, 2nd ed.

Philodemus. *On Piety*. Critical text with commentary, edited by D. Obbink. Oxford: Oxford University Press, 1996.

——— . *Philodemi volumina rhetorica*. Vol. 2. Edited by S. Sudhaus. Leipzig: Teubner, 1896.

——— . "Filodemo. Gli Stoici (*PHerc*. 155 e 339)." Edited by T. Dorandi. *Cronache Ercolanesi* 12 (1982): 91–133.

Plato. *Complete Works*. Edited by John M. Cooper. Indianapolis: Hackett, 1997.

——— . *Platonis Opera*. Edited by John Burnet. 5 vols. Oxford: Clarendon Press, 1900–1907.

——— . *Platon Werke: Übersetzung und Kommentar*. Vol. 5, *Lysis*. Translation and commentary by Michael Bordt. Göttingen: Vandenhoeck und Ruprecht, 1998.

Plutarch. *On Stoic Self-Contradictions and On Common Conceptions*. In *Moralia, vol.* 13, pt. 2. Translated by H. Cherniss. Cambridge, Mass.: Harvard University Press, 1976.

[Annaeus] Seneca. *Moral and Political Essays*. Edited and translated by John M. Cooper and J. F. Procopé. Cambridge: Cambridge University Press, 1995.

——— . *Philosophische Schriften*. Vol. 1. Dialogues 1–6. Translated with an introduction and notes by Manfred Rosenbach. Darmstadt: Reclam, 1989.

Sextus Empiricus. *Sesto Empirico: Contro gli Etici*. Edited and translated by Emidio Spinelli. Napoli: Bibliopolis 1995.

——— . *Sextus Empiricus*. Translated by R. G. Bury [SE]. Vol. 1 [PH 1–3] (1933); vol. 2 [M 7, 8] (1935); vol. 3 [M 9–11] (1936); vol. 4 [M 1–6] (1949). Loeb Classical Library. Cambridge, Mass.: Harvard University Press, 1933–49.

——— . *Sextus Empiricus: Against the Ethicists*. Translated with an introduction by Richard Bett. Oxford: Clarendon Press, 2000. First published 1997. Citations are to the 2000 edition.

——— . *Sextus Empiricus: Outlines of Scepticism*. Translated by Julia Annas and Jonathan Barnes. Cambridge: Cambridge University Press, 1994.

——— . *The Sceptic Way: Sextus Empiricus's Outlines of Pyrrhonism*. Translated with introduction and commentary by Benson Mates. New York: Oxford University Press, 1996.

Ioannis Stobaei Anthologii. Books 1 and 2. Edited by C. Wachsmuth. Berlin: Weidmann, 1884. Books 3 and 4. Edited by O Hense. Berlin: Weidmann, 1894–1909.

Collections of Fragments

Diehls, H. and Kranz, W., *Die Fragmente der Vorsokratiker*. Zürich: Weidmann, 1952.

Hülser, Karlheinz. *Die Fragmente zur Dialektik der Stoiker: Neue Sammlung der Texte mit Übersetzung und Kommentar*. Vols. 1–3 (1987); vol. 4 (1988). Stuttgart: Metzler, 1987–88.

Long, A. A., and D. N. Sedley. *The Hellenistic Philosophers*. Vol. 1. *Translations of the Principal Sources, with a Philosophical Commentary*. Vol. 2. *Greek and Latin Texts with Notes and Bibliography*. Cambridge: Cambridge University Press, 1992 [LS].

von Arnim, Johannes. *Stoicorum Veterum Fragmenta*. Vols. 1–4. Leipzig: Teubner, 1903–24 [SVF].

Secondary Literature

Alesse, Francesca. *La Stoa e la Tradizione Socratica*. Naples: Bibliopolis, 2000.

——— . "La *Repubblica* di Zenone di Cizio e la letteratura socratica." *Studi italiani di filologia classica*, 3rd ser., 16.1 (1998): 17–38.

Algra, Keimpe. "The Mechanism of Social Appropriation and Its Role in Hellenistic Ethics." *Oxford Studies in Ancient Philosophy* 25 (2003): 265–296.

——— ."Stoic Theology." In Inwood, *The Cambridge Companion to the Stoics*, 153–178.

——— . "Zeno of Citium and Stoic Cosmology." *Elenchos* 24 (2003): 9–32.

Algra, Keimpe, Jonathan Barnes, Jaap Mansfeld, and Malcolm Schofield, eds. *The Cambridge History of Hellenistic Philosophy*. Cambridge: Cambridge University Press, 1999.

Annas, Julia. "Aristotelian Political Theory in the Hellenistic Period." In Laks und Schofield, *Justice and Generosity*, 74–94.

——— . "From Nature to Happiness." Review of *Papers in Hellenistic Epistemology and Ethics* by G. Striker. *Apeiron* 31.1 (1998): 59–73.

——— . *The Morality of Happiness*. New York: Oxford University Press, 1995.

——— . *Platonic Ethics, Old and New*. Ithaca, N.Y.: Cornell University Press, 1999.

Annas, Julia, and Jonathan Barnes. *The Modes of Scepticism*. Cambridge: Cambridge University Press, 1985.

Athenassiadi, Polymnia, and Michael Frede, eds. *Pagan Monotheism in Late Antiquity*. Oxford: Clarendon Press, 1999.

Baldry, H. C. "Zeno's Ideal State." *Journal of Hellenic Studies* 79 (1959): 3–15.

Banateanu, Anne. *Le théorie stoïciennce de l'amitié. Essai de reconstruction.* Fribourg: Editions Universitaires Fribourg Suisse, 2001.

Barney, Rachel. *Names and Nature in Plato's "Cratylus."* New York: Routledge, 2001.

——. "A Puzzle in Stoic Ethics." *Oxford Studies in Ancient Philosophy* 24 (2003): 303–340.

Betegh, Gábor. "Cosmological Ethics in the *Timaeus* and Early Stoicism." *Oxford Studies in Ancient Philosophy* 23 (2002): 273–290.

Bobzien, Susanne. *Determinism and Freedom in Stoic Philosophy.* Oxford: Clarendon Press, 1998.

——. "Logic." In Inwood, *The Cambridge Companion to the Stoics*, 85–123.

Bonhöffer, A. *Die Ethik des Stoikers Epiktet.* Stuttgart: Frommann, 1894; reprint, 1968.

Brennan, Tad. "Reasonable Impressions in Stoicism." *Phronesis* 41 (1996): 318–334.

——. *The Stoic Life: Emotions, Duties, and Fate.* Oxford: Oxford University Press, 2005.

——. "Stoic Moral Psychology." In Inwood, *The Cambridge Companion to the Stoics*, 257–294.

Brittain, Charles. "Common Sense: Concepts, Definition and Meaning in and out of the Stoa." In *Philosophy of Language in the Hellenistic Age: Proceedings of the Ninth Symposium Hellenisticum*, ed. Dorothea Frede and Brad Inwood, 164–209. Cambridge: Cambridge University Press, 2005.

——. "Non-rational Perception in the Stoics and Augustine." *Oxford Studies in Ancient Philosophy* 22 (2002): 253–308.

——. "Rationality, Rules and Rights." *Apeiron* 34.3 (2001): 247–267.

Brouwer, René. "Sagehood and the Stoics." *Oxford Studies in Ancient Philosophy* 2 23 (2002): 181–224.

Brunschwig, Jacques. "The Cradle Argument." In Schofield and Striker, *The Norms of Nature*, 113–144.

——. "On a Book-Title by Chrysippus: 'On the Fact That the Ancients Admitted Dialectic along with Demonstrations.'" *Oxford Studies in Ancient Philosophy* supp. (1991): 81–95.

Brunschwig, Jacques, and Martha Nussbaum, eds. *Passions and Perceptions: Studies in Hellenistic Philosophy of Mind: Proceedings of the Fifth Symposium Hellenisticum.* Cambridge: Cambridge University Press, 1993.

Colvin, Matthew. "Heraclitus and Material Flux in Stoic Psychology." *Oxford Studies in Ancient Philosophy* 28 (2005): 257–272.

Cooper, John M. "The Emotional Life of the Wise." *Southern Journal of Philosophy* 43, supp. (2005): 176–218.

——— . "Eudaimonism and the Appeal to Nature in the Morality of Happiness: Comments on Julia Annas, *The Morality of Happiness.*" *Philosophy and Phenomenological Research* 55 (1995): 587–598.

——— . "Eudaimonism, the Appeal to Nature and 'Moral Duty' in Stoicism." In *Aristotle, Kant, and the Stoics: Rethinking Happiness and Duty*, ed. S. Engstrom and J. Whiting, 261–284. Cambridge: Cambridge University Press, 1996.

——— . "Greek Philosophers on Euthanasia and Suicide." In *Reason and Emotion*, 515–541. Princeton, N.J.: Princeton University Press, 1999.

——— . *Knowledge, Nature, and the Good.* Princeton, N.J.: Princeton University Press, 2004.

——— . "Moral Theory and Moral Improvement." In *Knowledge, Nature and the Good*, 309–334.

——— . *Reason and Emotion: Essays on Ancient Moral Psychology and Ethical Theory.* Princeton, N.J.: Princeton University Press, 1999.

——— . "Stoic Autonomy." In *Knowledge, Nature, and the Good*, 204–244.

Coulmas, P. *Les citoyens de monde: Histoire du Cosmopolitanism.* Paris: Albin Michel, 1995.

Couissin, P. "Le stoicisme de la nouvelle Académie." *Revue d'histoire de la Philosophie* (1929): 241–276.

Doty, Ralph. "*Ennoêmata, prolêpseis*, and Common Notions." *Southwestern Journal of Philosophy* 7.3 (1976): 143–148.

Dragona-Monachou, Myrtô. *The Stoic Argument for the Existence and the Providence of the Gods.* Athens: National and Capodistrian University of Athens, 1976.

Erskine, Andrew. *The Hellenistic Stoa: Political Thought and Action.* Ithaca, N.Y.: Cornell University Press, 1990.

Festugière, A. J. *La révélation d'Hermès Trismégiste.* Vol. 2. *Le Dieu cosmique.* Paris: Gabada, 1949.

Finley, M. I. "Utopianism Ancient and Modern." In *The Use and Abuse of History.* London: Hogarth, 1975.

Fortenbaugh, William W., ed. *Stoic and Peripatetic Ethics: The Work of Arius Didymus.* New Brunswick, N.J.: Transaction Books, 1983.

Frede, Dorothea. "Theodicy and Providential Care in Stoicism." In Frede and Laks, *Traditions in Theology*, 85–117.

Frede, Dorothea, and André Laks, eds. *Traditions in Theology: Studies in Hellenistic Theology: Its Background and Aftermath.* Papers presented at the eighth Symposium Hellenisticum. Leiden: Brill, 2002.

Frede, Michael. Introduction to *Rationality in Greek Thought*, ed. Michael Frede and Gisela Striker, 1–28. Oxford: Oxford University Press, 1996.

————. "Monotheism and Pagan Philosophy in Later Antiquity." In Athenassiadi and Frede, *Pagan Monotheism in Late Antiquity*, 41–69.

————. "On the Stoic Conception of the Good." In Ierodiakonou, *Topics in Stoic Philosophy*, 71–94.

————. "The Original Notion of Causes." In Michael Frede, *Essays in Ancient Philosophy*, 125–150. Minneapolis: University of Minnesota Press, 1987.

————. "The Stoic Conception of Reason." In *Hellenistic Philosophy*, ed. K. J. Boudouris, 2:50–61. Athens: International Center for Greek Philosophy and Culture, 1994.

————. "The Stoic Doctrine of the Affections of the Soul." In Schofield and Striker, *The Norms of Nature*, 93–110.

————. "Stoic Epistemology." In Algra et al., *The Cambridge History of Hellenistic Philosophy*, 295–322.

Frede, Michael, and Gisela Striker, eds. *Rationality in Greek Thought*. Oxford: Oxford University Press, 1996.

Gill, Christopher. "The Stoic Theory of Ethical Development: In What Sense Is Nature a Norm?" In *Was ist das für den Menschen Gute? Menschliche Natur und Güterlehre*, ed. Jan Szaif, 101–125. Berlin: de Gruyter, 2004.

Goulet-Cazé, Marie-Odile. "La Politeia de Diogène de Sinope et quelques remarques sur sa pensée politique." In Goulet-Cazé and Goulet, *Le cynisme ancien et ses prolongements*, 57–68.

————. *Les "Kynica" du stoïcisme*. Hermes Einzelschriften, vol. 89. Stuttgart: Franz Steiner Verlag, 2003.

Goulet-Cazé, Marie-Odile, and R. Goulet, eds. *Le cynisme ancien et ses prolongements*. Paris: Presses universitaires de France, 1993.

Henrichs, A. "Die Kritik der stoischen Theologie in *PHerc*. 1428." *Cronache Ercolanesi* 4 (1974): 5–32, 20.

Hirzel, R. *Untersuchungen zu Cicero's philosophischen Schriften*. Vol. 2, pt. 1. *Die Entwicklung der stoischen Philosophie*, 271–298. Leipzig, 1882.

Ierodiakonou, Katerina, ed. *Topics in Stoic Philosophy*. Oxford: Oxford University Press, 2001.

Inwood, Brad, ed. *The Cambridge Companion to the Stoics*. Cambridge: Cambridge University Press, 2003.

————. "Comments on Professor Görgemann's Paper: The Two Forms of *oikeiôsis* in Arius and the Stoa." In *On Stoic and Peripatetic Ethics: The Work of Arius Didymus*, ed. W. W. Fortenbaugh, 190–201. New Brunswick, N.J.: Rutgers University Press, 1983.

————. *Ethics and Human Action in Early Stoicism*. Oxford: Clarendon Press, 1985.

———— . "Getting to Goodness." In *Reading Seneca,* 271–301.

———— . *Reading Seneca: Stoic Philosophy at Rome.* Oxford: Oxford University Press, 2005.

———— . Review of *The Stoic Idea of the City* by Malcolm Schofield. *Bryn Mawr Classical Review.* http://ccat.sas.upenn.edu/bmcr/1992/03.03.13.html.

———— . Review of *Morality of Happiness* by J. Annas. *Ancient Philosophy* 15 (1995): 647–666.

———— . "Rules and Reasoning in Stoic Ethics." In Ierodiakonou, *Topics in Stoic Philosophy,* 95–127.

———— . "Seneca and Psychological Dualism." In Brunschwig and Nussbaum, *Passions and Perceptions,* 150–183.

———— . "The Stoics on the Grammar of Action." *Southern Journal of Philosophy* 23, supp. (1985): 75–86.

———— , with Donini, P. L. "Stoic Ethics." In Algra et al., *The Cambridge History of Hellenistic Philosophy,* 675–738.

Ioppolo, Anna Maria. *Aristone di Chio e lo Stoicismo antico.* Naples: Bibliopolis, 1980.

———— . "Decreta e praecepta in Seneca." In *La Filisofia in Eta Imperiale,* ed. Aldo Brancacci, 15–36. Naples: Bibliopolis, 2000.

———— . *Opinione e Scienza: Il dibattito tra Stoizi e Accademici nel III e nel II a.C.* Naples: Bibliopolis, 1986.

Janaçek, Karl. *Prolegomena to Sextus Empiricus.* Olomouc: N.p., 1948.

———— . "Skeptische Zweitropenlehre und Sextus Empiricus." *Eirene* 8 (1970): 47–55.

Kerferd, G. B. "What Does the Wise Man Know?" In Rist, *The Stoics,* 125–136.

Kidd, Ian. "Moral Actions and Rules in Stoicism." In Rist, *The Stoics,* 247–258.

Laks, André. "Legislation and Demiurgy: On the Relationship between Plato's *Republic* and *Laws.*" *Classical Antiquity* 9 (1990): 209–229.

———— . Review of *The Stoic Idea of the City* by Malcolm Schofield. *Ancient Philosophy* 14 (1994): 459–460.

Laks, A., and M. Schofield, eds. *Justice and Generosity.* Cambridge: Cambridge University Press, 1995.

Lesses, Glenn. "Austere Friends: The Stoics and Friendship." *Apeiron* 26.1 (1993): 57–75.

Lisi, Francisco L., ed. *Plato's "Laws" and Its Historical Significance.* In *Selected Papers of the First International Congress on Ancient Thought.* Salamanca: Academia Verlag, 1998.

Long, A. *Problems in Stoicism.* London: Athlone Press, 1971.

———— . "Sextus Empiricus on the Criterion of Truth." *Bulletin of the Institute of Classical Studies* 25 (1978): 25–49.

——— . "Socrates in Hellenistic Philosophy." *Classical Quarterly* 38 (1988): 150–171.

——— . "The Stoic Distinction between Truth and the True." In *Les Stoicienne et leur logique*, ed. J. Brunschwig, 297–316. Paris: Vrin, 1978.

Ludlum, Ivor. "Two Long-Running Myths: A Centralized Orthodox Stoic School and Stoic Scholarchs." *Elenchos* 24 (2003), pt.: 33–55.

Ludwig, Paul W. *Eros and Polis: Desire and Community in Greek Political Theory*. Cambridge: Cambridge University Press, 2002.

Mansfeld, J. "Diogenes Laertius on Stoic Philosophy." *Elenchos* 7 (1986): 297–382.

——— . "Theology." In Algra et al., *The Cambridge History of Hellenistic Philosophy*, 452–478.

Meinwald, Constance. "Ignorance and Opinion in Stoic Epistemology." *Phronesis* 50 (2005): 215–231.

Menn, Stephen. "Physics as Virtue." *Proceedings of the Boston Area Colloquium in Ancient Philosophy* 11, ed. John J. Clearly and William C. Wians (1995): 1–34.

——— . "On Plato's *Politeia*." In *Proceedings of the Boston Area Colloquium* 21, ed. John J. Cleary and Gary M. Gurtler (2005), 1–55.

Mitsis, Phillip. "Moral Rules and the Aims of Stoic Ethics." *Journal of Philosophy* 83 (1986): 556–558.

——— . "Seneca on Reason, Rules, and Moral Development." In Brunschwig and Nussbaum, *Passions and Perceptions*, 285–312.

——— . "The Stoic Origin of Natural Rights." In Ierodiakonou, *Topics in Stoic Philosophy*, 153–177.

Mitsis, Phillip, with J. DeFilippo. "Socrates and Stoic Natural Law." In Vander Waerdt, *The Socratic Movement*, 252–271.

Moles, John. "Le cosmopolitisme cynique." In Goulet-Cazé and Goulet, *Le cynisme ancien et ses prolongements*, 259–280.

——— . "The Cynics." In Rowe and Schofield, *The Cambridge History of Greek and Roman Political Thought*, 415–434.

——— . "The Cynics and Politics." In Laks and Schofield, *Justice and Generosity*, 129–158.

Nussbaum, Martha. " 'All Gods Are True' in Epicurus." In Frede and Laks, *Traditions in Theology*, 183–221.

——— . "Commentary on Menn." In *Proceedings of the Boston Area Colloquium in Ancient Philosophy* 11, ed. John J. Clearly and William C. Wians (1995): 35–45.

Obbink, Dirk. "The Stoic Sage in the Cosmic City." In Ierodiakonou, *Topics in Stoic Philosophy*, 178–195.

Reed, B. "The Stoics' Account of Cognitive Impression." *Oxford Studies in Ancient Philosophy* 23 (2002): 147–180.

Reydams-Schils, Gretchen. "Human Bonding and *oikeiôsis* in Roman Stoicism." *Oxford Studies in Ancient Philosophy* 22 (2002): 221–251.

Rist, John. *Stoic Philosophy*. Cambridge: Cambridge University Press, 1969.

——— , ed. *The Stoics*. Berkeley: University of California Press, 1987.

Roloff, D. *Gottähnlichkeit, Vergöttlichung und Erhöhung zu seligem Leben: Untersuchungen zur Herkunft der platonischen Angleichung an Gott*. Berlin: de Gruyter, 1970.

Rowe, Christopher, and Malcolm Schofield, eds. *The Cambridge History of Greek and Roman Political Thought*. Cambridge: Cambridge University Press, 2000.

Salles, Ricardo. "Determinism and Recurrence in Early Stoic Thought." *Oxford Studies in Ancient Philosophy* 24 (2003): 253–272.

Sandbach, F. H. "Aristotle's Legacy to Stoic Ethics." *Bulletin of the London University Institute of Classical Studies* 15 (1968): 72–85.

——— . "Ennoia and Prolepsis in the Stoic Theory of Knowledge." In Long, *Problems in Stoicism*, 22–37. London: Athlone Press, 1971.

Schofield, Malcolm. "Epicurean and Stoic Political Thought." In Rowe and Schofield, *The Cambridge History of Greek and Roman Political Thought*. 435–456.

——— . *The Stoic Idea of the City*. Cambridge: Cambridge: Press, 1991.

——— . *The Stoic Idea of the City*. With a foreword by Martha Nussbaum. Chicago: University of Chicago Press, 1999.

——— . "Two Stoic Approaches to Justice." In Laks and Schofield, *Justice and Generosity*, 191–212.

Schofield, Malcolm, and Gisela Striker, eds. *The Norms of Nature: Studies in Hellenistic Ethics*. Cambridge: Cambridge University Press, 1986.

Sedley, David. " 'Becoming Like God' in the Timeaus and Aristotle." In *Interpretation the Timaeus-Critias: Proceedings of the Fourth Symposium Platonicum*, ed. T. Calvo and L. Brisson, 327–339. St. Augustin, Germany: Academia Verlag, 1997.

——— . "The Stoic-Platonist Debate on *kathekonta*." In Ierodiakonou, *Topics in Stoic Philosophy*, 128–152.

——— . "The Origins of Stoic God." In Frede and Laks, *Traditions in Theology*, 41–83.

Stephens, William O. "Epictetus on How the Stoic Sage Loves." *Oxford Studies in Ancient Philosophy* 14 (1996): 193–210.

Stevens, John A. "Preliminary Impulse in Stoic Psychology." *Ancient Philosophy* 20 (2000): 139–168.

Striker, Gisela. "Antipater, or the Art of Living." In Schofield and Striker, *The Norms of Nature*, 185–204.

——— . "Ataraxia: Happiness as Tranquillity." *Monist* 73 (1990): 97–110.

——— . "Following Nature: A Study in Stoic Ethics." *Oxford Studies in Ancient Philosophy* 9 (1991): 1–73.

——— . "Origins of the Concept of Natural Law." *Boston Area Colloquium in Ancient Philosophy* 2 (1987): 79–94; reprinted in *Papers in Hellenistic Epistemology and Ethics*, 209–220. Cambridge: Cambridge University Press, 1996.

——— . *Papers in Hellenistic Epistemology and Ethics*. Cambridge: Cambridge University Press, 1996.

——— . "The Role of *oikeiôsis* in Stoic Ethics." In *Papers in Hellenistic Epistemology and Ethics*, 281–297.

Vander Waerdt, Paul. "Politics and Philosophy in Stoicism." Review of *The Hellenistic Stoa* by Andrew Erskine. *Oxford Studies in Ancient Philosophy* 9 (1991): 185–211.

——— , ed. *The Socratic Movement*. Ithaca, N.Y.: Cornell University Press, 1994.

——— . "Zeno's Republic and the Origins of Natural Law." In Vander Waerdt, *The Socratic Movement*, 272–308.

Vogt, Katja. "Anger, Present Injustice and Future Revenge in Seneca's *De Ira*." In *New Developments in Seneca Studies,* edited by Gareth Williams and Katharina Volk, 57–74. Columbia Studies in the Classical Tradition. Leiden: Brill, 2006.

——— . "Die frühe stoische Theorie des Werts." In *Abwägende Vernunft*, ed. Ch. Schröer and F.-J. Borman, 61–77. Berlin: de Gruyter, 2004.

——— . "Gibt es eine Lebenskunst? Politische Philosophie in der frühen Stoa und skeptische Kritik." *Zeitschrift für Philosophische Forschung* 59.1 (2005): 1–21.

——— . *Skepsis und Lebenspraxis: Das pyrrhonische Leben ohne Meinungen.* Freiburg: Alber Verlag, 1998.

——— . "Die stoische Theorie der Emotionen." In *Zur Ethik der älteren Stoa,* ed. Barbara Guckes, 69–93. Göttingen: Vandenhoeck und Ruprecht, 2004.

——— . "Plutarch über Zenons Traum: Ist die politische Philosophie der frühen Stoa kosmopolitisch?" In *Antike Philosophie Verstehen: Understanding Ancient Philosophy*, ed. Marcel v. Ackeren and Jörn Müller, 196–217. Darmstadt: WBG, 2006.

Wachsmuth, C. "Stichometrisches und Bibliothekarisches," *Rheinisches Museum* 34 (1879): 38–51.

Watson, G. "The Natural Law and Stoicism." In Long, *Problems in Stoicism*, ed. 216–238.

West, M. L. "Towards Monotheism." In Athenassiadi and Frede, *Pagan Monotheism in Late Antiquity*, 21–41.

White, Michael. "Stoic Natural Philosophy (Physics and Cosmology)." In Inwood, *The Cambridge Companion to the Stoics*, 124–152.

White, N. "Nature and Regularity in Stoic Ethics." *Oxford Studies in Ancient Philosophy* 3 (1985): 289–305.

——— . "The Role of Physics in Stoic Ethics." *Southern Journal of Philosophy* 23, supp. (1985): 57–74.

Index of Passages Cited

General Index

74810198R00153

Made in the USA
San Bernardino, CA
20 April 2018